Contents

Acknowledgements

To my father, whose generosity in selling Oldfield Nurseries to me at a fraction of its value enabled me to resign from the Royal Botanic Gardens at Kew, take my leave of botanical research when the time was ripe, and enjoy seven years as a nurseryman.

To Tom Wallace and Eric Hewitt, under whose tutelage at Long Ashton Research Station I first discovered connections between plants and nutrients – but did not discover till years later that plant nutrition was connected in any way with plant physiology.

To Christopher Lloyd, who as a lecturer at Wye College sustained my belief that gardening lay beyond horticulture, and that the calling of a gardener was one of life's most fulfilling professions.

To Louis Wain, one of the pioneers of the selective use of herbicides against plants, whose lectures at Wye yet taught me to be wary of claims that the effects of chemicals are restricted to the targets against which we use them, and who, later, as an examiner for my PhD thesis, was prepared to look beyond my antipathy towards statistical analysis of experimental results.

To Vita Sackville-West, whom I met once, friendly but formidable in britches and broad-brimmed hat, and Harold Nicolson, whose garden at Sissinghurst first compelled me to to see that a garden was a composition, not just a collection of plants; and to Pamela Schwerdt and Pauline Kreutsberger, who ensured that this garden continued to develop, and became an unique – though widely imitated – expression of a particularly vivid style of English gardening.

To Marjorie Fish, whom I never met, for her garden at East Lambrook Manor, which first sowed the seeds of matrix planting in my mind; to John Boyd-Carpenter who was willing to struggle to ensure that East Lambrook did not die with Marjorie Fish, and Andrew Norton, who has undertaken the garden's restoration without destroying its essential qualities.

To Phyllis Reiss, whose garden at Tintinhull first showed me the magical effects of setting informal planting in a formal frame, and to Penelope Hobhouse for reviving the garden I had carried in my mind from my earliest visits; to Major and Mrs Knox Finlay of Keillor Castle; to James Hancock at Powys Castle, to Gordon Collier at Titoki Point and Alison McCrae in New Zealand; to Phoebe Noble near Victoria in British Columbia, Canada; to Mrs van Bennekom and Ton ter Linden in Holland, and to a hundred other gardeners whose efforts, skill and imagination have given me pleasure and inspiration over the years.

To Thomas Swarbrick, Director of the Scottish Horticultural Research Institute, who changed the course of my life by offering me a job as a plant physiologist – a profession I had never suspected existed, in a post I had not applied for.

To George Taylor, who, as Director of Kew, appointed me Head of the Physiology Section on its revival after a lapse of fifty years, and gave unstinting support to my proposal to set up a Seed Bank in which to conserve seeds of useful, threatened or otherwise save-worthy species and populations of wild plants; to Dick Shaw, the Curator of the Royal Botanic Gardens, Kew, at that time, and George Brown, an Assistant Curator, without whose energetic goodwill the space, staff and resources for the embryonic Seed Bank would never have been found.

To Chris Philip for his imagination in devising 'The Plant Finder' – nurtured in infancy by the Hardy Plant Society, and kidnapped when a promising adolescent by the Royal Horticultural Society – without whose efforts I could never have begun to cope with the nomenclatural problems in this book, even though many of the name changes I have been persuaded to adopt horrify me.

To all those whose gardens in Britain, Holland, Canada, the USA, France, Spain, Australia and New Zealand have been the sources of the photographs that appear in this book.

To Trish Johnson, whose arrival in my garden turned a lost cause into a forlorn hope, and whose efforts since then have made a garden full of promise for the future.

Finally, to all those who have taken part in courses at the Garden School – many of whom have become friends – and who, while coming to learn from me, have taught me much of what I know about gardening and the ways of gardeners.

Introduction

This book explores the theme that, if we allowed them to, plants would do much of the hard work we have been taught is an essential part of gardening. But the pursuit of that theme leads to the discovery that many traditional practices actually prevent that happening. For better or for worse, our approaches to gardening are inherited from days when labour cost so little to hire that it was almost free, and endless supplies of horse manure were a disposal problem, rather than a valued resource. But a system that worked for a Victorian head gardener with eight gardeners and a boy to do his bidding has less appeal to those who garden single-handedly, with other interests to fill a busy life.

True gardeners are inclined to dismiss suggestions that gardening can be done without digging or forking the soil, raking it level or hoeing the weeds. Some feel affronted by suggestions that their skills could be replaced by anything as unreal as alliances with plants, and many will regard this book as an attack on the craft and traditions which they cherish most dearly. But the concept of matrix planting is not an attack on traditional gardening, any more than one face of a coin represents an attack on the other. They share a common background but have opposing viewpoints that depend on different approaches and ways of doing things. The long-established techniques of traditional gardening enable us to grow the widest possible range of plants in the widest possible variety of situations. Those of us who garden in parts of the world where every year, every month – sometimes it seems every week – produces a meteorological record of some kind (whether it is the wettest, driest, coldest or windiest) owe a great deal to a system which blesses our gardening with success year by year, almost irrespective of the records being broken around us. Matrix planting does not attempt to make all gardens all things to all plants. It is based, on the contrary, on matching plant to place, with the reward that, when done successfully, plants replace activity with spade, rake and hoe as the controllers of what goes on in the garden – for without control, gardening of any kind is impossible.

Matrix planting – of a sort – is familiar to most of us in the guise of half-forgotten, unconsidered corners of our gardens in which plants like ivies, periwinkles, London pride and comfreys establish self-governing communities amongst which snowdrops and daffodils appear each spring and honesty seeds itself in an erratic pattern of bold spikes. In warmer climates agapanthus, wild ginger and cinerarias may occupy similarly neglected corners, and onion weed and sparaxis may replace daffodils. These corner colonists survive because we leave them alone, failing to fulfil our good intentions to 'do something about them one day'. (Throughout this book there are situations where vernacular names seem more appropriate than Latin binomials. To avoid confusion, Latin equivalents of all vernacular names used will be found in the index).

Ivies, periwinkles, agapanthus and wild ginger may strike discerning gardeners as plants they would be sorry to swap their treasures for, and they might reasonably suggest that if that is the price of matrix planting they would prefer to stick to spade, fork, hoe and rake, thank you very much! But that is not the price of matrix planting. All plants that grow in gardens once grew wild. The ancestry of some is a tangled web of species and forms that almost conceals their wild ancestors. Others have changed little, if at all. But ancient or modern, garden plants still possess the genes that enable their wild counterparts to combine successfully into communities. All we have to do is provide the conditions they need to get on with it.

This book is written for those whose gardens are in temperate parts of the world – ranging from places where temperatures seldom drop more than a degree or two below freezing point to those where -25 °C (-13 °F) is not an unusual winter minimum. That covers the extreme range in which gardens are made in Britain, from the Isles of Scilly to the Cairngorms, most of western and southern Europe, parts of the USA from New England to the mid-Atlantic states in the east, and the north-west Pacific states, Western Canada, New Zealand, south-eastern Australia, Japan and parts of South Africa.

Inevitably, across such a range, plants recommended for one situation will be inappropriate for another; communities which live together in one place may be riven by incompatibilities elsewhere. Some problems are quite familiar. Gardeners from Britain who encounter cannas colonizing damp meadows in New Zealand are not tempted to try them in similar situations when they return home, because they are fully aware that these plants cannot tolerate freezing temperatures. Numerous plants are referred to in this book – those that are not frost-hardy are marked in the lists with an asterisk. But frost-hardiness is only one aspect of a plant's ability to do well, and others, equally critical, can be harder to define.

Gardens along the eastern seaboard of the United States share many of the same conditions as those in parts of Britain. Yet Ravenna grass grows to imposing heights and flowers regularly in New Jersey, but is seldom more than a stunted and flowerless dwarf in Oxfordshire. Crape myrtle adorns gardens in Virginia, but is a miserable thing in Virginia Water. Silver-leaved artemisias thrive in Wales, but collapse in the summer heat and humidity of the Carolinas. I have found no way to cover all these problems, and the credentials of plants referred to in the book should be examined to check their gardenworthiness under your particular conditions. Amongst many possible guides are the maps depicting hardiness zones prepared for different parts of the United States by the US Department of Agriculture. Similar maps have now been prepared for other parts of the world, but need to be used with caution. They would reveal the limitations of none of the plants referred to earlier in this paragraph.

2A

2A, B & C. A dozen North American woodland wildflowers growing harmoniously (above) within an area of 1 sq. m (11 sq. ft). Garden plants can develop similarly balanced communities, like the one at East Lambrook Manor (top right): or these opportunists from a neglected herbaceous border, which have formed a robustly colourful matrix on a sunny bank in a Herefordshire garden (centre). Brandywine Conservancy Wildflower Garden, Chadds Ford, Pennsylvania, USA. East Lambrook Manor, Somerset, England.

How Caple Court, Ross on Wye, Herefordshire, England.

3. Aloes, aeoniums and agaves thrive in the almost frost-free Isles of Scilly, but gardeners in colder situations would know better than to expect similar results. Less familiar aspects of hardiness, including drought-resistance, heat-tolerance and vulnerability to wet, are equally critical to the success of communities of plants in gardens. The Abbey Gardens, Tresco, Scilly Islands, Cornwall, England.

2B

2C

3

Chapter one

What does your garden grow?

Pukka gardeners might puzzle over that question, and suggest that *gardeners* grow plants: gardens are the places where plants are grown, and what grows depends on the skills and resources of the gardener. We use skill to grow dahlias, gladioli, begonias and other tender plants in places with cold winters by lifting them and protecting them from frost through the winter. Some invest in conservatories: small ones when we need to count the pennies, and gigantic, multi-domed, corridored and aisled ones for those with more expansive tastes and fortunes. Gardeners have always enjoyed the challenge of growing plants in places far from their natural homes, and sometimes this has gone beyond modest pride in home-spun skills.

Louis XIV, the Sun King, saw no reason why

promenades amongst the parterres at Versailles should be spoilt by the frailties of plants. Whatever the season, the beds had to be bright with flowers, and tender bedding plants would die in their thousands on frosty winter nights. The gardeners replaced them as a matter of course – again and again, from countless stocks in reserve in greenhouses. You need not be an eighteenth-century monarch to pit your skills against the limitations of your garden. Many gardeners would argue that half the fun of gardening lies in growing plants where nature never intended them to be.

Natural and garden habitats

There is another approach. That is to match the place with the plant. It depends on summing up the assets and limitations of a garden, or a corner of a garden, and ultimately, of a planting space within a garden. Then choosing the plants most likely to do well in the conditions on offer from the apparently bewildering array available to us. To do that, we first have to know something about the conditions in which they grow naturally. That covers an immense variety of situations, from Antarctic islands and high screes on mountains to luxuriant tropical rain forests.

Gardens too exist in extraordinary variety – even when we include only those in temperate regions of the world. But within most gardens, the range is quite small. It so happens that the geological formations in the part of the world where I live are exceptionally diverse and fragmented, and in a bare half hectare my garden contains soils which vary from acidic to strongly basic. It includes dry, free-draining, sunlit banks, and places bordering a stream

4

4. Traditional gardeners adapt conditions to suit the plant, enabling them to compose striking compositions, like these bird of paradise flowers in a conservatory with delphiniums and foxgloves of plants from very different situations. The skills of matrix planting, however, lie in matching the natural requirements of the plants with settings in the garden. The Winter Garden, The Domain, Auckland, New Zealand.

5A

5B

5C

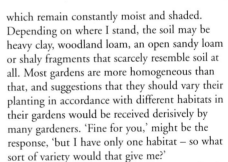

5D

which remain constantly moist and shaded. Depending on where I stand, the soil may be heavy clay, woodland loam, an open sandy loam or shaly fragments that scarcely resemble soil at all. Most gardens are more homogeneous than that, and suggestions that they should vary their planting in accordance with different habitats in their gardens would be received derisively by many gardeners. 'Fine for you,' might be the response, 'but I have only one habitat – so what sort of variety would that give me?'

But shade beneath an apple tree is woodland for the plants that grow there; a lawn mimics rabbit-grazed turf on a chalk hillside; perennials and shrubs in the mixed border experience some of the problems and opportunities of wildflowers amongst scrub. So instead of thinking of different parts of your garden as a series of *habitats* – a rather grand term that relates more

---

5A, B, C & D. Plants adapted to extreme conditions, like hot, arid bush (top left), perennially cool, wet, deeply-shaded temperate rain forests (top right), high alpine screes and snowfields (bottom left) or almost rainless deserts (bottom right) are specialists. In most gardens, they can only be grown in special situations. The ancestors of our garden plants are more likely to grow naturally in meadows, open woodlands, wetlands and other less demanding natural settings. Coomallo Creek, near Eneabba, Western Australia. Pukeiti Rhododendron Trust, New Plymouth, Taranaki, New Zealand. Mount Vrsic Slovenia, Sandveld, near Port Nolloth, Namaqualand, South Africa.

6A

6B

6D

6C

they remain wet or dry, and in many other ways. The plants likely to do best, and grow most easily in each, will be those that are found in natural habitats that provide similar conditions.

I am not suggesting that we dare not plant a thing without a detailed ecological survey of the conditions in which it grows naturally. Considerable progress is made by discovering that a particular plant grows in woodland or amongst grasses, in damp meadows perhaps, or in rocky, exposed places amongst small shrubs. We look for meadow flowers amongst grasses, woodland perennials amongst trees, and cornfield weeds – assuming herbicidal sprays have spared any – in fields of cereals. We can go further afield, to screes and snowfields at the tops of mountains, to arid places where sparsely scattered plants eke out a living amongst stones and rocks, and to the deepest recesses of heavily shaded forests. Plants will be there too, but these will have adapted to cope with the highly specialist conditions in which they live – few will be amongst the tolerant, easily grown, relatively accommodating garden plants we rely on to fill the borders in our gardens, which are also the ones most likely to settle down happily and form garden communities together.

The spring flowers in the Appalachian Mountains are beautiful; a bluebell wood in Britain must be one of the loveliest sights in

comfortably to the broad scale in which plants grow naturally – think of them as a series of *settings*. The smallest garden provides a variety of different settings, varying in the amounts of sun or shade, exposure or shelter, the extent to which

6A, B, C & D. A variety of settings (or habitats) can be found in any garden. They may share similar situations, yet be as different as the narrow, shaded north-facing border (top left) and the equally narrow, but hot, sunny, south-facing border (centre left), both against the walls of houses. Or they may be as obviously different as a hot, sunny, steeply-sloping bank

(right) and the level, soggy margins of a pool (bottom left). Success, in any setting, depends on choosing plants naturally adapted to grow well in that situation.
Benthall Hall, Shropshire, England. Powys Castle, Welshpool, Powys, Wales. Red Lion House, Horderley, Shropshire, England. Stourton House, Mere, Wiltshire, England.

nature; the brilliant displays of annuals and bulbs in Namaqualand or the intensity of colours and extraordinary shapes of the flowers on shrubs in Western Australia in springtime are worth travelling halfway round the world to see, and these are only a few of the dazzling spectacles wildflowers provide in natural settings. Nevertheless, even these spectacles lack the structure and evidence of deliberate intention that reveals the designer's hand in a garden – at worst, natural vegetation is a tangled chaos which no gardener could live with for a day. But wildflowers do not grow as haphazardly as a casual glance suggests, but in communities which are:

Ordered

The plants exist, one with another, in relationships, based on competition, through which they establish balanced communities in which every plant has its place, and from which each plant derives the support, shelter or protection it needs for survival.

Predictable

Particular species grow in particular situations. This extends beyond familiar examples like heathers on acid moorland, brooms on dry sandy banks or reeds along the edge of a pool. The wild flowers in any community are characteristic of the situation, depending on whether the soil is wet or free-draining, acid or alkaline, the climate cold or temperate, etc., and a botanist, given a description of the situation, would often be able to predict many of the species to be found there without going near the place.

Persistent

We may be taught that grassland is vulnerable to invasion by shrubs to form scrub, giving way in turn to woodland as trees establish themselves, but these transitions can be very slow. Soil types, grazing pressures, climatic extremes, fire and other influences – some of which correspond to forms of garden management – can delay or entirely prevent the evolution of one type of vegetation into another.

Stable

The mixture of species in a community can remain virtually the same for long periods. A return visit to a wood, or a riverside, or any other natural habitat which we knew in childhood, will renew our acquaintance with the same species – even the most insignificant ones – that we first got to know perhaps half a century or more previously.

'Ordered', 'predictable', 'persistent' and 'stable' are words with a more reassuring ring than the apparent chaos of untamed nature might suggest. They provide the foundation for matrix planting. If garden plants retain the responses of their wild progenitors, they too can form long-lived, self-sustaining communities that can be harnessed to make our gardens easier to look after.

Wild plants under the skin

That may sound like a big, big 'if'! Full-blown hybrid tea roses, cymbidiums with spikes like gladioli, and the great, round heads of exhibition dahlias are far from natural. Man-made creations like these could hardly be expected to survive without our protection. But garden plants are wild plants in disguise – their cover little more than the surface lustre and extra vigour conferred by high living and freedom from competition, amplified by selection for larger flowers with more petals and brighter, more varied colours than their wild counterparts.

In a brown, parched land, wild lilac bushes grow on low, rolling hills along the valley of the Vardar river in Macedonia. This river brings the influence of the Mediterranean deep into the Balkan Peninsula, and lilacs grow naturally in places like this, where winters have the cold severity of continental Europe and summers the torrid aridity that makes the Mediterranean a sun-baked paradise for holidaymakers. Shoots and flowers are produced in a few short weeks before the drought of summer closes a brief spring, and then growth stops and the leaves develop the heavy-duty guise they need to work effectively through long periods of hot, dry weather. They fall without delay – or time to develop autumn tints – as winter closes in, and are replaced by short, sturdy twigs, with buds encased in scales to protect them from cold winds. Dense networks of roots just below the

7A

7B

7C

surface collect water in spring from melting snow, and make the most of summer showers, and if unusually severe conditions – or outbreaks of fire – destroy the tops, they produce suckers to rebuild new plants.

Garden lilacs have more colourful, more sumptuous flowers, carried on more luxuriant trusses than the wild ones by the Vardar river, but in almost every other way they are the same. Superficial disguises lead us to suppose that the plants in our gardens are quite different to wild plants, and repeated unsubstantiated references in books, on television and in the gardening press to plants 'having been changed by cultivation' or 'having adapted to cultivation' reinforce that supposition.

If we believe only what we see, that is true –

but that does not mean that the physiological responses which control the ways plants react to their environments have changed too. Michaelmas daisies have been bred from two North American species, *Aster novae-angliae* and *A. novi-belgii*, that grow naturally in damp meadows. The wild plants are tall with quite small, pale-purple daisies; their rhizomes spread vigorously amongst the grasses at ground level, and eventually extend over large areas, becoming separated so that they look like numerous individual plants dotted over the meadow. Cultivated forms have larger flowers, more petals and many more colours; they range in size from dwarfs, barely 30 cm (1 ft) high, to tall forms that may reach 2 m (6 ft 6 in); they still produce rhizomes, but these are shorter and form compact clusters of stems that compete with one another for nutrients and water.

Most gardeners would think nothing of planting lilacs and Michaelmas daisies close to each other in a border, perhaps to provide similar colour tones at opposite ends of the season. And despite their very different origins and natural adaptations, these plants would grow quite happily, provided the ground was well prepared and they were cared for – pruned, watered, fertilized, sprayed for diseases, etc. – because, like most plants, they can tolerate a

7A, B & C. Garden plants are wild plants under the skin. Some, like the dahlia (top left) and hemerocallis (right), are highly-bred, exotic creations; others, like Meconopsis grandis (bottom left) are no different from their wild relatives. But, though appearances may change, plants retain the likes and dislikes of their wild ancestors in other ways. We can grow them only if we remember that all dahlias are vulnerable to frost; that hemerocallis are not tolerant of heat and drought, and meconopsis thrive only on moist, well-drained soils in humid atmospheres. Godspiece Leaze, Norton St Philip, Somerset, England. Little Norton Mill, Norton sub Hamden, Somerset, England. Threave Castle, Castle Douglas, Galloway, Scotland.

8A

8B

much wider range of conditions than those they are specifically adapted to cope with naturally. But even under exemplary conditions, Michaelmas daisies are so prone to mildew in most garden settings that many people have given up growing them. Their appearance may have changed, but physiologically, they still depend on the moist soils they are adapted to naturally, and without them become stressed and vulnerable to infection.

Many trees, shrubs, perennials and bulbs widely grown in gardens appear identical to their wild counterparts; others have been selected for trivial changes – variations in flower colour, increase in numbers of petals, variegated foliage. Some are hybrids between two species, and when these species occupy different habitats, their offspring may inherit the attributes of both parents. Primroses grow naturally on neutral to acid soils, cowslips on those that are well drained and strongly basic. Hybrids between the two have produced polyanthus which are equally happy in both conditions. More complex hybrids like roses, with a network of lineages leading back to several different species, are the inheritors of so many different responses that connections with any particular wild ancestor

may be more difficult to draw.

But simple or complex, the responses of garden plants stem from the adaptations of their wild ancestors. Their suitability for different situations, their compatibility with other plants and their prospects of settling down to form a community are all directly attributable to these adaptations. Normally many different plants live together, filling a variety of niches – some provide shade and shelter, others ground cover; some are permanent residents, others ever-ready to fill spaces that become available; some are active at one season, others at another.

So there will be many answers to the question, 'What does your garden grow?' – there will be areas of shade and sunshine; places where the water fails to drain in winter, and others where it drains too freely in summer. There may be trees to contend with, hedges to accommodate, shrubs to be planted and particular features – a rock garden, a pool, a bank covered with heathers and dwarf conifers – which you would like to include in your repertoire. Each poses different problems and opportunities, and each provides a setting within which a particular community of plants will be at home.

8A & B. Russell lupins (left) were deliberately introduced into the high, dry grasslands of central South Island in New Zealand, and now maintain themselves in a range of colours that would be the envy of most gardeners. (Lupins flourish in these infertile soils because they are able to form symbiotic associations with bacteria which fix nitrogen from the air, and with fungi whose mycelia can obtain phosphates from insoluble compounds unavailable to other plants.)

Primula hybrids (right) seed themselves along a wet ditch in the mild, humid conditions of the west of Scotland. Plants self-sow like this only when conditions match those which they are naturally adapted to survive. In gardens, with a little assistance from the gardener, a much wider variety of plants can become self-sufficient. Near Lake Tekapo, South Island, New Zealand. Achnacloich Gardens, Taynuilt, Argyllshire, Scotland.

Chapter two

Partnership with plants

Buy a house, and ninety-nine times out of a hundred you buy a plot, a section or a yard as well. Whatever you call it, whatever size it may be, you will quickly discover that the neighbours expect that space around your house to be turned into a garden. Your skills as a gardener may be wanting; you may have little inclination and no time to be a gardener; you may share your life with forces that are hostile to gardens – children who play games and want to ride bicycles with their friends; dogs and cats; the need for somewhere to park cars, caravans, even a boat; your own talent for relaxing and watching the world go by. You may have other plans for your plot, section or yard, but few resist the expectations of neighbours, the conventions of upbringing and the pressures of spouses. Before long most of us find ourselves out there mowing the lawn and trimming the hedges. We puzzle about planning and planting the borders, and, on Sunday afternoons lose ourselves amongst a maze of Latin names in the nearest garden centre.

We discover that the harder gardeners work, the more problems seem to multiply. This is not because plants are difficult to grow. Many manage quite well in our gardens, with or without our help, and weeds (which, like it or not, are still plants) appear in spite of everything we do to destroy them. Could we be creating our own problems? Rather than repeatedly assaulting our gardens with spades and hoes, could we not try to find ways to make the superabundant energy of plants work for us by enrolling them as partners? Gardeners regulate the ways they garden, and what goes on in a garden, within narrow limits. They restrict membership of that select group they call 'Garden Plants' to a narrow range of acceptable kinds, waging war on all others as weeds. The higher the state of gardening the narrower the definitions, the stricter the rules, the more exclusive the range of suitable plants, and the harder we must work.

Even today, when few have help in their gardens, and other interests compete for our time, we retain nostalgic visions of kitchen gardens, formal rose beds, herbaceous borders, lawns and rockeries, and, if transported on a temporal flying carpet – it might be on television or by virtual reality – to a garden of a century ago, many people would say they had seen perfection.

They would not be the first to take it for granted that gardening in Western Europe during the early twentieth century provided an example to be followed wherever gardening was practised. The model was adopted, as a matter of course, in the United States and Canada, as well as in more distant parts of the world, wherever European influences and traditions were predominant. The package, combining a garden flora and gardening techniques derived directly from European gardens, spread equally to places that were suitable, as to those where climates, conditions and traditions bore no resemblance to the lands of its origin. Identical rose beds were planted and tended with equal care in Kensington, Kashmir and Kenya. Herbaceous borders based on similar plans were the pride of Philadelphia, Perth and Paris. The annuals to be seen in bedding schemes in Cape Town made borders bright and beautiful on Isola Bella, in San Francisco, in Darjeeling and in St Petersburg. In North America, South Africa, New Zealand and Australia vastly diverse native floras were more or less ignored. A few species and their hybrids – pelargoniums, rhododendrons, heaths and hebes amongst others – became accepted players in the repertoire of European gardens, and cultivars of these were repatriated as garden plants to their native lands.

For much of this century, Western garden styles existed as a worldwide Pangaea, within which a select – though still enormous – band of garden plants circulated, and into which others were introduced, granted the honour of garden citizenship, and in their turn, distributed to play similar roles wherever gardening was practised. Now this supercontinent is breaking up. Early signs of the rift appeared in California, where climate and circumstances combined to create a a vision of a New Eden which stimulated innovation; later, a surfeit of the 'English Garden' in the eastern states led to the idea of the 'New American Garden'. That term

9A

find less demanding ways to garden. Roseraie de l'Hay-les-Roses, Paris, France. Oxford University Botanic Garden, Oxford, England.

10A

10C

10D

10B

from them, which are not only better adapted to grow in the gardens of these countries, but introduce forms and textures – and sometimes intensities of colour too – which were seldom or never seen in the gardens of Europe.

As this horticultural Pangaea breaks up, and the conventions that bond different parts together become less strong, the limits of what constitutes a garden, and the ways gardening should be done are being redefined – both globally and locally. Today, no one who sees gardens in different parts of the world can fail to notice how plants and practices vary from one place to another. While the Royal Horticultural Society in Britain makes a new garden at Rosemoor in Devon, steadfastly maintaining the

10A, B, C & D. In New England a simple foundation planting of ferns and ground elder is preferred to more complex 'English' styles. Bromeliads and monsteras create a woodland stage set in New Zealand (bottom left). The introduction of proteas from South Africa like *Leucodendron strobilinum* 'Waterlily' (top right) force us to change traditional approaches to cultivation and soil fertility. The spiky accents of cordylines, astelias and grasses (bottom right) stimulate imaginative new ways to combine plant forms. Weston, Vermont, USA. Felix, Mark & Abbie Jury's Garden, Waitara, Taranaki, New Zealand. Regional Botanic Garden, Manurewa, Auckland, New Zealand. Brian & Diana Anthony's Garden, Kauri, Whangarei, New Zealand.

planting patterns and garden features of the past in a broad, wooded valley which, for all one can tell, had never been visited by the garden's designer, Soka University in the Santa Monica Mountains near Los Angeles opts for a garden in which the themes and plants used are based on local plant communities of oak woodland, chaparral and coastal sage scrub. Plants and the methods used are chosen to match the needs of individuals in different places, and the conditions in which they garden, rather than some carry-over of Edwardiana from a distant land.

The developing interest in the new garden flora forces us to take another look at hallowed gardening principles, and review the opportunities plants offer garden designers. The introduction of proteas and their hybrids into gardens in their native South Africa as well as in Australia, California and New Zealand, has done more than present gardeners with new versions of evergreen shrubs. The aversion of these plants to even moderate levels of phosphates in soils, their sensitivity to disturbance of their roots and competition from other plants, forces gardeners who want to grow them to abandon traditional techniques of high-fertility gardening, forking between shrubs and composing mixed groups of different kinds. The introduction of cabbage trees and flaxes from New Zealand to gardens in many parts of the temperate world has provided novel plant forms of a kind not available before to garden designers and border composers. The interest in North America, Holland, Germany and other parts of Europe in establishing semi-natural communities in gardens based on the native flora or on plants carefully chosen to match their origins with conditions in the garden has led to new ways of looking at gardens and appreciating what they have to offer. These require major changes in perception from those accustomed to the carefully composed and often stilted forms of traditional styles of planting.

We are accustomed to borders and other forms of planting consisting of plants of many origins brought together solely for their visual impact – the ways the colours of the flowers match or contrast; the impact of their varied forms and foliage. We are less conversant with the effects of planting together those that share common qualities which enable them to do well in the particular conditions of the places where they are grown. Matrix planting aims to develop self-sustaining communities of plants based on a matrix of roots, stems, foliage and flowers, which provides protection for its members and resists invasion by outsiders. The guiding principle behind this book is that gardening is simplified by working within the limitations of the places where we garden. This might seem so obvious that it does not need to be stated, but it marks a decisive departure from the creed that underlines traditional gardening, based on the deployment of skills intended to enable gardeners to grow almost any plant almost anywhere, whatever the natural adaptations and preferences of the plants themselves.

Matrix planting calls for entirely different skills. It aims to use plants as allies that occupy ground and the space above it so effectively that intruders cannot find a way in – in a way that is as appropriate to the setting of the garden, and as decorative as possible. Because it is modelled on the ways plants grow naturally, it is easy to conclude that it is a style of planting designed for use with native plants or wildflowers, and therefore not applicable to garden plants in more ordered garden settings. That is not so: as we have seen, all garden plants are wild plants under the skin, and any plant can be planted in combination with others with the intention of forming a self-sustaining community. There is no reason why these principles should not be applied to almost any garden setting.

These aims spell redundancy for well-tried methods and tools. Hoes, rakes and forks have no part to play in disturbing soil between plants. The spade is no longer the inevitable, or even desirable, means of preparing ground before planting. The use of fertilizers before and after planting, and the control of pests and diseases with pesticides are more restricted, and even likely to be harmful. Plants and the communities in which they grow become the agents through which control is exercised – and in the pages which follow, a great many plants are mentioned by name.

Plant names always raise problems. Vernacular names are imprecise and open to misinterpretation, especially when used in an international context. Latin names are precise but can be intimidating, and in some situations

IIA

IIB

look stilted or pretentious. In this book I have used vernacular names freely in the text. To resolve confusion, for example between the British cowslip, *Primula veris*, and the American, *Caltha palustris*, the Latin equivalents of all common names used appear in the index. In tables and in the lists of plants used in the examples of gardens I have stuck to Latin names. Almost all these follow the nomenclature used in the *Plant Finder*, following the 1995/96 edition published by the Royal Horticultural Society. In a few cases, where familiar, old friends seem to me to be disguised beyond recognition by new names, I have added the older name in brackets.

Few of the plants referred to are described in detail, and some readers may feel they are being offered a feast of good food – all in cans – without a can-opener. However, there is no need to rise hungry from the table, and their predicament is easily solved. Descriptions of every plant would have submerged the message of the book beneath a redundancy of information – a redundancy, because information about almost every plant that is mentioned here can already be found, at whatever level of detail is needed, in countless encyclopedias, monographs and manuals. In addition, other garden writers have provided personal and often graphic impressions of a host of plants:

Reginald Farrer – vividly;
Gertrude Jekyll – artistically;
E. A. Bowles – eruditely;
Marjorie Fish – beguilingly;
Christopher Lloyd – elegantly;
Frederick McGourty – humorously;
Beth Chatto – naturally;
Rosemary Verey – perceptively;
Anne Lovejoy – intuitively;
Penelope Hobhouse – familiarly,
and Graham Thomas – authoritatively.
What untapped qualities of wit or wisdom could I hope to bring to a field already so well supplied?

11C

11D

11A, B, C & D. Effective matrices consist not only of several tiers of vegetation, but of plants which occupy space at different times of the year. Multi-tiered combinations of trees, shrubs and ground cover (left), including evergreen and deciduous species, form the strongest matrices. Shrubs, such as roses (right), grow through dense, interlocking mats of perennials. Hydrangeas and fuchsias planted amongst spring-flowering woodland perennials (opposite top) develop into an upper tier of the matrix later in the season. Perennials, alone, form more fragile matrices, like this combination (opposite bottom) in which rodgersias grow through and over bluebells and trilliums. Van Dusen Botanical Garden, Vancouver, British Columbia, Canada. De Kempenhof, Zeeland, The Netherlands. Bev, Stuart & Susan Davison's Garden, Auckland, New Zealand. Savill Gardens, Windsor Great Park, Berkshire, England.

Chapter three

Control in the garden

Plants are the vocabulary we use to express our dreams or create an atmosphere in gardens. Picked impulsively from garden centre displays, they are no more likely to create the effects we want than words chosen at random from a dictionary. On a Sunday afternoon's tour of garden centres, a golden-leaved hosta and a dahlia with crimson foliage and bright-red flowers tempt us to buy; we pick up three pots of aubrieta going cheap after their flowers have faded, and take away a conifer on a promise that it is the perfect thing to screen us from a neighbour's view. Skin-deep eye appeal, inability to resist 'bargains', and belief in promises of quick solutions – that is how we all start buying plants. Finding places for this little collection in the garden is like trying to make a sentence from 'elephant' because we like the word, 'iridotomy' because the sound intrigues us, even though we are baffled by its meaning, and 'manufacture' and 'bread' because they sound reassuringly useful.

We use qualifying or linking words to connect collections of nouns and verbs like these together and define the relationships of one with another. Natural plant communities, are also formed in structured ways in which different members have different roles. Some play prominent parts; others are unobtrusive fillers of spaces. Some will come and go with the seasons; others will be permanently visible. Prominent, eye-catching plants may be chiefly responsible for immediate impressions, but those that are woven between them are no less essential for the long-term success of the community and the atmosphere of the garden.

Matrix planting aims to construct a syntax in a garden, unlike, for example, a herbaceous border, in which the plants, arranged perhaps by size or colour, all have essentially the same value – each intended to contribute equally to the impact of the border, without lesser plants that fulfil linking and qualifying roles, fill spaces, extend the season and provide a background to the display. The plants we use will depend on the places where we garden, and on our inclinations and interests, but many parts of the world, and many different gardeners share a broadly similar vocabulary based on relatively tolerant, adaptable plants that have proven to be amenable to cultivation without special skills or the need for elaborate or specialized facilities. These are the plants, and theirs is the vocabulary on which this book is based. Numerous dialects – often almost incomprehensible to those who are not dedicated to alpines, orchids, the mysteries of xeric gardening, cacti and succulents – are more rarefied, and enter the syntax of matrix planting only in unusual situations.

Successful planting depends on a simple equation:

$$People \times Place = Planting$$

'*People*' is us (domestic harmony improves when we include the family) and what we need. Neighbours may expect every plot to be a garden. Convention may suggest a lawn, a patio, a border here, and a carefully placed small tree there – not forgetting a screen for the dustbins. Your spouse may insist on a pergola, yearn for a conservatory or a pool, and demand space for the children to play. In no time at all, the space around the house has become a garden of a particular, familiar kind that follows a general and civilized view of what a garden should be. Before that happens, reflect on your

12A & B. This variation on the herbaceous border theme (opposite top) is like a sentence composed of nouns and verbs. Each plant makes an equal contribution to the display and plays the same role in the community. It is an open invitation to weeds. The plants beside the path (opposite bottom) weave a matrix like a sentence in which major words are qualified by lesser, linking words. Plants mingle together, some stand out, others weave through the community, filling every available space and leaving no room for weeds. Savile Garden, Windsor Great Park, Berkshire. England. George Radford's Garden, Victoria, Vancouver Island, Canada.

12A

individual needs, limitations, or temperament, and your right to do what you like within that space, as long as it falls within the law, and hopefully, does not outrage neighbours to the point of conflict.

'*Place*' is where the garden is, and the opportunities and limitations that imposes on the ways it can be used and the plants that can be grown in it. You can, at your peril, ignore these pointers and insist on growing the plants you want, irrespective of their natural needs. After years of trial and error, sweat, tears and damning frustration, you might triumph at last and enjoy the spectacle of blue poppies flowering beside the Mediterranean, or burst with pride as friends admire your tree ferns arching gracefully over the Hudson river. Alternatively, you can try matching conditions in your garden with the places that plants grow naturally, and construct a garden in which communities come up, year after year, with few demands on your time or efforts.

12B

13A

13B

13A & B. Vivid displays of bedding plants (top) depend on annual digging, incorporation of humus and fertilizers, and careful spacing to ensure every plant gives of its best. Even in the more relaxed setting of a mixed border (bottom), the ground between the plants is forked over annually to root out weeds, and the perennials are repeatedly dug up and divided, in a routine in which control depends on periodic returns to bare earth. The Quarry Garden, Shrewsbury, Shropshire, England. Tedstone Court, Bromyard, Worcestershire, England.

The essence of gardening lies in control. Traditional gardeners rule in brutally direct ways, measuring success by visible evidence of the gardener's hand. Judges in gardening competitions expect lawns to be trimmed, with well-defined edges, hedges to be immaculately formed and closely shaved – all the better when imaginatively embellished by peacocks, pyramids or poodles. They like to see shrubs pruned and paths and borders kept scrupulously weed-free. Empty ground is dug over as much to maintain a neat and tidy appearance as from practical necessity, and the hoe is regularly used between plants – to destroy weeds, certainly, but also for the reassuring impression of authority produced by finely-tilled soil. Relax the controls, and unpleasant impressions of neglect appear as weeds grow, quickly followed by the disappearance of most of the garden plants. Clearly, we cannot make a garden by doing nothing. We must find alternative ways to control developments, such as the self-sustaining matrices through which plant communities survive under natural conditions. In brief, we can rule our gardens directly through the spade, the hoe and the shears, or indirectly through associations of plants that are compatible one with another, and with the conditions in which they grow.

The penalties of interference

Fashions come and go in gardening – driven by whim and novelty, but also by expediency. So, when the beach, or holidays abroad or the squash club beckon, we ditch the delphiniums, and plant easy-care day lilies to avoid hours of staking, tying, dead-heading, forking and slug-hunting. Then we discover that astrantias, geraniums, lady's mantles and Lenten roses also have certificates of proven self-sufficiency and add them to the day lilies. But, conditioned by our dependence on familiar, traditional methods, we start to fuss over them and tend them like the delphiniums, phloxes, sidalceas and lupins whose places they have taken. We set them out singly, or group them obediently in threes and fives, maintaining *cordons sanitaires* of hoed earth round every plant. When they meld

together, we dig them up and subdivide them to keep them in order. If the soil looks dry after three days without rain, we feel compelled to water it. We spray them with insecticides against nameless, imaginary pests, and sprinkle artificial fertilizers between them as offerings to the gods of gardening. We find so many things to do with our easy-care plants that we are faced with resigning our membership of the squash club, foregoing visits to the beach and curtailing our holidays – we might as well have stuck with our delphiniums.

What trifid complex lies behind all this? Why should gardeners be so fearful of independence in their plants? Spades and hoes are ruthlessly deployed as weapons of counter-insurgency whenever plants – cultivated as well as weeds – threaten to make themselves at home without servile reliance on artificial support. But plants take over only in exceptional circumstances. They exist naturally within controlled and self-controlling limits, within a framework of opportunity provided by the conditions in which they grow, and interactions with their neighbours in the community. Matrix planting sets out to reproduce conditions that impose similar limits, replacing control by the gardener with control by the plants themselves.

The first essential is *the plant mix*, based on species and cultivars that can share space compatibly, within limits set by the soil, climate, exposure etc of the place itself.
The second essential is *time*, during which plant communities grow together and develop a matrix of roots, stems, leaves, etc.
The third essential is *competition*, through which species and individuals ill-equipped to survive are eliminated, and the survivors establish a harmonious and balanced community.

Harnessing competition

Amongst the most notably invasive plants we sometimes kid ourselves we would like in our gardens is the yellow archangel, *Lamium galeobdolon*. Its variegated forms provide precisely the effect of dappled shade on a woodland floor that those with dim corners to illuminate long for. But unless you do not mind

your smaller shrubs and precious woodland plants being reduced to mounds beneath its shrouding foliage, you would be wiser to leave this archangel in the woods where it belongs.

Yet, within those woods, this is seldom a rampaging monster, but a plant that is rather vulnerable to disturbance, though scarcely a shrinking violet, and liable to be lost when woodlands are cleared and replanted. It is a natural occupant of shaded corners in my own garden amongst native stitchworts, wild roses and red campions, with woodlanders from further afield including tellimas, goatsbeard, dicentras, pulmonarias and bright-blue navelwort. It weaves amongst them; it does not smother, and each spring I welcome its pale-yellow chamois leather-coloured flowers.

Parkinson's Law, in a lighthearted expression of a serious economic principle, states that work expands to fill the time allotted to it. A similar principle applies to plants:

Plants expand to consume the resources at their disposal.

In reduced circumstances, plants may scarcely grow at all, though still managing to complete the essential processes of flowering and producing seeds. The effect can be seen when trays of annuals left unplanted long past their sell-by date – starved, barely watered and neglected – contrive to produce a few flowers, and eventually seeds, by recycling the meagre resources garnered by their first few leaves. Each one, set out, widely-spaced, in due time, in fertile soil and hoed and watered, would have been more productive than the whole starved trayful together. So competition between plants is competition for the resources which they need

to function properly and develop to maturity. These resources are:

Light – from which green plants derive energy. The more they receive, the more actively they photosynthesize and the more energetically they grow. Chlorophyll is the essential pigment in this case, but a variety of pigments, responding to other wavebands, control plant development in other important ways.

Nutrients – a dozen or so chemical elements are essential for the healthy growth and development of plants. Limited supplies in the soil have to be shared amongst members of the community.

Water – plant tissues function effectively only when hydrated. Under natural conditions competition for water is a major factor affecting the vigour, variety and nature of plant communities.

Oxygen – the fuel of respiration and the utilization of energy in all plant tissues. It is available more or less on demand to aerial parts of plants. Below ground level, the condition of the soil, the activity of worms and other fauna, and the presence and density of plant roots have considerable affects on availability.

Carbon dioxide – this combines with water during photosynthesis to produce sugars: like oxygen, it is more or less freely available to the leaves, and in most gardens is unlikely to be a competitively limited resource.

Orthodox gardening teaches us to dig, hoe, feed, water, and space out plants to ensure that each obtains its full share of these resources and grows into a large and productive individual. The yellow archangel in the corner of my garden, mercifully, does not achieve its full potential because it has to share these resources

Fig. 1. Matrix of trees, shrubs, perennials, ferns and bulbs
A natural woodland community provides the basis for the planting in this garden. The layered effects of plants growing above, beneath or through their neighbours create vital, constantly changing communities. The deep, three-dimensional matrix of trees, shrubs and perennials seen here ensures that there is always something new every day. In this view the layers are made up by:
a) an overhead canopy of kanukas.
b) a sub-canopy of immature kanukas, lancewoods and pittosporums, supplemented with planted deciduous trees like the young Norway maple.

c) climbing plants including Hydrangea petiolaris.
d) tall deciduous shrubs and small trees like Japanese angelica, flowering cherries, smoke bush amd flowering nutmeg.
e) evergreen shrubs including rhododenrons, hebes, schefflera and viburnums.
f) perennials at ground level include paeonies, euphorbias, epidemiums, tellimas and tiarellas, and shifting, self-sown carpets of forget-me-nots.
g) numerous woodland bulbs such as bluebells, camassias and daffodils appear before the lilies.
h) ferns and mosses.

14B

14A

with neighbouring woodland herbs and the oak trees below which it grows.

Competition may be anathema to traditional gardeners, but in matrix planting it becomes the balancing mechanism through which neighbours share resources – a balance that works only within limits and under the right conditions. The geraniums, day lilies and dicentras that grow with the archangels are natural inhabitants of deciduous woodlands. In sunlit, fertile, well-watered garden borders, they could develop into impressive occupiers of space. In the shadow of large trees, their vigour is curbed as they compete for and share limited resources, and all survive – not as a few large and productive clumps or spreading masses of stems, but as an integrated carpet of relatively small plants.

Plants like these with similar lifecycles and seasons of activity compete directly for resources. However, plant communities are usually much more complex than this. The lifecycles and growth forms of individual kinds will complement one another; some members grow actively at one season, others at another;

some will exploit soil at deeper levels than their fellows. The result is a garnering and partitioning of resources that ensures a widespread distribution and also uses what is available very efficiently by diversifying the seasons when peak demands are being made. The plants in my woodland garden grow beneath fifty-year-old oak trees. They compete with one another, but to a large extent avoid direct competition with the trees. Their cycles of root growth and development in late summer and autumn occur when the roots of the oaks are least active; they produce their foliage when the leaves have fallen from the oaks, and flower in late spring just as the oak leaves begin to expand – completing the processes most dependent on light before the leaf canopy overhead develops. They cannot entirely escape competition, and it remains a moderating influence on the extent to which they can grow, but they can reduce its intensity, and while doing so, take advantage of the shelter and protection of the trees through the winter.

But what on earth has all this to do with all those millions of gardens which bear no resemblance to a wood at all? Throughout this book, comparisons will be drawn between familiar garden features and the places where

14A & B. The woodland flowers on the right form a tight-knit community in which forget-me-nots are short-term occupants of spaces, and more perennial plants intermingle in a competitive balance which keeps them all in check. On the left, the gardener exercises control based on herbicides, which have been used to restrict the plants to reassuringly manageable, groups. Knightshayes Garden, Tiverton, Devon, England. Red Lion House, Horderley, Shropshire, England.

wildflowers grow naturally. Many gardens have lawns, some have meadows – the affinities of both with natural grasslands are obvious. Herbaceous borders seem to be giving way to so-called 'mixed borders' – a combination that can be compared with the communities of shrubs, grasses and herbs known as scrub; rockeries provide modest imitations of alpine peaks; gravel gardens, garden pools and herb gardens introduce elements of mountain screes, wetlands and the Mediterranean garigue or Californian chaparral, and the shaded space beneath a tree brings woodland into a garden. Even the smallest garden has room for one tree – when carefully chosen, for several. Neighbour's trees that overshadow boundaries and defeat attempts to grow plants in borders become assets when the space is filled with woodland plants. The pergola above the patio, the hedge along the boundary, and the sides of the garden shed create strips of woodland edge within their shadows.

Managing weeds

Cowslips grow in a flower bed by my back door. They attracted the attention of a friend, who looked intently at them, at first with interest and then, as though venturing to express a forbidden thought, turned to me and said, 'Aren't those things weeds?'

Proper gardeners maintain two mutually exclusive lists. One bears the names of the select – the plants which figure in regular gardening books and qualify for approval as 'Garden Plants'. The other is a catalogue of the damned – numerous recognized weeds, anything which grows wild, anything which has not been seen before, and anything which crops up spontaneously and causes surprise. Lumped together and labelled 'Weeds', good gardeners blush when caught in their company. But one day they find themselves making excuses and saying, 'Well, it may be a weed but it's quite pretty, and seems to be doing no harm – so I thought I'd leave it for now.' Gradually, excuses for accepting plants which hitherto were instantly condemned become more frequent and more ingenious, and one plant after another slips from one list to the other or hovers uneasily

between the two. Eventually, this schizophrenic situation seems to be resolved by the discovery of the well known dictum:

'A weed is a plant in the wrong place.'

If so, any plant growing where we happen to like it – whether we put it there or it just appeared – is growing in the right place. It is not a weed, and *can* (should be!) left where it is. When we object to its presence for any reason – and it might be a garden plant which has outstayed its welcome – it is in the wrong place, and should be destroyed.

So far so good, but no sooner has the undear departed been dumped on the compost heap than its space is filled by another plant, and we have to decide whether that is right or wrong. We can spend many happy hours, year after year, destroying 'plants in the wrong place', as one generation of weeds succeeds another in the spaces we have prepared for them. Essentially, a place is a space; an open invitation to weeds, and it is more constructive to think about weediness than split hairs trying to define a weed.

The recognition that our gardens are *weedy when spaces are filled by plants we do not want* is the key to successful weed control. The answer is to replace plants we do not want with those we do – and as one hand stretches out to pull up a weed, the other should be holding an approved successor to take its place. Sometimes the season and conditions may be just right for planting or we happen to have a suitable replacement. But an opportunist, piecemeal approach like this could raise more problems than it solves. More radical and more purposeful approaches could serve us better.

Dealing with weediness

We can tear weeds out by hand. It will take a long time to cover much ground, and dandelions, ground elder, onion weed and oxalis seem to find it rather stimulating, but direct action of this sort appeals to those who like to see results – and many gardeners find it a soothing, relaxingly therapeutic way to spend

15A

15C

15D

15B

time. We can make for the tool rack and arm ourselves with a hoe. Hoes are pleasant to use, and if you possess several different kinds, you can experience several different pleasures. They can cover a great deal of ground remarkably quickly, and produce a satisfyingly professional-looking result. But the fine tilths they leave in their wakes make comforting beds for seedlings, and a familiar green haze will cover their surfaces soon after the first shower of rain. We can resort to chemical warfare – after all, paraquat has been dubbed the 'chemical hoe'. An approach of devilish cunning is to combine an instantly effective herbicide with another that acts residually; we can then watch the weeds that first attracted our attention curl up and shrivel in a few days, and enjoy the satisfaction

15A,B,C & D. A garden need not be in a wood to provide woodland settings. Trees in a corner (top left) form a spinney for the plants in their shade. An ornamental orchard (lower left) provides shaded spaces separated by grassy 'rides'. Bulbs and woodland perennials flourish in the 'woodland edge' beneath a pergola (upper right), and patterns of sunlight and shadow produced by walls, structures and shrubs (bottom right) simulate a woodland glade.
John & Susan Wallace's Garden, Taumarunui, New Zealand. Phoebe Noble's Garden, Sidney, Vancouver Island, Canada. Heale House, Nr Salisbury, Wiltshire, England. Newby Hall, Ripon, Yorkshire, England.

of knowing that for weeks, or even months, any others that germinate will be dead before we even see them. These are all short-lived remedies. None are radical solutions, and unless we use the time we have gained constructively, we can be sure that before long, act two of Operation Weed Control will simply be a repeat of act one.

Somehow we must break the cycle of space creation and space occupation. Mulches fill gaps and exclude weeds, and under the high-input/high-return conditions of a kitchen garden, can be economical and productive as a regular, permanent method of weed control. In less intensive situations, mulches are better used as stopgaps pending the development of a complete plant cover.

Every garden has its own weed mix. My first was saturated with annual mercury (known locally by the curious name of butcher's bacon weed), and it has never bothered me since. Elsewhere I have met groundsel, ground elder, shepherd's purse, popping weed, dandelion, creeping thistle and other members of the international brigade which crop up wherever ground is regularly turned over. Sometimes I have had to contend with more specialist plants like nipplewort, creeping buttercup and hairy vetch, and once, to my astonishment and discomfort, with the Roman nettle. This rare alien infested my kitchen garden in Scotland. Dealing with it was an unpleasant, painful experience until, to my delight, my particular colony of this rare plant followed others that had grown in Britain down the path to extinction. But whatever their nature, weeds exist as a direct result of what has happened in the past and what we do today. Change what is going on, and the weeds too will change.

We can hoe unremittingly between the vegetables for years on end, for decades even, and the hordes of groundsel, chickweed, sow thistles and fat hen seedlings destroyed each time may be no less at the end than at the beginning. But if we make the vegetable patch into a lawn, all those weeds will disappear. Their seeds continue to lie in the ground, but none grow amongst the turf that covers the soil. That sward will be infiltrated within a few years by hoary plantains, hop trefoils, white clovers that attract bees that sting bare feet, daisies, the ferny eruptions of yarrow, brown and yellow tufts of field woodrush, cocksfoot, Yorkshire fog and mosses. If you find these blemishes disturbing, you might let the grass grow long in the hope of turning lawn weeds into meadow flowers. But as the grasses grow, many plants that were happy under the mower's rule will disappear. Ribwort plantain, birds' foot trefoils and buttercups, hawkweeds, red clover and moondaisies, field scabious and lady's bedstraw will take their place. Crested dog's tail, timothy and other meadow grasses will replace the fescues that made the lawn. In time, we may overplant the meadow with trees to turn it into a spinney. Their shade will gradually suppress the grasses and wildflowers, and as these depart, brambles and wild roses will appear from seeds dropped by birds; old man's beard will begin to drape the young trees; stinging nettles will make an unwelcome appearance; ground elder, foxgloves, red campion, celandine and cow parsley will appear – from heaven knows where – and if you are lucky, primroses, sanicle, sweet woodruff and violets.

Change your gardening, and you change your weeds. The choice is yours – but few of us would be keen to design our gardens simply with the need to weed in mind. You may want to keep your vegetable garden; you may enjoy roses growing formally in their beds; the children would protest if you dug up the lawn. But if you want lawns and potagers, which make heavy demands on your time and energy, you can balance them with meadows and spinneys that can be left more to their own devices. When the demands of the garden become too pressing, and ways must be found to reduce the pressure – or move to a house with a smaller garden – you can take advantage of the strong matrices formed by mixtures of trees, shrubs, perennials and bulbs growing together to save you work, and eventually produce a garden that is almost self-sustaining.

Garden management

Matrix planting depends for success on the competition and interactions between one plant and another. The key to this kind of control lies in the choice of plants. Ill-judged choices result in excessive dominance by one or two species, and the disappearance of those that cannot cope. Well judged choices lead to the establishment of persistent communities of plants which are self-renewing, resistant to invasion by weeds and look attractive. But this is not a simple matter of planting and walking away – these matrices take time to develop, and depend on positive, rather than neutral management.

The twin aims appear to be so simple that I hesitate to write them down:
Encourage the plants you *do* want.
Discourage the plants you *do not* want.

You can achieve this by providing conditions in which the plants you do want can compete successfully with the ones you don't. Management is by manipulation rather than the brute force of hoes or forks, which destroy rather than encourage the development of matrices. No gardener with any imagination – or even the most unimaginative with any experience – expects every plant to survive, every combination to perform as expected, or even effects that looked good one year to look presentable the next. Initial plantings, however well conceived, always lead to surprises – plants which were thought certain to do well will fail, others which were included on an off chance may settle down unexpectedly well. Only you can decide how insistently to plant and replant those that make a faltering start, how actively to push forward management towards a particular ideal, or how tolerantly to accept developments as they turn out.

Familiar management routines that identify this as a weed and that as a garden plant become

Table 3.1 Nine point management scale for weed control

	Description	Management
1	An out-and-out weed with vigorous powers of regeneration and tenacity; clearly not wanted.	Must be singled out for destruction, and no effort should be spared to eradicate it as quickly as possible.
2	A plant that is out of place and would pose a threat to the planting unless kept under close control.	Successful methods of control needed to reduce/eliminate existing plants and prevent their regeneration.
3	A weedy, though not threateningly invasive plant that contributes little and is better out than in.	Complete control is unnecessary, but numbers should be reduced as and when opportunities can be found.
4	A wild or garden flower with attractive qualities appropriate to the situation, but with invasive tendencies.	Regular attention will be needed to remove surplus plants and reduce seed production or vegetative renewal.
5	A long-lived, tenacious plant, suitable for the site and capable of holding its own more or less unaided.	Little or no direct attention should be needed.
6	An appropriate plant, able to self-sow or regenerate, but likely to need some assistance to ensure its survival.	Support needed may include introduction of further specimens, reduction of local competition, etc.
7	A plant whose long-term survival will depend on infrequent but repeated care and attention.	Some preparation of of planting sites necessary, plus removal of competition in early years; possibly replacement of failures.
8	A plant dependent on regular attention of some kind for an indefinite period if it is to survive and thrive.	Attention needed may include periodic pruning, long-term reduction of competition, feeding, etc.
9	A plant that will grow successfully in the situation only if given repeated, time-consuming attention.	May require annual replanting, frequent radical pruning, or protective measures against pests and diseases.

16A

16B

16C

16A, B & C. Bold groups and the repetitive use of colour, form or texture are effective ways to introduce atmosphere, especially when the plants used have strong individual characteristics, such as the umbrella-like foliage of rodgersias (top), the brilliantly glossy leaves of galax (lower left) in a woodland setting, or the repetition of the plump forms of cacti (lower right). Abbotsbury Gardens, Dorset, England. The Garden in the Woods, Framingham, Massachusetts, USA. Le Jardin Exotique, Monte Carlo.

inadequate – especially in meadows, ponds, woodlands and other semi-natural garden settings. It becomes unproductive, often impossible to make simple distinctions between weeds and garden plants, and a more analytical approach to the roles of different plants within the developing matrices is needed.

In any planting scheme, there will be pernicious weeds to destroy; there will be desirable plants that need little attention, and there will be others which we have to pay to possess with lavish care and skilful treatment. There may be wildflowers we should like to encourage, and garden plants whose take-over bids need to be restrained. Management has to be based on the qualities plants possess, and their contribution to the garden and the developing community. Table 3.1 (see page 30) sets out a nine-point scale that provides a working guide to the development and maintenance of a matrix in a garden. Plants that conform to descriptions towards the centre of the table require relatively little management; those at the extremities require frequent attention either to keep them under control or to ensure their continued presence.

Forming alliances

Botanists long ago recognized the tendencies of plants to form communities, naming them after the most conspicuous or characteristic plants present. Gardeners need not be concerned about the passionate disputes over the minutiae which distinguish one community from another, let alone feel obliged to christen the patch of heathers by the back door an erecetum. It is enough if they recognize that plants can form stable, long-lasting alliances, and that the conditions in which they are growing will define which plants are fit to join the club.

The most significant steps towards building a community are the choice of plants and the way they are planted:

a) The plants chosen should be compatible one with another and with their situation.
b) They should be planted in a way which facilitates the formation of a self-sustaining matrix.

The knack of living together harmoniously is

the essence of compatibility – a simple enough idea, but a complex and challenging matter in practice. Until recently, few gardeners paid much attention to the situations where the ancestors of their plants grew naturally. Most plants, apart from extremes such as aquatics, alpines and the frost-tender, would do well enough provided the soil was well prepared and fertilized and they were hoed or hand-weeded from time to time to eliminate competition, and dead-headed or sprayed when necessary. Without this support, compatibility between plant and plant, and plant and situation become vitally important. We see this in an extreme form in gardens devoted to native wildflowers, but it also applies to much more 'domestic' garden features, like rose beds, mixed borders and the herb garden.

The developing interest in the use of native plants in gardens sometimes leads to an extreme purist view that favours those that grow naturally in the locality and condemns exotics. It seems an unnecessary restriction to me – and one that goes against the spirit of gardening – to limit the choice of plants to the native flora when we plant our gardens. Woodlands, meadows, ponds, etc. recur throughout the temperate world, each providing similar conditions,and each with its own muster of plants. There is no reason why grassland plants like liatris and coreopsis from North America should be excluded from garden meadows made in Britain, nor anything to be gained by confining the cimicifugas used to embellish a woodland setting in Connecticut to those that grow naturally in New England, while disregarding those from Ussuriland.

Establishment of a matrix

Ready-made woods, pools, meadows, screes or bogs are garden rarities. Most of us must make such settings from scratch if we want to enjoy them and, when first made and planted, these are less than pale imitations of the final result. The smallest pond takes time to establish a balance; newly-planted mixed borders favour pioneering species that will later give way to more durable alternatives; freshly-sown meadows change progressively for decades; whips and maidens, supported by a scattering of standard or even semi-mature trees, are not a forest this year, nor will they be in ten years.

We have to accept that spaces on plans labelled 'meadow'; 'woodland garden', 'mixed border', etc. reflect hopes rather than actualities. The character and composition of any planting changes as it develops and matures and we must allow for this. Annuals and short-lived perennials can sometimes be used as fillers in the early stages of development, dying out within a few years as the vegetation matures. Commercial mixtures of meadow seeds frequently contain poppies, cornflower, love-in-a-mist, larkspur and corncockle. These are not meadow plants but cornfield weeds that add colour and excitement (and customer satisfaction!) in the first year, and also serve as nurse plants, giving shelter and protection to perennials that take over within a year or two. Similarly, short-lived perennials from the woodland edge – foxgloves, rose and red campion, toadflax, fringe flower and columbine – can be sown beneath newly-planted trees to provide shade and shelter for woodland perennials, and hold grasses at bay, until the overhead canopy of leaves starts to develop. In mixed borders, sun-loving annuals like cosmos, hares' tail grass, spider flower, shoo fly plant and pot marigolds will occupy spaces between shrubs and perennials in the first year or so, and short-lived, self-sowing perennials including Jacob's ladder, Miss Wilmot's ghost, peach-leaved bellflower and violettas, can maintain themselves in suitable conditions – finding and occupying gaps in the matrix for many years.

The strongest matrices are not only deeply three-dimensional – made up of a succession of layers of vegetation through which sunlight filters, until at ground level there is enough only to support plants that can cope with very little light – but also four-dimensional, in the sense that different plants contribute to the matrix at different times. The most complete development of such matrices can be seen in woodlands, but that does not mean all gardens have to become micro-forests. Effective matrices can be formed by shrubs and perennials in mixed borders. Those who are convinced that no garden is complete without a rose bed need not sacrifice

their convictions, but can take advantage of the fact that roses inherit the rough, tough, pioneering qualities of their wild progenitors, which are amongst the first to infiltrate meadows – in company with thorns and brambles – and prepare the way for other shrubs, and eventually, trees. They need no coddling in segregated beds, but thrust their way above weed-excluding perennials including many geraniums, hybrids of *Viola cornuta*, lamiums, hostas and grasses.

The essential quality of a plant matrix is the occupation of space, through a spectrum that ranges from the multi-layered canopies of forests to single, ground-covering layers no more substantial than a spreading mat of pearlwort or mosses. These latter make fragile matrices, and in gardens they need special conditions to be effective, but between the two extremes we have endless options open to us. Shrubs can emerge like islands, surrounded by a sea of perennials; perennials can be planted to interlock like jig-saw puzzles, or as intimate mixtures of foliage and flowers; underplantings of bulbs occupy spaces amongst deciduous plants during winter and early spring; tussock (bunch) grasses can be interplanted with annuals and bulbous plants; sub-shrubs and mat-forming perennials can be combined to contour-carpet the ground on banks and rocky slopes; ferns will colonize densely dark corners close to buildings or under evergreens.

Maintaining the balance

In an ideal world, the choice of plants and the manner of their planting would be so well contrived that they would inevitably proceed to form self-sustaining communities. There are situations and combinations of plants where that can and does happen. More often, some intervention is needed to maintain a balance. This balancing act may seem a precarious form of gardening, but it is not an unfamiliar idea. Lawns provide a commonplace example of matrices, in which complex mixtures of grasses, wildflowers and mosses live together without any question of hoeing or forking between the plants. The balance in these communities is kept

MATRIX PLANTING

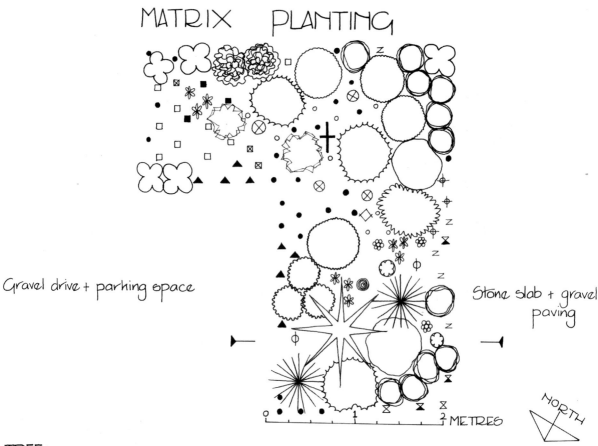

Gravel drive + parking space

Stone slab + gravel paving

METRES

NORTH

TREE:

✝ Rhus typhina

SHRUBS + EVERGREEN PERENNIALS:

⚡	Arabis ferdinandi-coburgii Variegata	3
❀	Bergenia Abendglocken	5
❁	Fuchsia versicolor	3
❀	Hebe Country Park	3
❀	Hebe Pagei	2
❁	Helleborus argutifolius	2
◎	Lavandula Munstead	11
◯	Salvia officinalis	2
•	Saxifraga umbrosa	26
◯	Spiraea Anthony Waterer	4
⋈	Stachys byzantina	2
✳	Yucca filamentosa	1

GRASSES + HERBACEOUS PLANTS:

✿	Achillea Cerise Queen	2
○	Aquilegia McKanna Hybrids	6
z	Chamaemelum nobile Flore Pleno	4
▲	Dicentra Stuart Boothman	8
⊗	Digitalis purpurea	4
▱	Geranium cantabrigense	3
▫	" dalmaticum	6
⊠	" ibericum	3
■	" Kashmir White	3
◇	" psilostemon	1
✳	Helictotrichon sempervirens	2
◎	Knautia macedonica	1
φ	Sedum Autumn Joy	2
⟊	" Ruby Glow	2
✿	Verbena bonariensis	3

BULBS:

✳	Tulip White Triumphator	5
	Lilium Regale	1
	Allium sphaerocephalum	5
▱▢⊠○⊗	Scilla bifolia	10
	Narcissus Tete a Tete	10
	Tulip Red Riding Hood	10
✿	Allium christophii	3
	" sphaerocephalum	5
φ	Tulip Scarlet Baby	10
✿	Tulip Westpoint	5
◎	Allium sphaerocephalum	5

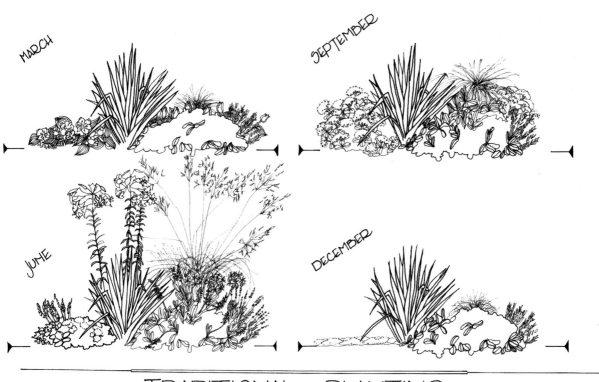

TRADITIONAL PLANTING

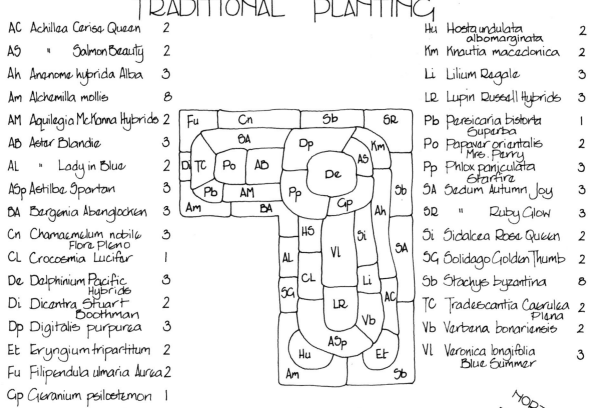

AC	Achillea Cerise Queen	2
AS	" Salmon Beauty	2
Ah	Anemone hybrida Alba	3
Am	Alchemilla mollis	8
AM	Aquilegia McKenna Hybrids	2
AB	Aster Blandie	3
AL	" Lady in Blue	2
ASp	Astilbe Spartan	3
BA	Bergenia Abenglocken	3
Cn	Chamaemelum nobile Flora Pleno	3
CL	Crocosmia Lucifer	1
De	Delphinium Pacific Hybrids	3
Di	Dicentra Stuart Boothman	2
Dp	Digitalis purpurea	3
Et	Eryngium tripartitum	2
Fu	Filipendula ulmaria Aurea	2
Gp	Geranium psilostemon	1
HS	Hemerocallis Stafford	2

Hu	Hosta undulata albomarginata	2
Km	Knautia macedonica	2
Li	Lilium Regale	3
LR	Lupin Russell Hybrids	3
Pb	Persicaria bistorta Superba	1
Po	Papaver orientalis Mrs. Perry	2
Pp	Phlox paniculata Starfire	3
SA	Sedum Autumn Joy	3
SR	" Ruby Glow	3
Si	Sidalcea Rose Queen	2
SG	Solidago Golden Thumb	2
Sb	Stachys byzantina	8
TC	Tradescantia Caerulea Plena	2
Vb	Verbena bonariensis	2
Vl	Veronica longifolia Blue Summer	3

0   1   2 METRES

NORTH

by routinely running the mower over them, and
that works very effectively, saving us the effort
of bothering about the individual needs of
different plants within the community.
Similarly, we are also quite accustomed to the
idea of mowing meadows to maintain the
balance between grasses and wildflowers, of
pruning shrubs to limit their spread and make
them more inclined to produce flowers, and
dead-heading or cutting back perennials after
they have flowered to encourage renewed
flowering or to give neighbours space. Selective
cutting back plays a vital part in balancing
competition within any plant community,
developing or mature. It can be used to:

Regenerate the plants – resulting in a flush of new
foliage, freshening their appearance and eye
appeal, and helping to maintain close ground
cover.
Reduce competitive effects of foliage – particularly
important beneath trees, but the stronger grasses
and broad-leaved perennials also overshadow
lesser plants, and annual reductions allow closer
and more diverse planting.
Reduce height at flowering time – cutting back
the stems of some of the late-flowering daisies,
including heleniums, sunflowers and
Michaelmas daisies when about half-grown to
make staking unnecessary and produce a greater
concentration of flowers on shorter plants.
Prepare the way for winter mulching – removing
mats of foliage in late autumn identifies the
positions of individual plants more clearly.
Remove blight-infested foliage – interrupting
cycles of infection, also reducing cover for

insects, etc., both beneficial and pestiferous.
Control the size of shrubs – maintaining the
production of new growth, and/or improving
flowering performance.
Provide a means of dead-heading – preventing
competition for resources between developing
seeds and other parts of the plant, or preventing
overenthusiastic self-sowing by ardent colonizers.

Controlling pests and diseases

Stock plants of alpines on my nursery used to be
grown on a rock garden, and at night, slugs
emerging from crevices would dine on the
shoots of the choicest. Eventually, these feasts
went too far; the area was saturated with slug
pellets, and for several mornings we collected
the corpses, quietly satisfied with our success. A
few months later, Kanji, my affectionate and
gentlemanly tom cat, died of kidney failure,
hedgehog droppings on the lawn became a thing
of the past, and the following spring, for the
first time in memory, no thrush's nest could be
found in the hornbeam hedge. By then the slugs
were back in strength, and continued so in ever-
increasing numbers until nothing survived on
the rock garden except the coarsest, hairiest,
most slug-repellent plants.

After that, I gave up slug pellets and
insecticides and fungicides of all sorts, and for
twelve years, in two quite different gardens, have
not used them at all. The shoots of my plants
are seldom laden with green fly; leather jackets
and destructive caterpillars seem to be quite

Fig. 2a. Matrix planting
This planting is an open, sheltered, sunny, front garden. There is
no lawn and no precisely defined drive or parking space.
Instead the garden is composed of gravel, stone and brick
paving combined with beds and borders. These are planted in a
manner which produces dynamic, constantly interesting effects.
The trees, shrubs and evergreen perennials provide a
permanent framework within which other plants produce
shoots and flowers, change colour and come and go with the
seasons. Some plants grow side by side as neighbours; others
grow through each other – e.g. bulbs are planted in the same
holes as compatible herbaceous companions. In this way the
dying stems and leaves of early spring bulbs are concealed by
developing foliage, and summer bulbs are supported and shown
off by the foliage of the perennial plants. Management relies on
restraint but constant attention throughout the growing season.

Fig. 2b. Traditional planting
If the bed was planted in the traditional manner shown in the
other plan – the effects produced and the management
needed would be very different. From early November to early
June there would be little to see. Everything would then come
in a whoosh – early spring growth would be accompanied by
urgent efforts to provide support. A blaze of showy summer
flowering would decline, into, with luck, a mellow autumn
display – but more often a descent into a matted, dank mass.
This incites premature and overzealous clean-ups and forkings
between plants and a sterile-looking winter garden, in which an
impression of neatness is the only claim to merit.
(See illustrations on pages 34 and 35).

rare, and slugs are no more than a passing nuisance on a few susceptible plants in spring. I am convinced that mixed collections of plants, like those used in matrix planting, do not need protection with poisonous chemicals to keep them healthy. Occasionally individual plants, or a particular species or cultivar, will be repeatedly crippled by an insect or fungal infection. Sometimes this seems to be due to their situation – they may be too dry or too shaded, and mulching, the removal of overhanging branches or a move elsewhere provides a cure. Sometimes they die and are replaced with something else. Otherwise, the plants are remarkably free from damaging attacks of any sort, and over the years it has become rarer and rarer to come across attacks by insects or fungal infections that could justify a return to chemical warfare.

'Biological pest control' is one of today's gardening ploys. We can buy mites to control mites, bacteria to destroy caterpillars, and eelworms to devour weevils – even fungi to attack other fungi. Farmers, having destroyed

the hedges that sheltered the predators of slugs, now construct beetle banks covered with coarse grasses to serve the same purpose. A perusal of the literature leaves the impression that biological pest control is a smart new idea thought up by scientists – but of course, it is *natural* pest control, and until we interfere, our gardens are the haunt of beetles, wasps, mites, eelworms, bacteria, fungi and other organisms which hunt, trap, infest and otherwise destroy most pests and diseases before they ever become a problem.

Natural balances between predators and prey are the best possible guarantee of a disease- and pest-free garden, and far safer and more effective than chemical insecticides and fungicides. But over and beyond that, the success of a plant matrix is fundamentally dependent on the well-being of the soil's fauna and flora, through which nutrients are recycled and the structure and profile of the soil maintained. Unwise use of poisonous chemicals interferes with the ways these function and destroys the foundations on which matrix planting depends.

17

17. Chemical control of pests and diseases can seriously damage the soil fauna and flora. Natural balances between predators and prey are the most effective ways to avoid problems in mixed plantings, supplemented, if necessary, by the recruitment of additional predators like this slug patrol. Erddig, Wrexham, Clwyd, Wales.

Chapter four

Down to basics: care of the soil

Anyone who has bought a house and garden will know the feeling. The hassles and traumas of Removal Day are over; the cat did not make itself scarce before the day dawned nor escape during the journey, and the first night has been spent in makeshift fashion. In the morning, after stepping gingerly through a muddle of possessions and packing cases, the curtains are pulled aside to reveal not a garden, but a bewilderness calling for attention. All but the incorrigibly insensitive shudder, draw the curtains and return to bed.

Newly-acquired gardens demand attention when our minds are full of the business of settling into unfamiliar houses, discovering unknown districts, finding new routes to work and feeling our way in untested relationships with neighbours. This is no time for urgent action: better to dream about possibilities and turn things over in the mind. Otherwise, we plunge too eagerly into the trite and trivial. We do not even need to wrestle with the problems ourselves – advertisements in glossy magazines offer computerized solutions for those seeking paradise on prescription.

Such concoctions are as personal as cans of baked beans – space-fillers, that will never satisfy your appetite for a garden of your own. Wait, first, to see how the patterns of your life develop in new surroundings. Second, to discover more about the garden's limitations and assets, and how these fit in with the things you like to do, and the time you have to spare. You can be as traditional or radical as imagination, time and resources allow. You can base your garden on age-old methods of tilling the soil, or manage it by approaches that depend on understanding the natural processes through which soil fertility is conserved and maintained indefinitely.

To dig or not to dig?

History relates that revolting peasants who had never heard of 'Here we go/here we go/here we go' chanted a moralistic little ditty about Adam delving and Eve spinning, before removing the Archbishop's head in their attempt to establish a people's proletariat in 1381. An unlikely story, but an illustration of the age-long link between gardening and digging. Spade, fork, digging stick or hoe – these and the plough have been the tools used to make successful gardens since gardening began. Forking between the shrubs in winter, regularly tickling the ground between plants with a hoe through the summer, and double trenching every patch of spare ground by

Fig. 3. Profile of a woodland soil

1. **Surface layer** Dead and dying leaves, twigs, animal droppings etc.
2. **Bacterial zone** Fungi, bacteria and small creatures break down organic remains to form humus. Dark in colour with a spongy texture and high organic content.
3. **Mixing zone** Activity of worms and other soil fauna mix mineral components with humus washed down from above. Usually a dark loam, maybe slightly acid due to rain water.
4. **Leaching zone** Mainly mineral particles from which nutrients and particles of clay are lost by leaching, especially under acid* conditions – often a light colour. (*Acid conditions may develop in areas of high rainfall, because rainwater contains weak solutions of carbonic and sulphuric acids. The effects are reduced by the presence of basic rocks which provide calcium, and most pronounced above acidic rocks, beneath coniferous trees, and in areas where temperatures are low and rainfall low).

5. **Accumulation zone** Clay particles leached from above accumulate and clump together, holding nutrients and iron washed down from above. This is where the major nutrient reserves of many soils are conserved – held at a level where they are still within easy reach of roots, deep enough to remain constantly moist, and within range of worms and other soil fauna.
6. **Subsoil** Filled with weathered and decomposing mineral fragments – penetrated by the larger roots in search of water and anchorage, but low in bacterial activity and usually relatively infertile.
7. **Bed rock** Acidic (e.g. granites and millstone grits) or basic (e.g. chalk and limestones). Penetrated only by the largest roots. The nutrients derived from the rocks dissolve in ground water and percolate into the layers above – contributing to their fertility, acidity/alkalinity and their qualities.

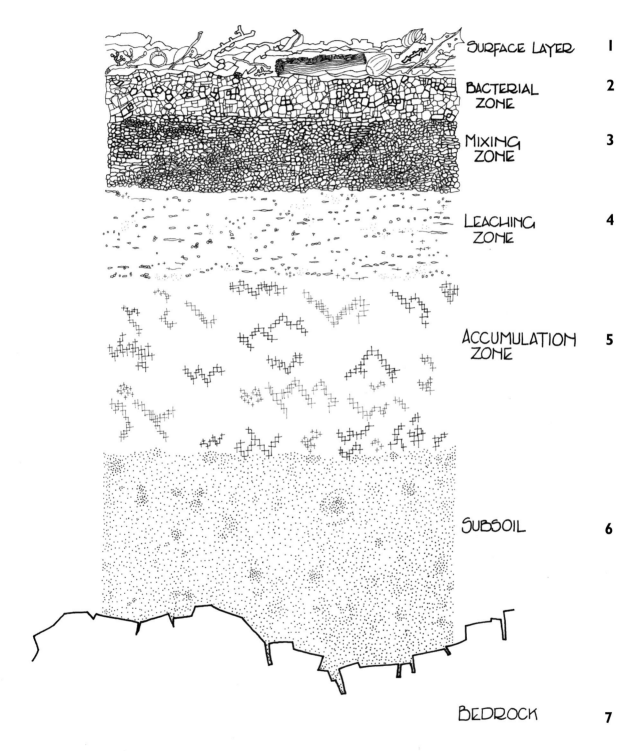

SURFACE LAYER | 1

BACTERIAL ZONE | 2

MIXING ZONE | 3

LEACHING ZONE | 4

ACCUMULATION ZONE | 5

SUBSOIL | 6

BEDROCK | 7

dawn on the day of the winter solstice are widely-accepted signs of the well-run garden.

But there are those who will tell you that these activities are unnecessary, adding that they are a waste of time and energy, because plants grow perfectly well without their aid; and warming to their theme, they will end by asserting that they do more harm than good. These are fundamental issues for anyone with a garden to look after. We can choose between a system that commits us to endlessly repeated cycles of hard physical labour, or a process that is much less onerous and more sustainable. The issue is a critical one for those who attempt to base their gardening on self-sustaining communities of plants because, once established, the matrices of stems and roots make it impossible to work between the plants with spades, forks, hoes or anything else. Other ways must be found to conserve the soil in a condition that will support the healthy growth and development of plants.

That depends on maintaining:

Fertility – This is a measure of the nutrients available in the soil. Under natural conditions, the level and availability of particular nutrient elements varies widely. Traditionally, gardeners aim to produce soils with high levels of nutrients, all present in so-called 'balanced' proportions – a shadowy term that indicates that plants are able to obtain what they want in more or less the proportions they need.

Satisfactory pH – The balance between alkalinity and acidity (referred to as the pH) of a soil is vitally important. Roots take up nutrients between relatively narrow ranges, and the availability of some nutrients is critically affected by pH. Soils may have a natural balance (they are more or less neutral), and display a resistance to change that makes them easy to manage. Others have tendencies towards excess acidity or alkalinity, and need careful management to maintain healthy growing conditions.

Structure – This vitally important quality refers to the way that small and ultra-small particles in the soil combine to form what are known as 'crumbs'. In poorly-structured soils, clay and silt form layers so compact that they are almost impenetrable to water and roots.

Drainage and water-holding capacity – 'Free-draining' and 'water-retentive' are descriptions frequently used approvingly in relation to soils. This apparent contradiction in terms depends on a well-developed structure in which particles of clay and humus are aggregated together by physical forces to form irregularly shaped crumbs within which nutrients and water are conserved, and between which water and air move freely.

Aeration – Roots need oxygen, and cannot grow without it. They obtain it from air diffusing through the soil from the surface. Adequate diffusion depends on spaces between the particles of soil – the result of a good crumb structure – or the presence of large particles of sand, grit or small stones, between which air can diffuse and products of respiration like carbon dioxide and ethylene can disperse before reaching harmfully high concentrations.

Well-being of the soil fauna and flora – The soil fauna and flora, ranging from bacteria to earthworms, are the key to well-structured, fertile soils. Their activities break down plant and animal residues and recycle them as nutrients, or build them into the soil as humus.

A perfect soil might be defined as one that contains a complete range of nutrients in readily available forms; and is water-retentive, free-draining, deep, homogeneous and neutral.

Digging – especially when practised as double trenching – attempts to reduce the natural diversity of soils to a common mean, and aims directly at this ideal. It is a mechanical process which is part of a system intended to maintain fertility by regular additions of nutrients – organic, inorganic or both, depending on preference – and to counter tendencies towards increasing acidity by applications of lime or chalk when necessary. Crumb structure is maintained by digging in partially decayed – usually described as 'well-rotted' – organic matter each year. Aeration and drainage are promoted by turning over, loosening and breaking up the surface soil, at least to a depth of 20 cm (8 in), and to three times that depth in the gardens of the most enthusiastic delvers. The reward is a soil which is as independent as can be from the variations produced by natural conditions, in which plants naturally adapted to widely varying conditions – maize, asparagus, cabbages and lettuce, for example – can be set out side by side in rows with every hope of success.

Non-diggers aim to modify and improve soils, rather than change them totally. Fertility is maintained, by applications of fertilizers, but these are likely to be used in different forms, less frequently, and in lesser quantities than by those who dig. Regular applications of organic matter are used in a less decayed condition and spread over the surface of the soil, relying on the activity of the soil fauna and flora to break them down and eventually incorporate them in the soil below. Soil acidity is balanced by applications of minerals containing lime – often in forms which release it relatively slowly, rather than as an immediate boost. The overall aim is a progressive, steady incorporation of organic matter and nutrients to form a soil that is not only well structured but varies at different depths below the surface – unlike the homogenized effects produced by digging. Nutrients released by decay in the upper layers move down to, and are held in the lower layers, where they are conserved and become available for uptake by the plants' roots. Fertility may seldom, or never, reach the peaks attainable by fertilizing and digging, but under good management, it remains at more steady levels fully capable of supporting plant growth. Aeration is favoured by a residual layer of open, undecayed organic matter on the surface of the soil, and by undisturbed channels to deeper levels produced by the tunnelling of worms and the disintegration of roots. The soil fauna and flora play a major part, and the lack of disturbance, and regular inputs of organic matter, encourage a diverse and very active community.

Foundations of soil fertility

Plants absorb nutrients dissolved in water in the soil, and insoluble forms of phosphorus, nitrogen, potassium and other vitally important nutrients are of little use to most plants, though they may provide reserves for future use. But nutrients in solution can be carried away in water and eventually lost to rivers or reservoirs of ground water far beyond the reach of roots.

This loss goes on all the time and is known as 'leaching'. It would have catastrophic affects on soil fertility but for the fact that most soils contain particles that hold nutrients by physical forces that prevent them being washed away. This is possible because nutrient minerals occur in one or other of two forms: Some, for example calcium, potassium, magnesium, ammonium and iron, exist as positively-charged *cations* that bind to negatively-charged particles in the soil. Others, for example phosphorus, nitrate nitrogen, and sulphur, exist as negatively-charged *anions* that bind to positive charges. Stones, sand and silt carry few effective charges, and do little to prevent loss of nutrients through leaching. Clays and humus are the vital components which lock on to nutrients and conserve soil fertility.

Care of the soil

Recipes for fertile, easily-managed soils contain sands, silts and clays combined with humus. These form the rich, responsive mixtures we call *loams*. Throughout much of Europe, the eastern parts of the United States, Japan and large parts of China, the natural soils are loams of one kind or another originally nurtured beneath deciduous forests. These areas – so significant to gardeners – have moderate rainfalls, temperatures high enough for much of the year to promote effective bacterial activity, and generally fertile soils. The processes which once fashioned them into the foundation which sustained the deciduous forests continue, and can still be called upon by those who want to make use of them. Nevertheless, we abandon spades at our peril, unless the natural processes we expect to do the work for us can operate effectively. In summary these depend on:

A supply of organic matter – This can be compost, or any other organic residue, spread on the surface between the plants. The amounts needed depend on the nature of the underlying soil. Light (sandy) soils and heavy (silty) soils need heavy, repeated applications to make significant improvements. Well-balanced loams containing 10–30 per cent clay, mixed with sand and silt, respond to lower levels. Established plants produce annual residues of organic matter from

Make-up of the soil

Soils are complex mixtures of minerals, organic matter, nutrients and living organisms. Their nature, condition and proportions directly affect the ease with which soils can be cultivated; the plants which grow on them, and the care needed to maintain them in a fertile condition. Table 4.1 details the constituents of soil, with brief notes on their origins and functions.

Table 4.1 Soil make-up

Constituent	Origin and description	Function
Minerals, including: stones, grit, sand, silt, clay	Result from the weathering and breakdown of rocks; may be acidic or alkaline, depending on origin; soils of different types derive their properties from varying proportions of these minerals.	Form the foundation of the soil and are responsible for its major characteristics, including: porosity, fertility, rate of loss of nutrients by leaching, liability to erosion, and water-holding capacity.
Organic residues, e.g.: humus, peat, plant and animal remains	Consist of the remains of plants and animals, either close to the surface, or within the soil itself; may decay partially or completely, depending on soil and climatic conditions.	Partially decayed remnants provide nutrients and hold water; humus is a product of organic decomposition, which alone, or in combination with clays, improves soil structure and the availability and retention of nutrients.
Inorganic nutrients, e.g.: nitrogen, potassium, phosphorus, calcium, magnesium, sulphur, iron, etc.	All derived from the rocks from which the soil was formed, except for nitrogen, which is obtained from air by bacterial activity; present as ions in the soil solution, and absorbed by plants through membranes of root hairs by a process known as cation exchange.	Nitrogen, calcium, magnesium, sulphur and iron are tissue-building nutrients; potassium balances ionic concentrations in cell sap; phosphorus is involved in energy transfers; calcium plays a major part in processes involved in stabilization of soils.
Gases, including: carbon dioxide, nitrogen, ethanol	The first three are obtained from the air and from the respiration and decay of living animals and plants; ethanol is produced by plant and bacterial metabolism.	Nitrogen is fixed by bacteria to produce nitrate ions in the soil solution; oxygen is taken up by roots and soil organisms during respiration, carbon dioxide by algae and green plants during photosynthesis.
Water	Predominantly from dew, rainfall or snow; ground water can rise by capillarity to 30 cm (1 ft) in sand and more than 2 m (6 ft 6 in) in silt; water vapour condenses on the cool undersurfaces of stones.	Provides the liquid medium within which nutrients and gases dissolve, are transported and absorbed by the roots of plants; the basis of life on which almost all living organisms depend; without it, the soil seems dead.
Living organisms: roots, worms, slugs and snails, insects[2], algae, fungi, bacteria	The soil microflora and fauna form a hidden world of mutually dependent, interacting organisms; some live only within the soil; others do so for part of their lifecycles or during particular seasons.	These sustain a balance between destructive and constructive activities in myriad ways, turn over and aerate the soil mass, recycle nutrients, improve soil structure and porosity, and maintain or build up soil fertility.

Notes: 1 This includes micro-elements (trace elements) including manganese, copper, zinc, molybdenum and boron, which plants use in minute quantities, often as catalysts in enzyme reactions.

2 Used here as an all-embracing term that includes a great variety of creatures other than insects, e.g.: springtails, mites, nematodes, crustaceans, etc.

falling leaves, decaying stems and roots that may
be be enough to maintain well balanced soils in
good condition.

A vigorous and active soil fauna and flora – Top
dressings of compost and occasional applications
of lime, when necessary, usually produce high
biological activity in soils. The presence of large
numbers of worms, insects and other small
animals is a good sign, and the presence of a few
known or suspected plant pests should not be
taken as an excuse to blunder in with poisonous
chemicals which have unpredictable and harmful
effects far beyond their intended victims.

Effective drainage – Most plants abhor
waterlogged soils, and particularly in the winter,
short periods of excessive wet kill many
otherwise fully hardy plants. Water fails to drain
freely for two reasons: (1) it has nowhere to run
to; (2) spaces are clogged by silt or badly-
structured clays, which prevent the movement of
water. If ditches need to dug, they should be dug
before any other kind of garden-making is
attempted. Badly-structured silts and clays can
be treated by digging in as much bulky organic
material as possible. This will produce
immediate improvements, but remedial
treatment must continue after the plants are in
position. No further digging or forking should
be attempted, but top dressings of compost and
lime between the plants will lead to increases in
soil fauna, particularly worms. Their passage
through the soil produces drainage channels, and
even more significantly, they ingest and mix
together calcium, humus and clay particles.
These mixtures are excreted and help to form the
open, crumbly structures which make soils easy
to work, free-draining and well aerated.

A source of calcium – Calcium is one of the
agents that bind clay particles together to form
clusters which are the foundation of a good
crumb structure. Soils lose calcium by leaching
due to the acidity of rainfall, but in soils derived
from alkaline rocks, it is replaced by natural
weathering. Neutral or acid soils lack natural
sources of replenishment, and levels will need to
be topped up from time to time by applications
of lime, finely-ground limestones or gypsum
(but see 'Calcifuge plants' below).

Managing acid and alkaline soils

Nowadays, when it rains, a host of organic
vapours, pollutants and fumes return to plague
us in that sinister-sounding potion, acid rain.
But rain has always been acid; only the degree of
acidity is new – and threatening. Rain from the
cleanest, most unpolluted skies was never pure
water, but extremely dilute carbonic acid, which
betrays nothing of its acidity to our tongues, but
is so powerful that it has been one of the great
shapers of our landscapes. Limestone and chalk,
both calcium-containing minerals and amongst
the most widespread building materials of
mountains, are dissolved by carbonic acid, which
destroys their structure and washes them away in
solution. Long after the rocks disintegrate, soils
made from their remains continue to lose
nutrients as rain leaches calcium and other bases
out of the upper layers, moving them down into
lower levels of the soil profile, where they are
bound on to particles of clay, which prevents
their total loss. The consequence is that the
surface layers of natural soils become
progressively more acid, particularly when a
covering of plants supplies a steady input of
organic matter, which itself produces acids as
it decays.

Digging prevents this increase in the acidity of
surface layers, but acidification occurs in gardens
where soil processing follows more natural lines.
That can be a good thing – under natural
conditions, the effects can be so marked that
rhododendrons, heathers and other calcifuge
plants sometimes grow immediately above
limestone rocks, their shallow roots confined to
the acid surface layers of the soil. This can
happen in gardens too, allowing calcifuge plants
to be grown above soils that are, potentially, too
limy for them to thrive.

But unless that is your deliberate intention, or
you garden on alkaline soils with a pH above
about 7.5, with natural reserves of lime, you may
need to counter steadily increasing acidity from
time to time with dressings of ground limestone,
chalk or other minerals that contain calcium.

Effects of acidity on soil fertility

Acid rocks tend to contain lower levels of plant
nutrients than alkaline rocks, and available levels
of some elements – including phosphorus and
manganese – are further reduced as acidity

18A

18B

18C

18D

increases because of their conversion to insoluble compounds unavailable to most plants. However, some acid-loving plants, for example lupins and members of the Protea family, secrete citric acid from their roots, which enables them to absorb phosphorus from these insoluble forms.

Worms need calcium to perform effectively, and bacteria and fungi function less well as acidity increases. In very acid conditions, the recycling of nutrients from the remains of animals and plants slows down, supplies

18A, B, C & D. Amongst the calcifuge plants that cannot cope with base-rich soils are many of the most glamorously splendid shrubs and trees, like rhododendrons and azaleas (top left), most magnolias (top right), proteas (bottom left) and waratahs (bottom right). Hergest Croft, Kington Herefordshire, England. The Arboretum, Westonbirt, Gloucestershire, England. Regional Botanic Garden, Manurewa, Auckland, New Zealand. Regional Botanic Garden, Manurewa, Auckland, New Zealand.

becomes restricted, and production may practically cease. Reduced bacterial activity inhibits the production of humus from organic remains, and these are only partially decomposed – peat is a familiar example, but leaves of trees may also hang in a limbo of unfulfilled decay.

Lack of humus, with its high cation exchange capacity, leads to the loss of nutrients from silty and sandy soils by leaching. Clays, deprived of calcium and humus, degenerate into poorly-structured minerals that restrict the movement of water and air.

This catalogue of ill-effects could lead to an unbalanced view of acid soil as a problem which any gardener could do without. That is not usually the case at all, as most people with gardens on acid soils who enjoy the pleasures of growing rhododendrons, camellias and heathers will testify. Many acid soils are light and easy to work, free-draining and rewarding to garden, but they also have their weaknesses and particular problems.

Calcifuge plants

Books warn us that rhododendrons are not for soils that contain lime – these plants, we learn, are *calcifuge*. In reality, they cannot turn and flee in the face of lime, but their leaves go pale, diminish in size and soon cease to be produced at all. Yet many rhododendrons grow naturally on limestone formations, and when that enduring plant collector, George Forrest, found them in Yunnan, growing out of the fissures in limestone rocks and on screes formed from piles of lime-rich fragments, he voiced his doubts about their inability to thrive in gardens where soils contain lime. Eventually, a series of trials were carried out to investigate this, but the results did little more than convince gardeners that, whatever wild rhododendrons might get up to, they do not do well in gardens on lime-rich soils.

The distinction between calcifuge and calcicole (lime-loving) plants is an ancient and significant one, deeply rooted in their evolution. It can be vitally important for gardeners too, especially in Britain, where many gardens are made on soils derived from chalk and limestone, and to a lesser extent, in parts of France, Spain and Italy. It is much less significant in the eastern United States, where limestone formations are comparatively unusual, and is

something which those who garden in Japan or New Zealand seldom need to think about.

In practical terms, calcifuge plants fail to thrive on soils rich in chemical bases, amongst which calcium (or lime, as a gardener would say) is usually by far the most common. But, like other plants, calcifuges do need calcium to stiffen their cell walls and play its part in cell division. The trouble is caused by chemical groups associated with calcium and other bases that reduce the acidity of water. Iron becomes insoluble as acidity decreases, and calcifuge plants can no longer take it up and use it as a catalyst in the production of chlorophyll.

The problem can be solved by using solutions of iron combined with organic molecules known as *chelates* (or *sequestrenes*), which maintain the iron in an available form under alkaline conditions. These provide an effective treatment when simply watered over the soil around plants on marginally lime-rich soils: more severe cases have to be treated by spraying the foliage several times a year.

Limy soils

Heather and azalea addicts cast by fate into gardens with lime-rich soils are amongst the saddest sights in gardening. At first, an inconsolable refusal to accept their loss leads to an exploration of the possibilities of making peat beds, or growing their darlings in containers. Desperate efforts follow, including rebellious sallies, and surrenders to the impulse to plant or be damned – pinning hopes on potions of iron sequestrene to restore green leaves to the plants they love so dearly. Despair lightens as winter-flowering heaths appear in neighbours' gardens, and realization dawns that there are heathers able to thrive in this damned soil. As the seasons bring renewed light and warmth, the diversity of the plants that fill the gardens comes as a revelation to those previously enthralled by heathers and dwarf conifers, and the flamboyant but limited charms of rhododendrons. They discover that the flowers that grow naturally on soils containing lime are at least as rich and varied an assembly as those to be found on acid soils.

The limestone floras of the world include: Many silver-leaved plants – including species of *Anthemis, Artemisia, Argyranthemum,*

19A

19B

Helichrysum, Lavandula, Santolina and *Phlomis*.
Many herbs and shrubs with fragrant foliage –
including *Calamintha, Cistus, Hyssopus,
Origanum, Ruta, Salvia, Rosmarinus, Satureja*
and *Thymus*.
Some of the brightest and most vigorous alpines
– including *Achillea, Alyssum, Arabis, Aubrieta,
Campanula, Dianthus, Erysimum, Gypsophila,
Pulsatilla, Saxifraga, Sedum* and *Sempervivum*
Some of the most striking shrubs – *Ballota,
Buddleia, Caesalpina, Clematis, Coronilla,
Daphne, Genista, Halimiocistus, Helianthemum,
Iberis, Psoralea, Punica, Spartium, Syringa* and
Viburnum.
Many of the most attractive wildflowers of
meadows – especially of the short grasslands
found in well-grazed situations on thin soils
above chalk and limestone.
Plants that in the wild grow only on limestone
formations (calcicoles) are almost all tolerant

enough to grow on acid soils under the protected conditions of a garden. They may grow less well where soils are acid, and many are more susceptible to adverse conditions – usually cold or wet – but they *can* be grown. Nevertheless, they are naturally adapted to lime-rich conditions, and this very often shows in the freedom with which they grow and flower, their longevity and their air of well-being, and the success with which they can be induced to form sustainable communities.

Some natural indicators of acid and alkaline soils in Europe

Wildflowers can often be used as a guide to soil acidity. Some conspicuous plants that are characteristic of acid or alkaline soils are listed below. Many of these are widely distributed throughout temperate parts of the world, and are useful indicators wherever they are found.

19C

19D

19A, B, C & D. Lime-loving plants – known as calcicoles – include cistuses (opposite top), the garden pinks (opposite bottom), bearded irises (top) and butterfly bushes (bottom). Almost all will also grow on acid soils, usually in sunny, well-drained situations, though they may then be less long-lived and less inclined to form successful matrices. Powys Castle, Welshpool, Powys, Wales. Godspiece Leaze, Norton St Philip, Somerset, England. Powys Castle, Welshpool, Powys, Wales. Red Lion House, Horderley, Shropshire, England.

Coping with clay soils

Clays exist in a world almost beyond imagination in which seemingly infinitely small particles dance in a complex of physical forces separating or combining one with another in ways which almost defy representation in familiar terms. Sand and silt particles are more

Table 4.2 Indicator plants

Acid soils: pH < 6.5	Alkaline soils: pH > 7.5
Aruncus dioicus	*Anthyllis vulneraria*
Athyrium filix-femina	*Campanula glomerata*
Calluna vulgaris	*Cirsium vulgare*
Campanula barbata	*Clematis vitalba*
Cytisus scoparius	*Cornus mas*
Dianthus deltoides	*Cornus sanguinea*
Digitalis grandiflora	*Dictamnus albus*
Digitalis purpurea	*Fragaria vesca*
Erica tetralix	*Galium verum*
Osmunda regalis	*Geranium sanguineum*
Oxalis acetosella	*Lactuca perennis*
Potentilla erecta	*Lathyrus aphaca*
Potentilla sterilis	*Ligustrum vulgare*
Primula vulgaris	*Lotus corniculatus*
Pteridium aquifolium	*Muscari botryoides*
Raphanus raphanistrum	*Origanum vulgare*
Rumex acetosella	*Plantago media*
Saxifraga granulata	*Primula veris*
Spergula arvensis	*Scabiosa columbaria*
Stellaria holostea	*Silene vulgaris*
Trifolium arvense	*Sorbus aria*
Vaccinium myrtillus	*Trifolium campestre*
Vaccinium oxycoccos	*Tussilago farfara*
Viola canina	*Viburnum lantana*

or less rounded, more or less impervious, more or less stable and more or less inert. Clays are none of those things. They have scarcely more substance than electrical charges, but arranged in layers stacked one upon another and cemented together by calcium and humus like bricks in a wall, they form the large and vitally important structures referred to earlier as 'crumbs'. Water molecules sandwiched between these layers cause clays to expand when wet and contract as they dry out. Clays are not inert, but super-active, and the most vital part of the

complex material we call 'soil' or 'dirt'.

Clay soils have:

Natural high fertility – due to their ability to retain nutrients, and prevent their loss by leaching.
High cation exchange capacity – making them very receptive to treatments intended to increase fertility.
High water-holding capacity – relieving the effects of drought on the plants that grow on them.

Clay soils can be fertile, open and a pleasure to work – though many gardeners may be surprised to read this – but deteriorate rapidly if neglected, and the sins of omission weigh heavily. The crumb structure collapses, and particles of silt pack the spaces between the coarser grains of sand, impeding the movement of water and air. A crust forms on the surface, preventing water draining away after rain, while the soil below remains waterlogged and airless. The recycling of resources, and the production of humus is reduced as poor aeration inhibits biological activity, leading to further deterioration in soil structure. Roots grow less vigorously, accentuating the effects of reduced fertility, leading to restricted plant growth and a downward spiral in the rate of accumulation and recycling of organic matter and nutrients.

Keeping on top of clay

A ride on Barry Brickell's railway into the hills above Coromandel in New Zealand is an entertaining way to discover the rewards and problems of managing clay soils. Originally designed to bring down clay for his pottery, the home-made trains of Driving Creek ascend a steep, narrow-gauge track between the shuttlecocks of tree ferns, and trundle on trestle bridges over deep, shaded gullies, as they zigzag up his clay mountain. Beside the track, and all over the hill, thousands of trees have been planted, and it is hard to believe that, following the logging of the kauri and rimu trees and the burning of the rest of the bush a century ago, this land was farmed for many years. Early in this restoration, kauri tree seedlings were planted into holes laboriously dug in the clay, and summers were spent struggling to bring them water – most died by autumn. Now the kauri seedlings are lightly dapped into heaps of decaying vegetation piled on top of the clay – they are no longer watered, but they flourish.

Digging in organic matter and lime is the traditional way to deal with clay soils. Alternatives, equally effective in their long-term results, improve clay soils bit by bit, starting with the parts that are most accessible to the roots; taking advantage of their high water-holding capacity, and thriftily conserving the reserves of nutrients which they hold. Organic matter is not dug in, but spread over the surface – the place where it is found naturally. This creates conditions which lead to progressive improvements by:

a) Encouraging the activity of the soil fauna and flora;
b) Providing an absorbent surface that does not form a crust, and avoids loss of water and nutrients by run-off;
c) Preventing the development of surface cracks by maintaining the water content of clay particles;
d) Restoring and improving soil structure by providing a source of humus;
e) Conserving nutrients by restoring effective soil structure and reducing loss by leaching;
f) Suppressing weed growth;
g) Maintaining aeration by protecting the surface of the soil from compaction by trampling or the effects of the weather.

Results depend on the generosity with which these surface layers of organic matter are spread. In new gardens and on unplanted beds, they should be applied lavishly – 30 cm (1 ft) of strawy manure is not too deep, and layers of compost, bark, wool waste, grass cuttings, or whatever may be available, should be spread as thickly as can be afforded – even straw or spoilt hay is effective. Plants can be set out directly into these top dressings, and as worms and other creatures carry humus and recycled nutrients into the clay layers below, the plants' roots will follow.

The leaves, shoots and roots of the plants themselves provide a source of humus as they decline and decay, which can be supplemented by annual or less frequent applications of organic matter, with additions of lime if needed.

A great many perennial plants (especially woodland perennials) and bulbs not only tolerate, but benefit from dressings of organic matter – proto-humus – spread over their tops while they are dormant during the winter. In the spring their shoots grow through deep layers of such top dressings, and fallen leaves, compost, strawy manure, etc. applied in this way ensures the long-term maintenance of soil structure, and the health and vitality of the plant communities that depend on it.

Management of sandy soils

Those whose gardens are mostly sand struggle to conserve water and maintain fertility. The most positive way to do both is to follow much the same approach as described for clay. Light, open-textured, sandy soils may be more tempting to dig than solid clays, but surface dressing is more economical and makes better use of organic materials than digging them into the ground. There will be differences in degree – for example, the surfaces of sandy soils are not easily compacted and mulches have little effect on aeration; nor will they increase the rate of water movement through the soil – on the contrary, they will tend to retain water and counter too rapid loss. Humus does not combine with sand in alliances that build up structure and retain nutrient ions as it does with clays, but humus itself retains nutrient ions and prevents their loss by leaching.

Sandy soils are infertile because nutrients are easily and rapidly lost from them by leaching. But their infertility is more fundamental than that. Often they consist of almost pure quartz, the last remnants of rocks which never contained more than low levels of the elements that contribute to plant nutrition. Unlike soils which contain stones and rocks, let alone clays, they hold practically no untapped reserves of nutrients. Applications of organic materials help build up nutrient levels: the addition of humus to the soil reduces losses by leaching; more effective recycling of dead leaves, roots, etc. by an enhanced soil fauna and flora conserves nutrients more effectively. But even allowing for these benefits, sandy or gravelly soils are much more likely to need regular additions of fertilizers than more balanced loams containing significant proportions of clay.

Effects of adding fertilizers

Applications of fertilizers can do more than simply boost nutrient levels. They can also effect:

a) *The pH of the soil* – lime and chalk result in immediate and rapid decreases in acidity, which can adversely affect calcifuge plants; less active forms, including ground limestone, break down slowly and result in smaller changes over longer periods. Calcium applied in the form of gypsum has little effect on soil acidity. Sulphates, widely used as sources of ammonium (nitrogen), potassium and magnesium, increase acidity. This may be beneficial, but on soils which are already acid, it can lead to loss of calcium and other bases, reduced rates of humus formation; deterioration in the structure of clays, and loss of nutrients by leaching, or conversion to unavailable forms.

b) *The structure of soils* – may respond to changes in pH, and increases or depletions in calcium levels in the soil. Chlorides, sometimes applied as economical sources of potassium, can adversely affect the structure of clays.

c) *The activity of soil fauna and flora* – this

20

20. These shrubs growing in dry stony soil in Western Australia are well adapted to make the most of such situations. Improving the soil would be no help to them, but would merely increase competition from plants less well equipped to cope with drought, low fertility and high temperatures. Management is often simplified by going for the right plants, rather than changing the conditions.
'The Wildflower Way', between Perenjori and Wubin, Western Australia.

responds in complex, often obscure ways to changes in pH, to nutrient status and the presence or absence of particular chemicals. For example, worms use calcium as a digestif for organic residues, and it is essential for their well-being.

d) *The relative proportions of nutrients in the soil* – these are directly affected by those applied in fertilizers, which have beneficial effects when used to increase levels of nutrients which are deficient, but a build-up of high levels of individual nutrients can reduce the availability of others. For example, magnesium becomes deficient when potassium is applied too liberally or too frequently.

e) *The nutrient status of the plants* – this is governed by ion uptake from the soil. Plants take up nutrients selectively and can function effectively in spite of widely varying levels in the soil, but many plants are 'greedy' for nitrogen, and high levels in the soil can result in unbalanced, excessively luxuriant growth.

Traditional vegetable and flower border gardening practises intensive systems of management with the aim of maximum productivity – an aim quite different from the more passive approaches of matrix planting, when overabundant fertility can be a problem. Plants can grow too well! A self-sustaining community depends on a competitive balance between its component plants, and the vigorous growth made possible by heavy applications of fertilizers produces specimen plants – little emperors – that overwhelm those unable to keep up, rather than integrating to form a matrix.

The desirability of increased fertility may be less clear cut in other ways too. For example, infertile, sandy soils are the natural habitat of many species, which are well adapted to cope with their problems. In similar garden settings, it is usually much easier to set up successful matrices by using well-chosen, appropriate plants than attempting to change the soil to accommodate a broader range. Before attempting to improve nutrient-deficient, water-restricted, sandy soils or gravels, we should ask ourselves:

Is high productivity – as in a vegetable garden – a priority?
Is optimal growth of individual plants the aim? Are we aiming for high-maintenance planting, in which success depends on constant intervention?

When the answers to all those questions are 'yes', the soil should be managed to maintain high levels of available nutrients: fertilizers will need to be added at an early stage and replenished regularly, and the easiest, quickest way to do that is by dipping into a bag – most cheaply and rapidly, into a bag of inorganic fertilizers; or, if you avoid the use of 'artificials', into similarly concentrated organic alternatives. Irrigation will almost certainly be needed during dry spells.

But when maximum productivity is not the prime aim; when balanced communities of plants rather than individual performance is the intention, and when a low level of interference by the gardener is the hope, then less drastic approaches are called for. This approach depends on more restrained and much more specific use of fertilizers from a bag – whether artificial or organic – and dependance on deep-rooted, drought-resistant plants that do not need, and like ceanothuses and Californian live oaks, may even be killed by overwatering.

It may be possible to rely almost entirely on natural sources of nutrients, such as the bacterial and fungal associations with roots through which many plants obtain nitrogen from the air, and phosphorus from otherwise unavailable sources. These associations are most familiar in plants of the pea family, but also occur extremely widely amongst other plants – especially under the conditions of matrix planting, in which lack of disturbance favours symbiotic associations.

Chapter five

Setting up

My brother once had a dog called Fido – a scrap of a thing, but, like other Jack Russell terriers, that was beneath his notice – and on his outings, he would court disaster by assaulting every large dog he met. His attempts at suicide failed because his 'victims' refused to take him seriously, fending him off with their chests, or kneeling on the squirming Fido until he was quiet. Eventually, while maintaining his right of way down the white line in the middle of a road, he met his match – a car that also lacked a sense of size, but had no sense of humour either. Gardens, too, are sized by attitude rather than area. They are small when time is ample, rather

than where space is limited, and grow large, whatever their dimensions, when we cannot control what goes on inside them.

That applies whether the garden is a new one, on a so-called 'green field' site (though there are likely to be precious few traces of green fields after the builders have finished their work) or a well-established garden with its quota of well-established plants. Houses with mature gardens can be dubious bargains, beguiling purchasers with promises of off-the-peg convenience. But what we buy is somebody else's garden – never our own. Our predecessor may have been a manic rhododendrophile, or a dedicated plantsperson whose pernickety, aristocratic beauties make demands beyond our skills. Perhaps we succeed a lawn addict who erased every crinkle, displaced daisies and dandelions, banished bitches and preferred to rake moss than go fishing. Sometimes, the trees and shrubs in the garden we buy have grown old and tired together. Their skin-deep beauty barely hides the need for drastic face-lifts to restore vitality and balance. Other people's gardens, like other people's clothes, seldom fit. Sooner or later, we have to accept that the finery is not for us. Then we discard it, bit by bit, or in one dramatic disrobing, replacing it with something we can slip into more comfortably.

The vision and ability to see when changes are needed, and the confidence to make them, are amongst the less widely recognized skills of gardening. Never assume that anything is where it is wanted, or should be left just because it is there. Nothing – including trees – should be sacrosanct because of a feeling that 'the previous owner must have had a reason for putting it there'. At best, most of the garden can be left as it is, and be made to fit with a nip here or a tuck or two there. At worst, established gardens are assets to be stripped.

21. Lawns create quiet horizontal spaces in gardens that set off neighbouring vertical features. But paving or gravel, or a pool, can do this as effectively, need less maintenance, and offer more scope to the imagination. Chateau Courances, Essonne, near Fontainebleu, France.

22A

22C

22B

First steps

Plants steal the show on television programmes about gardens, and in the alluring photographs we find in magazines, because they make wonderfully attractive pictures, and the impression that comes over is that gardens are places for *plants*. Plants are fine – when they are wanted – but first and foremost, gardens are places for *people*. Places to sit or stroll around, places to play or work, places to entertain friends or relax, to ride a bicycle, fly pigeons or breed

rabbits – places to do a spot of gardening even. The things that you and your family want from the space around the house that we call a garden should have priority; then fit the plants in according to your needs.

The starting point in most gardens will be close to the house – making a place to sit out to enjoy a cup of coffee, or for children to play; somewhere for breakfast in the morning or a G&T, a dry Martini or a share of a six-pack in the evening. First thoughts are likely to insist that it must be sunny, but shelter from the wind, and shade in hot weather are just as important for comfort, and lead to thoughts of screens and cover overhead – trellises and pergolas perhaps – on which climbing plants can be grown. Warm places close to the house provide settings for plants that would not survive elsewhere in the garden: somewhere to grow the tender perennials whose colourful flowers fill patios and terraces with colour for months on end during the summer. The shade beneath a pergola provides a woodland setting – and many of the woodland plants that are evergreen in winter, and flower in spring will do well there – complementing the summer displays of the tender perennials.

22A, B & C. Boundaries are too important to waste, but should enhance neighbouring planting, like this little arbour (top left) at the back of a rose garden, or a trellis (lower left) behind a mixed border, covered with clematis, honeysuckles and other climbers. A high fence treated as a woodland edge (top right) with a dense, vertical matrix of shrubs, climbing roses, bamboos, ground-covering perennials and ferns, is more interesting and provides just as much privacy as a monotone hedge. Shirley Beach's Garden, Victoria, Vancouver Island, Canada. Godspiece Leaze, Norton St Philip, Somerset., England. Phoebe Noble's garden, Sidney, Vancouver Island, Canada.

Next, think of the garden as a playground – for children certainly, but for adults too. Plants and play can be a troublesome combination. Sand pits and paddling pools create local wear and tear; their contents spread out, and toys accumulate in and around them. Ball games involve lethal missiles, flailing legs, hurtling bodies and dogs in hot pursuit that destroy fragile, tender or special plants. More ambitious projects like a netball pad, a tennis court or a swimming pool need ample space and freedom from unwanted nuisances like falling leaves or shade at the wrong times of day. These activities are incompatible with gardens dedicated to plants alone. It is better to take them into account, using plants to provide screens or shelter that resist or tolerate damage from balls, or are clean to live with – try planting oleasters, or many kinds of eucalyptus close to a swimming pool to discover what a nuisance falling bits and pieces from a tree can be! Bright and cheerful displays from plants in flower are likely to be less satisfactory than carefully-placed, well-chosen shrubs and small trees, particularly those that are evergreen, dense and compact. This should not involve sacrificing all that makes a garden attractive, nor need it be difficult to look after. Many of these evergreens lend themselves to strong structural effects, and their dense growth readily forms weed-excluding matrices with little help from the gardener.

The belief that lawns are the indispensable resort of children at play and adults at rest makes them popular. But other features in a garden serve these purposes as well, or better, and many lawns are never used in these 'indispensable' ways. They provide quiet, open, horizontal spaces from which to view the surrounding planting, and contrast with the vertical forms of plants, buildings and features such as hedges and walls. Other types of surface may be preferable when time for gardening is limited. Paving or gravel, even a broad path down the centre of a garden, are options that not only need less maintenance, but stir the imagination more seductively. Materials can be varied or combined; plants can be used between paving, in walls or planters, or in other ways, to create shade, localized spots of colour or contrasts between textures and effects. They also

provide all-weather surfaces, free from the problems of wet or frozen grass in winter, and they do not become dessicated apologies for a green sward in hot summers. Pools and garden ponds are another way to introduce horizontal surfaces, with all the imaginative possibilities they bring with them.

Privacy is valuable in a garden, and if we are to judge by boundary hedges and fences, many people are prepared to pay a high price for it – aesthetically if not financially. Field hedges are still exciting places, even today, after half a century of herbicidal sprays have done their worst, where shrubs, some with flowers, some with berries, some with glowing autumn foliage, combine with wildflowers growing in their shelter. How many garden hedges display such interest and variety? Too often they are mere screens, planted without considering their affects on the garden, their demands on maintenance or the alternatives available. The hedge bottom is written off as sterile space beneath the sterile foliage of Castlewellan gold or scarlet-leaved photinias, neglectful of the possibilities of hawthorn, blackthorn, dogwood and wild rose beneath which primroses, violets, wood anemones and other spring flowers will thrive.

It is perverse to choose to surround our gardens with dull monocultures and disregard the opportunities these mixed communities offer for changing effects throughout the year – a perversion carried to extremes when every boundary around a garden is uniformly treated, producing a dreary monotony that pays no attention to aspect, situation or viewpoint, and diminishes the impact of every planting by the irrelevant regimentation of its backcloth. Boundaries form the backdrops to the planting and in small gardens, in particular, are too conspicuous and occupy too much precious space to be wasted unimaginatively. Screening can be provided in many ways: with hedges, with fences, with trellises and arbours, with groups of shrubs and carefully-sited trees. Any or all of these can be deployed along a boundary to complement the planting and contribute to the matrix of the community.

My earlier comments questioning the importance of plants in gardens were made

23A

23B

tongue in cheek, disregarding the fact that the main interest of almost everyone reading this book will be plants and how to make the best use of them. Places to play and places to sit are all very well, but for most of us, the ways the plants perform make or mar our gardens.

Matrix planting starts with bare earth, but then aims to establish long-lived communities which knit together to exclude unwelcome outsiders. Traditional gardening techniques almost invariably depend on bare earth as an essential element in the processes of control. Growers of vegetables, annuals and bedding plants start and finish and then start again with bare soil. Less ephemeral forms of gardening, like herbaceous borders, are based on periodic renewals and a return to bare soil. The ground in rose beds and between shrubs is hoed or forked according to the season. The mounting complexities of the mixed border are once in a while resolved by wholesale clearances and new starts to reduce the strength of the strong and encourage the weak. Only lawns and meadows are managed without regular resort to open space, and even in these, the option to destroy and start again from scratch is often the first response to serious problems.

Yet most gardens are made in places where bare earth is a rare and fleeting natural phenomenon. The tight sward in communities of meadow grasses may open up after flowering – especially during droughts – to let in seedlings; and mole hills and ant heaps, worm

casts too, provide other opportunities for colonists. Spaces appear each spring amongst plants on the woodland floor, and are reoccupied as the foliage of established plants develops, or provide points of entry for a tiny proportion of their offspring to grow up and replace their parents. Land slips, floods or windblown trees expose ground which is quickly occupied by new plants, and in time develops a cover indistinguishable from the surrounding vegetation. But regularly-recurring expanses of bare earth are characteristic of places where intense droughts and periods of rain succeed each other seasonally or at more erratic intervals, and it is only in such places that natural events follow the traditional gardener's cycle of seeding, maturation, destruction and resurrection from the seeds of the previous generation.

Baring the soil

Digging destroys established soil profiles and structures, and disrupts natural balances within the soil fauna and flora. In established gardens where the borders have been dug for many years, a final flourish of the fork, a last delve with the spade in a fond farewell to digging will

23A & B. The bottom of a hedge need not be sterile space. Spring-flowering woodland perennials (left) grow happily amongst the roots of blackthorn, hazel, dogwood, hawthorn, hornbeam and other shrubs that make excellent hedges.

More exotic plants, especially busy lizzies (right), co-exist colourfully with ivies, periwinkles and ferns during the summer. Red Lion House, Horderley, Shropshire. England.

do no further damage. But it is not necessary, and in other situations is likely to be a backward step. The soil beneath a meadow, and even under lawns, will have horizons and structures that may be embryonic or very well developed. Soils may be infertile and dry beneath established trees – one of the bogey areas of gardening – but often have a good structure. The same goes for long-established, neglected and overgrown borders and shrubberies. In every case, the structure of the soils, and the integrity of their fauna and flora, should be preserved and built on, rather than destroyed.

Some preparations will be needed:

Clearing the surface – unwanted garden plants should be lifted and moved elsewhere, and perennial weeds destroyed with herbicides, or in other ways: sheets of black polythene used as covers can be very effective when time allows. Standard and worthy advice to destroy every fragment of perennial weeds should be followed, but it is dangerous optimism to act as though that were the end of the matter. Their seeds will still be in the ground, and they will return, if allowed, to plague you later. Outbursts of annual weeds may shame conscientious gardeners into their removal, but these have no long-term future. Conversely, it will always be necessary to maintain a sharp watch for intrusive perennial seedlings, and their destruction is a vitally important ploy in the development of a successful matrix.

Supplying organic matter – this aims to improve the soil structure, encouraging the soil fauna and flora and assisting newly-planted plants to establish themselves. This is essential for success in most situations, but especially when attempting to establish plants beneath trees. Anything that will break down into a source of humus can be used, spread in as generous a layer as can be afforded (in material and financial terms) over the surface.

Boosting soil fertility – this may be an urgent necessity or something that can be pursued gradually. The former calls for applications of fertilizers – either organic or inorganic – out of the bag. The latter may be satisfied by using sources of humus like garden compost, farmyard manure and other animal derivatives, such as cocoa shell, etc., which contribute significant quantities of nutrients.

Adding calcium – either to bring acid soils closer to neutrality, or to provide for the needs of earthworms. The most readily available source is agricultural lime; alternatives are chalk, which, depending on the size of particles, becomes available more gradually, or ground limestone – including magnesium limestone – which slowly release calcium over periods of several years. All these will raise the pH of acid soils, and can pose hazards for calcifuge plants, which can be avoided by using gypsum (calcium sulphate).

Planting patterns and rhythms

Like the cornerstone of a building, the placing of the first plant in a new garden or flower bed deserves celebration with champagne, the cutting of ribbons or discreetly muted fanfares of trumpets. It is the last chance to discard most of what we have been taught to do when planting a border, and think about the ways that plants form communities when growing under natural conditions. It is still almost standard practice to set out groups of plants in discrete blobs, though some follow Gertrude Jekyll's principle of planting in narrow drifts. Tall plants to the back, short to the front is a rule, but one that may be broken in the interests of added excitement. Few can resist packing in as many different plants as possible, rationalizing the diversity by attention to colour theming, harmonies and contrasts, and excusing excess on the grounds of a prolonged flowering season.

An oft-repeated gardening dictum proposes that we plant in threes and fives. The source and sense are equally obscure, and it is dubious advice even when applied to traditional patterns of planting. But plant matrices are not formed by plants growing in threes or fives, or even fifteens. Small plants grow naturally under and weave amongst the larger ones; relatively few kinds, but large numbers of each, combine better than extreme diversity, and, the ability to thrive in a particular setting is more critical than contrasts, harmonies and colour theming.

Matrix planting draws inspiration from the ways plants grow together naturally, but should not be a mere imitation of nature any more than maps are copies of the countryside they

24A

24B

represent. Map-makers adapt reality by simplification and organization; accentuating some features and eliminating others to produce a comprehensible, serviceable and agreeable result. The same landscape can be represented in a hundred different ways, depending on the intended use of the map and the art of the cartographer. Similarly, gardens depend for success on visual logic and intentional combinations of colours, shapes and textures that combine to form enjoyable – even inspiring – impressions.

Newly-planted borders possess no matrix of any kind, and invite occupation by weeds. However skilfully plants are chosen, and however effectively they will combine eventually, stopgaps are needed at first, either in the form of weed-excluding mulches, or as short-lived plants to fill space between more permanent residents.

Trees and shrubs can be grown to produce canopies so dense that no perennials – weeds or otherwise – can survive beneath them, but this mode of planting is usually the mark of neglected gardens, or badly-conceived public parks, and much more attractive effects are obtained when overhead canopies are open enough for perennials and bulbs to make their contribution to the garden. Whatever the ultimate aim, perennials are likely to be the

24C

main matrix-formers during the first few years, and underestimating the contribution of perennials was the crucial, strategic error of the twentieth-century gardener's retreat into the shrubbery.

Garden plants, used in familiar fashions, will create a good impression on most observers, however chaotic the planting or lacking in

24A, B & C. Mulches fill spaces in newly-planted beds simply and effectively. A pond has been dug out in the garden under construction (top left), and the soil used to build up beds elsewhere. Thick layers of fresh, strawy horse manure have been spread over beds in the foreground, and between newly-planted roses in the middle distance. Trees and shrubs (top right) are thickly mulched with dried pea haulms until they grow large enough to provide shade for woodland perennials. Even vegetables can be grown in deep layers of annually replenished hay or straw (bottom right) (a method developed by Ruth Stout and fully described by her in numerous articles and books). Godspiece Leaze, Norton St Philip, Bath, England. Speight Gardens, Arrowtown, Queenstown, New Zealand. Phoebe Noble's Garden, Sidney , Vancouver Island, Canada.

of particular plants, and bold planting based on relatively few kinds.

First and future colonists

Annuals might seem the obvious starting point for a planting destined to become a matrix – and they can be used in this way. Many perennials, especially those naturally associated with grasslands, tolerate their presence, and after their disappearance grow away strongly. But such annuals are, in effect, weeds – more decorative and enjoyable than fat hen and annual nettle, but competitors for water, light and nutrients nevertheless. Unless there is good reason for a display of flowers during the first year, better results are likely, and life is simpler, without the annuals, using mulches to fill temporary spaces, exclude weeds, conserve water and provide a source of humus and some nutrients.

The vivid displays of annuals that attract people to places like Springbok in South Africa and Morawa in Western Australia, and colour the landscape round the Mediterranean and in California each spring, are seldom part of a succession that leads progressively to a close community of shrubs and perennials. More often they occupy gaps that become vacant year after year between long-lived shrubs and perennials.

The tontine effect

An annual matrix may seem to be a contradiction, since matrices are usually associated with plant communities capable of holding their own in a sustainable, semi-permanent fashion. But under natural conditions, annuals, more than most plants, have to cope with the problems of finding a roothold and establishing themselves, and frequently do this through the formation of a matrix. These are short-lived, in the sense that each lasts only during the short lifespan of its members, but more permanent in that they recur in the same area year after year.

The great majority of our garden annuals

25A

25B

rhythm the mishmash of different plants may be: especially when the affects are sanitized by mown grass, clipped hedges and freshly-turned soil. In more relaxed situations, the familiar cues that identify a place as a garden are subdued or more easily misinterpreted. It becomes more necessary for the planting itself to provide the visual logic and the rhythm and co-ordination that make a garden. The most effective way to achieve this is by the well-placed, repetitive use

25A & B. Many soils have a naturally-developed structure, which is destroyed by digging. Banks in a recently-cleared woodland (top) were not dug over – or even mulched – before planting with shade-tolerant perennials. Two years later (bottom), the plants had formed an intricate matrix that almost completely covered the ground. Both Red Lion House, Horderley, Shropshire, England.

26A

26B

occur naturally in places where periods of
adequate rainfall alternate with drought. The
latter destroys much of the existing vegetation –
an effect often accentuated by mankind's
reduction of the more permanent plant cover –
so that large areas of bare ground are available
for colonization by annuals at the start of each
rainy season. Seeds of the annuals that grow in
these areas fall to the ground beneath their
parents at the end of each growing season. The
regular recurrence of drought and wet creates a
single optimum time for germination, at the
start of the rains, and then masses of seedlings
appear. There is no room for most of them, but
those that die before maturity also play a vital
role. The numerous seedlings produced by each
species occupy space, denying it to others, and
conserving nutrients in the upper layers of the
soil which might otherwise be lost by leaching
during the wet season. Weaker plants die, but
bequeath their space and nutrients to others
until eventually – as in a tontine – the survivors
inherit the resources once shared amongst a
large number.

In gardens, similar processes can be harnessed
to make annual 'meadows' by departing from
the traditional gardener's insistence on giving
every plant ample space to develop. Space
sowing, pricking or thinning out are time-
consuming but essential chores when large
specimen plants are required for formal bedding.
In less formal, more relaxed situations –
especially when filling spaces between more
permanent plants, whether in gardens in dry
areas where such spaces are annually-recurring
features or in more temporary situations – the
natural abilities of annuals displayed in the
tontine effect will produce a successful result
with much less effort on the gardener's part.
Mixtures of seeds of annuals can be sown thinly
in rows, or broadcast over the spaces to be
occupied, and apart from the removal of weeds,
can be left to develop with little other attention.

Spaces for annuals are likely to be transient at
best in gardens on fertile soils in well-watered
situations, but in drier settings, annuals,
biennials and short-lived perennials that are able
to sow themselves successfully year after year are
a colourful way to fill spaces – between
unsociable shrubs and tussock grasses, for
example – at seasons when these would
otherwise be occupied by weeds. Suitable
candidates for these positions will vary from one
garden to another depending on soils, situations
and climates, and the following are just a few
representative examples: columbines, red orache,
larkspur, quaking grass, marigolds, squirrel and
hare's tail grasses, candytuft, poached egg plant,
Moroccan toadflax, crown campion, honesty,
foxgloves, forget-me-nots, evening primrose,

26A & B. Annuals in Namaqualand (right), growing between
low, drought-tolerant shrubs, form temporary matrices of
seedlings, many of which die before maturity, but yield their
space and nutrients to the survivors. This 'tontine effect' goes
against the grain for gardeners accustomed to thinning out
plants to give each one space, but can be used in gardens –
especially in dry situations – to form annual meadows (left).
Kirstenbosch Botanic Gardens, Cape Town, South Africa.
Skilpad Wildflower Reserve, Namaqualand, South Africa.

27A

27B

poppies, Jacob's ladder, our lady's thistle, nasturtiums and pansies.

The gardens

Starter pack for a small garden

This back garden of about 300 sq. m (3,200 sq. ft) is on a development of small, detached houses near High Wycombe in southern England. The soil is a light woodland loam overlying chalk. Summers are usually cool, winters are seldom severe, and spring frosts are unusual, but the site has little shelter from the prevailing westerly wind. The owner is in her mid-thirties and practises locally as an architect. She has a nine-year-old daughter, who goes to school nearby. The mother likes gardening, has a basic knowledge of the principles of garden design, and has picked up quite a good general knowledge of plants from her parents, who are keen gardeners and live nearby. She has little spare time, and insists that she does not want to spend too much of it doing the garden. The daughter finds gardening 'dead boooring' and has no intention of becoming involved.

Review

A
Building activities had left the ground in a bad state. First priority was to reinstate surface drainage, and start on the restoration of the structure of the soil.
B
The soil has a high pH and moderate fertility, which needed boosting before planting began.
C
Privacy and shelter were both lacking, and were needed urgently to make the garden more relaxing to be in.
D
There were no plants, paths or features of any kind. The sooner a start could be made on doing something about this the better.
E
Much of the initial work could be done by contractors. After that, the aim was to make low-maintenance garden.

27A & B. Short-lived plants can be used to fill gaps amongst perennials and shrubs by self-seeding. Verbascums (top) self-seed in well-drained, calcareous soils in open, sunny situations. Foxgloves (bottom) are more likely to oblige in humus-rich, neutral to acid soils, in the shade of trees, shrubs or herbaceous perennials. Both Red Lion House, Horderley, Shropshire, England.

Outcome

A & B

a) The surface was thoroughly forked over to remove builder's rubbish and restore surface drainage and a more or less level working surface.

b) A top dressing of inorganic fertilizer made up of equal parts of sulphate of potash, sulphate of ammonia and superphosphate was broadcast over the soil at the rate of 100 g/sq. m (this produces an NPK ratio of 10:8:24 – a fertilizer made up pf 10% nitrogen:8% phosphorus:24% potassium). No lime was added, as the soil already contained ample reserves of calcium from the underlying chalk.

c) The garden was then covered with a 7.5 cm (3 in) layer of mulch. Farmyard manure was avoided for fear of upsetting the neighbours; mushroom compost was unsuitable because of its chalk content, and was available only in inconvenient bulk loads. The owner disliked the coarse appearance of wood chips or stripped bark, and quotations for composted bark exceeded her budget. Eventually, sources of shredded bark and composted town refuse were found at more or less the same price, and the owner's 'green' tendencies led her to choose this option.

C

The owner was determined to avoid the boxed-in effects of lines of fences and hedges along the boundaries of small gardens, and composed her boundaries using carefully-sited trees, trellises and arbours, with short lengths of fencing and groups of shrubs to give her shelter and privacy.

D

a) Six months after laying the mulch, the paths and other surface features were dug out and beds formed for plants. Topsoil excavated from the paths was used to make raised beds close to a small terrace behind the house, providing changes in level and contributing a comfortable sense of enclosure.

b)More fertiliser was broadcast over the beds, and raked in, using a mixture of two parts of ammonium sulphate and one part each of superphosphate and potassium sulphate to boost nitrogen levels in preparation for planting.

c) Trees and shrubs were planted first, and a 5 cm (2 in) layer of shredded bark was laid down between them. Perennials and bulbs were planted through this mulch, and more was used to patch up spaces between them.

E

a) In the interests of low maintenance, no lawn was laid, and short-lived plantings of annuals, etc. were restricted to one or two easily-managed raised beds close to the house.

b) Paths and broader areas of paving and gravel were designed to make every part of the garden accessible and to form spaces amongst the densely-filled beds.

c) Spaces between the plants were kept topped up with shredded bark until they had grown into a more or less complete ground cover.

The planting

Plants were used to form weed-excluding matrices of two kinds. Most of the garden – particularly parts away from the house – was planted with a mix of bushy trees, shrubs and shade-tolerant perennials to form strong, three-dimensional matrices, which also contributed shade and shelter. Other parts close to the house and on the sunlit sides of beds were planted with sun-loving, unsociable shrubs, interplanted with a close carpet of evergreen perennials overlying numerous bulbs. A few trees used to provide height amongst the shrubs included *Aesculus parviflora*, *Clerodendrum trichotomum* var. *fargesii* and *Hippophae rhamnoides* – all trimmed and trained to develop tree forms. Climbers were used freely on structures along the boundary, especially hybrids of *Clematis viticella* for the ease with which they can be controlled by hard pruning, and one or two more burgeoning species, like *Akebia quinnata* for rapid cover, grown with climbing roses, backed by ivies such as *Hedera colchica* 'Dentata Variegata' and 'Sulphur Heart' for foliage and shelter in winter.

Gregarious deciduous shrubs planted amongst the trees included *Buddleia fallowiana* 'Lochinch', *Deutzia* x *hybrida* 'Mont Rose', *Forsythia giraldiana*, *Leycesteria formosa* and *Viburnum farreri*, supplemented by evergreen shrubs including *Choisya ternata* and *Viburnum tinus* 'Eve Price' towards the boundaries. Groups of small, shade-tolerant, evergreen shrubs like *Sarcococca hookeriana* var. *digyna*, *Viburnum davidii* and *Ribes laurifolium* were used to reinforce the matrix close to the ground.

Unsociable shrubs were planted individually

near the house and on sunlit margins of borders, with the spaces between them filled with evergreen carpeting perennials. The former were mostly evergreen, many with fragrant foliage, including *Lavandula angustifolia* cvs, *Rosmarinus officinalis* 'Sissinghurst Blue', *Ruta graveolens*, *Salvia officinalis* 'Icterina', 'Purpurascens' and broad-leaved, *Santolina incana* 'Oldfield Hybrid' and *S. pinnata* 'Edward Bowles' and *Satureja hortensis*. Beneath the trees and shrubs, relatively few kinds of shade-tolerant perennials were planted in mixed groups and drifts to develop into a ground-covering matrix. Amongst these were: *Aegopodium podagraria* 'Variegatum', *Brunnera macrophylla* 'Hadspen Cream', the long-flowering *Geranium* 'Johnson's Blue' and *G. X riversleaianum* 'Russell Pritchard', amongst others, and pulmonaria spp. and cvs, *Dicentra* 'Langtrees', a number of hostas, *Fragaria vesca* 'Multiplex' *Tellima grandiflora* 'Purpurea' and *Waldsteinia ternata*.

The spaces between the unsociable shrubs were planted with drifts of carpeting evergreen perennials such as *Acaena novae-zealandiae* and *A. glabra*. *Artemisia schmidtiana* 'Nana', *Dianthus* 'Pike's Pink', *Oreganum vulgare* 'Aureum' and *Thymus citriodorus* and *T. serpyllum* with occasional upright plants of *Verbascum chaixii* 'Alba' and *Digitalis ferruginea* for contrast.

Bulbs were used liberally throughout the garden, with cyclamen and narcissus cvs in the more shaded parts, and *Allium christophii*, *Crocus chrysanthus* cvs, and *Tulipa sprengeri* hybrids beneath the carpets of evergreen perennials.

The captain's little love nest

This garden around an Edwardian villa in Bishop Auckland in County Durham is sheltered from wind at the foot of hills, but lies in a frost pocket and suffers from late frosts in spring and early ones in autumn. The soil is a poorly-drained,

poorly-structured clay loam overlying limestone. The owner, formerly a merchant seaman and master on container ships operated by a company registered in Cyprus, now shares his house and his retirement with the two women who each expected to be his sole companion. After initial ructions, the *ménage à trois* has settled for a wary truce. One 'wife' takes care of the garden; the other the house, and the two have developed a mutual respect bordering on fondness for one another.

The captain at first congratulated himself on an arrangement which looked likely to revolve around his every need, but now has second thoughts, as two capable and stubborn women rule the roost, leaving him little choice but to fall in with what they suggest. One problem about which they cannot agree is what to do with a row of three large flowering cherries that dominate most of one half of the back garden. He says they look good only when in flower for about ten days a year, and would like to take them out. They regard them as one of the glories of the neighbourhood and are determined to preserve them.

Review

A
The short burst of flowers from the cherries is a poor return for the ground they occupy. Over the years their shade has progressively suppressed shrubs, roses and miscellaneous garden plants that once grew beneath them.
B
The ground has been neglected for years. Even the fallen leaves – the one source of humus – have been carefully swept up every year. It lies wet all winter with a slimy surface, and ranges from damp to bone dry during the summer. The soil is infertile, and despite the underlying limestone, has become very acid. Before it can be

---

Fig. 4. Starter pack for a small garden
The design and style of planting in this garden avoids a 'fenced in' feeling. Low, shade-loving plants run under and through taller, open-branched shrubs and trees. This produces layered effects which are more lively than hedges or fences fronted by a mass of shrubbery.

The appearance of the boundary changes around the garden – trellis panels merge into weathered old floorboards that give way to strained wire on which trained fruit trees and

climbers grow. Elsewhere shrubs, trees and evergreen perennials provide informal screens.

The management of the planting relies on observation and interpretation of the ways plants grow and relate to their neighbours. It becomes a much more creative and imaginative form of gardening than the outdoor housework involved in keeping hedges trim, shrubs confined to their allocated spaces and herbaceous plants uniform, upright and trim.

replanted, lost humus and nutrients must be replaced, and the soil structure and fertility improved.

C

The cherries' roots lie almost on the surface, and any attempts at digging would damage them and lead to a profusion of suckers.

D

Attempts to plant annuals in the spring have been miserable failures, and delphiniums and lupins optimistically proposed by an assistant at the local garden centre did no better. Ivies are now spreading over the surface, which makes it look green, but one thing they all agree on is that they would prefer something more interesting.

Outcome

A

a) His hopes of doing away with the cherries were brushed aside by his wives' declaration that if they went, he would follow them! They decided to take advice about making the ground beneath the trees more amenable to plants.

b) As a start, despite the possibility of infection from bacterial canker, the lower limbs of the cherries were removed – this was done in spring to minimize the risk – to let more light reach the ground below them.

B

a) The border was then top dressed with ground limestone broadcast at 500 g/sq. m and covered all over with a 20 cm (8 in) deep layer of mushroom compost to provide humus and more lime in the form of chalk.

b) During the late summer, 7.5 cm (3 in) of good quality topsoil was spread over the remains of the mushroom compost, and a general-purpose fertiliser – 7:7:7 – was broadcast over it at 100 g/sq. m and lightly raked in. This was then covered with a layer of shredded bark 5 cm (2 in) thick through which the plants were set into the topsoil below. Mushroom compost was used to fill in spaces between the plants, leaving

many of them partially buried – an effect which was reinforced when the leaves of the cherries dropped soon afterwards, and were left where they fell.

C & D

a) Early the following spring, 150 g/sq. m of blood, fish and bone manure was scattered between the plants, and the following autumn – after the leaves had fallen – a mulch of mushroom compost 7.5 cm (3 in) deep was spread over the bed – partially submerging many of the plants.

b) These applications of blood, fish and bone and a mulch (mushroom compost, rotted stable manure or shredded bark, depending on cost and availability) were repeated annually, but after the second year the bed became almost self-maintaining, needing virtually no other attention.

The plants

This situation represents a garden spinney – and apart from its darkest, driest corners, provides tolerable conditions for ground-covering woodland shrubs and perennials, provided that species which would suffer from the prevalent spring frosts are avoided. Bulbs are likely to be easy to establish and to do well, and a great many were put in during September, about a month before the other plants.

The fully-developed roots and canopy of the cherries formed an unbalanced matrix which made it difficult to establish plants beneath them. This was countered by the methods described above, and the border was planted with shade-tolerant plants – including a high proportion of semi-evergreens – in mixed groups, alternating with drifts or clumps of a single kind. Preference was given to plants with persistent, decorative foliage and textures that combined or contrasted attractively, planting some of the more striking forms in large drifts for bold effects.

Some clumps of *Ruscus aculeatus* had

Fig 5. The captain's little love nest
'A' shows the three cherry trees before their lower leaves were removed. The ground beneath them is uninviting, even hostile, to plants and not readily accessible to gardeners.

In 'B' the lower branches have been carefully and cleanly cut off, making it more comfortable to move about beneath the trees, and allowing light and rain to reach the ground beneath them. Substantial improvements to the surface layers of the soil and careful choice of suitable shade-loving, woodland plants make it possible to transform the space under the trees into a very inviting part of the garden.

survived, and these were left to emerge above the rest of the planting. Other more procumbent evergreen shrubs used to form a pattern at ground level and enfold perennials were *Cotoneaster* X *suecicus* 'Coral Beauty', chosen for its regular crops of bright berries, and *Euonymus fortunei* 'Dart's Blanket' and 'Emerald 'n' Gold for their foliage. *Lonicera pileata*, in spite of some sensitivity to spring frosts, was used for its fresh spring foliage and to provide slightly bolder clumps, and varieties of *Vinca minor* were planted amongst small-leaved, variegated ivies for foliage effects and flowers, even in the darkest, driest areas.

A few perennials were also used in these 'difficult' areas, mainly large groups of *Asarum europaeum* and *Lamium maculatum*, interplanted with the broad, glossy leaves of *Iris foetidissima* var. *citrina* and 'Variegata'. In lighter areas towards the edges, *Campanula poscharskyana*, *Epimedium pinnatum* subsp. *colchicum* and *E.* x *versicolor* 'Sulphureum', *Convallaria majalis* and *Viola riviniana (labradorica)* 'Purpurea' were planted around clumps of ferns, including forms of *Dryopteris affinis* and *Polystichum setiferum* 'Acutilobum'; the latter were 'home-grown' from buds produced on their fronds.

Aquilegia vulgaris, *Digitalis grandiflora*, *Lychnis coronaria* and *Myrrhis odorata* were included in the original planting as self-seeders to plug gaps in the matrix.

Amongst the bulbs were large numbers of *Scilla bifolia* (many unfortunately turned out to be the unsatisfactory dirty-pink form rather than the bright-blue), *Galanthus nivalis* 'Flore Plena', *Hyacinthoides hispanica*, several narcissus cvs including 'Beersheba', 'Flower Carpet', 'Golden Harvest', 'Ice Follies' and 'Mrs R.O. Backhouse' (the women both insisted on these large and florid hybrids rather than the smaller species hybrids preferred by the captain), and *Camassia cusickii* and *C. leitchlinii* 'Alba'.

Garden take-away in Auckland

This garden is a 1,000 sq. m (10,000 sq. ft) section around a cream-and-blue-painted wooden house in Birkenhead on the North Shore of Auckland Harbour in New Zealand. It is owned by the former head of the PR department of a large company, who has recently retired, and following an enjoyable day

out, in spite of the queues, at the first Ellerslie Flower Show, she has decided the garden is in need of a face-lift. She lives with her father, formerly a green-keeper for the city council, who also helped his wife with the family's Indian take-away restaurant at weekends and in the evenings. The garden has been his baby, and almost all of it has been turned into lawn, which he has tended with great pride, totally absorbed in a perpetual cycle of mowing, edging, rolling, feeding, watering, sweeping and a dozen other tasks. He has acceded to her plans, 'provided there are no shrubberies and absolutely no aciphyllas!'.

Review

A
The owner's father is secretly pleased by his daughter's interest. He is beginning to find the garden hard work, and is not unwilling to allow her a small part in its care.

B
Winters are practically frost-free, summers tend to be hot and sometimes humid, and droughts are unusual. It is possible to grow an unusually wide variety of plants. But the favourable conditions encourage weeds to grow with exceptional vigour and persistence.

C
The ban on 'shrubberies' is an echo of old rivalries between the green-keeper and other gardeners in the city's parks department, and should not be taken too seriously. This is just as well, since shrubs of some kind – and trees too – are almost essential here as part of a strong, weed-resistant matrix.

D
A visit to the Regional Botanic Gardens at Manurewa has drawn the owner's attention to the hitherto unsuspected possibilities of native plants, revealed in collections of coprosmas, pseudopanax, manukas and phormiums, amongst others. These provide plenty of choice for matrices formed by dense, evergreen, weed-excluding plants.

Outcome

A
a) Hopes of restricting his daughter to a few beds tucked away in a corner proved to be unrealistic. She had not been in public relations

for nothing, and quickly persuaded him to let her do things her way.

b) Trees and shrubs were planted to mask the boundaries of the garden, and provide a setting for a much-reduced lawn sharing space with a pool along one of its sides.

B

a) The structure of the soil beneath the lovingly-maintained turf was excellent, and could only have been damaged by digging.

b) Instead, the positions of new beds were marked out on the grass and sprayed with glyphosate to kill the turf, then covered with 10 cm (4 in) of shredded tree fern mulch.

c) Bonemeal at 150 g/sq. m was broadcast over the surface of the mulch before planting.

C

a) Trees and shrubs were planted through the mulch. The father suggested planting them through sheets of woven plastic, to reinforce the effects of the mulch – following the practice he had seen used on roadside plantings of native trees and shrubs.

b) His daughter objected to the appearance of the plastic sheet, and preferred to keep spaces mulched with organic matter. She supplemented this with annuals to brighten up the garden, which worked very well for the first year, but an unusually severe drought during the following year reduced the annuals to a less than exhilarating performance.

D

Following heavy rain in the autumn of the second year, blood, fish and bone meal was broadcast over the ground at 100 g/sq. m before planting shade-tolerant, ground-covering perennials and ferns beneath the developing canopy of trees and shrubs.

The plants

Nearly all the trees and shrubs used were evergreens. Amongst the the former were fast-growing native pioneer species like *Knightia excelsa* and *Leptospermum ericoides* to provide a quick impression of height and cover, combined with other fast-growing, but ultimately quite small exotics, including *Agonis flexuosa*, *Callistemon salignis*, *Embothrium coccinea*, *Michelia* x *foggii* 'Touch of Pink' and the Australian frangipani, *Hymenospermum flavum*. Also used were small groups of cultivars of

Cordyline australis and *Griselinia littoralis*, with *Meryta sinclairii*, chosen for their contrasting foliage textures and forms.

Few conifers were used, but an existing pair of *Agathis australis* were given a prominent role in the design, and a *Podocarpus totara* was used to screen a corner. Several tree ferns, including *Cyathea dealbata* and *Dicksonia squarrosa* were planted to add variety to the treescape.

Shrubs were planted as a dense evergreen cover between the trees, and carefully composed to make the most of the patterns of variegation on the glossy leaves of *Coprosmas* like 'Kiwi Gold', 'Copper Shine', 'Pride', 'Beatson's Gold' and *C. repens* 'Pink Splendour', with contrast provided by the broad foliage of *Macropipum excelsum* 'Variegatum', the dark, leathery leaves of *Pseudopanax* 'Adiantifolium' and *P. discolor* 'Rangatira', and the soft greys and crimsons of *Brachyglottis repanda* 'Purpurea'.

Other shrubs included *Camellia japonica* cvs, because they perform too splendidly to do without them; *Hebe* 'Inspiration', 'Snowdrift', 'Wiri Charm' and 'Wiri Dawn'; to provide rapid front of border substance, and *Leptospermum* 'Crimson Glory', 'Martinii', 'Rosy Morn' and 'Wiri Joan'; for their deep-crimson, pink and white flowers during late winter and spring.

The dense evergreen foliage of the shrubs afforded few opportunities to plant perennials, grasses or bulbs beneath them, and these were used sparingly, some as dot plants like cultivars and hybrids of *Astelia nervosa* and *A. chathamica*, a couple of groups of *Cortaderia richardii* and clumps of agapanthus to contrast with the shrubs. The peppermint-scented *Pelargonium tomentosum* and *Arthropodium cirrhatum* were planted in drifts in semi-shaded parts, and *Acaena inermis* and *A. microphylla*, and other species and cultivars, carpeted more open spaces. As overhead cover developed, groups of ferns were planted, using, amongst others, *Blechnum* 'Capense' and *B. penna-marina* in the less shaded spaces, and *Asplenium bulbiferum*, *Polystichum vestitum*, *Blechnum discolor* and *B. fraseri* in shadier situations.

The old man finally rebelled, and delivered the firmest possible veto, when his daughter proposed to plant freesias and sparaxis in what was left of his lawn.

Chapter six

Variations on grassy themes

Not long ago a visitor drew me aside and whispered, 'Of course, you can always tell a proper gardener by his lawn' – a splendid assertion of the pivotal role of mown grass in people's minds, all the more pointed since my garden lacks a lawn of any kind. A million gardens, large and small, in Britain and New Zealand, and the summer-long rattle and whirr of contractor's mowers criss-crossing the private prairies around houses in the countryside of the mid-Atlantic states of the USA testify to the widespread appeal of lawns.

Patch or prairie, lawns bring matrix planting to us in a familiar guise. Whether a choice selection of fine-leaved, low-growing grasses on bowling greens or a score or more mixed wildflowers and grasses in a rough sward, they are examples of tight-knit, sustainable communities of plants. Both these and meadows depend on highly-developed systems of management and control that teach us valuable lessons about matrix planting in general:

1. Where we garden and what we do are more critical in matrix planting than in traditional forms of gardening that control events more closely. The situation, the climate and pattern of use, as well as management, decisively affect the composition of the species that eventually form the matrix.
2. It is extraordinarily difficult to forecast precisely which species will form the matrix – even on lawns sown originally with similar mixtures of seeds. In this, as in other applications of matrix planting, the gardener must view alliances with plants as co-operative ventures in which developments may take unexpected turns.

The most hide-bound traditional gardeners approve of grasses in lawns, but are inclined to extend a more leery welcome to those met elsewhere in the garden. Attempts to disentangle couch grass from clumps of herbaceous plants, the all-investing, surface nastiness of annual meadow grass, or the penalties of seduction by the gaily-variegated foliage of gardeners' garters planted in a treasured place in the garden instil a deeply embedded distrust of the entire breed. But grasses, and their cousins the sedges, reeds and rushes, include good garden plants and bad – and those that are good can be very, very good indeed.

28

Grasses are free spirits. Their wind-born motion transforms the atmosphere of a garden, but the traditional suspicion of the orthodox for the free has some justification. Marram grasses may be priceless to those who contend with shifting sand dunes, and Gertrude Jekyll may have doted on lyme grass for its striking silvery-blue foliage, but she and her clients employed gardeners to restrain its wanderings. Most of us should be deeply wary, or ban totally, those grasses – including some bamboos – whose insinuating, pervasive rhizomes invade territory unseen beneath the ground. Apart from these space-eating rhizomatous infiltrators, grasses can be divided into two main groups: some grow intermingled as well-knit swards; others develop independently as tussocks.

28. Lawns and meadows are popular because they can be kept under control by simple routines. Less familiar is the fact that the character of the community depends on the frequency, timing and height of mowing. Imaginative variations on these would produce a much more attractive landscape than these sterile, domestic prairies.
Near Rose Haven on Chesapeake Bay, Maryland, USA.

Swards provide the matrices within which flowers exist in lawns and meadows. The grasses in them dominate these communities, and their management defines which flowers thrive and which die out. Change the timing or frequency of mowing, and conditions within the matrix change too, leading inevitably to additions and subtractions amongst the plants that live amongst the grasses. These meadow wildflowers are a great source of garden plants. Brought to us from wet meadows and dry, salt marshes by the sea and alpine grasslands high in the mountains, they grow side by side in borders wherever gardens are made. Divorced from their natural association with grasses, and free from their competition, they flourish in open, sunlit, fertile borders – the natural preferences that restricted them to particular niches in particular habitats rendered largely redundant by the gardener's care and the undemanding conditions. We will return to them later.

Tussock (or bunch) grasses also often dominate their communities under natural conditions, but gardeners tend to use them as accent plants amongst other perennials or shrubs. Then their growth cycles and management do not decide the fate of the plants that grow with them, whether used to create affects on the grand scale of bamboos, pampas grasses, cultivars of *Miscanthus* and *Arundo donax* – or more modestly, within the framework of a border, where stipas, chionochloas, helictotrichons, digitarias, fescues, themadas and poas introduce a change of texture, or a focal point. Only very recently have attempts been made to plant these grasses in gardens as they grow in nature, where plants, sometimes arranged so evenly that they might have been set out by hand, cover enormous areas – the spaces between them filling with a bright variety of flowering herbs and bulbs at particular times of the year. The bunch grasses of the American prairies and Russian steppes, or the tussocks of New Zealand and South Africa could be used much more in dry gardens, including those in colder, more exposed

29A

29B

situations, where the overarching foliage of the grasses not only shelters the plants between them from wind, but also from the cold in winter.

Natural grasslands

Where grasses once stretched from horizon to horizon, it is easy to suppose that conditions are too dry for woody plants to grow well. But that is not necessarily so. Grasses and herbs that extend over country-sized expanses of steppes and prairies do not depend on rainfall alone, but develop as the result of alliances between

29A & B. Grasses and wildflowers (top) grow intimately mixed together in meadows, or grasses may form discrete tussocks (bottom), separated by spaces occupied by bulbs or annuals, or, as here, by tussock-forming perennials like astelias and celmisias. Inverewe Gardens, Polewe, North-west Highlands, Scotland. Jack's Pass, Hanmer Springs, South Island, New Zealand.

30

desiccating effects which favour grasses, and create oases of forest and scrub, which can even attract woodland birds and insects which are unable to survive in the surrounding grasslands.

Garden grasslands

Selected forms of fine-leaved grasses are the pride of those who seek the perfect lawn, because of their appearance and exceptional ability to withstand wear and tear. Their leaves resist damage, and grow quickly to repair any that they do suffer, and nothing serves better than the traditional lawn in situations exposed to daily use and abuse. Other grasses and broad-leaved flowering plants can also form very attractive communities in less demanding situations – roles that would make any self-respecting green-keeper weep, but can be very attractive and rewarding to less dedicated gardeners.

Weedy lawns

During the Second World War, when the whole garden lay neglected due to lack of labour, my grandfather would pay me threepence a hundred (pocket money for the week was tuppence) for plantains removed from his lawn. Today, a quick tour of shelves in garden centres laden with herbicides, lawn sand, fertilizers and every kind of sward cosmetic confirms that the jealous preservation of turf from contamination by wildflowers survives as a major gardening preoccupation.

Yet my grandfather's lawns consisted almost entirely of 'weeds', and if every plantain had been removed, speedwells, buttercups, field woodrush, mouse ears, medicks and white clovers would have far outnumbered the grasses. Butterflies, bees, burnet moths and other insects attracted to their flowers throughout the summer made them much more lively and interesting places than pure swards of fine-leaved grasses could ever have been. Those lawns overlaid perfectly-drained, calcareous loams above deep beds of gravel, and when mown they

rainfall, wind and fire: decreasing rainfall favours the transition from forest to savanna to prairie, but this is a progression in which fire and wind are allies of the grasses.
1. Initially, thinning of the tree and shrub cover leads to reduction of shelter. Air movement increases, and with it the desiccating effects of wind on the landscape.
2. Dryer conditions and increased wind speeds increase the frequency and intensity of fires started by lightning or other causes, destroying remaining trees and shrubs. The grasses with well-protected ground-level buds are designed to recover quickly after fires.
3. As the grasses take over, their dry stems and leaves, and increased movement of unimpeded air, accentuate the effects of fire to the benefit of the grasses, which gain from the recycling of nutrients, the elimination of plant litter and the removal of overhead shade.

Grasslands can dominate a landscape in places where trees and shrubs are able to grow quite well so long as they are protected from fire. Woody plants planted in gardens made in such situations reduce wind speed, reversing the

---

30. Alliances of wind, fire and drought can maintain grasslands indefinitely by preventing the regeneration of trees and shrubs. It may be possible to establish them in the protected conditions of a garden, when they will provide shelter and shade for other plants.
View across the Orange River, Fort Hartley, Near Quthing, Lesotho.

developed a sward not unlike that on the Downs of southern England, where intensive grazing by sheep or rabbits produces a close turf of fine-leaved grasses, herbs and orchids on thin soils above chalk.

Plants for floral lawns on well-drained calcareous soils.

Numerous plants associated naturally with short grass will form well knit matrices in sunny open situations. The essentials of success include excellent drainage and generally low levels of fertility. Occasional sparing applications of fertiliser may be necessary and on neutral soils regular applications of ground limestone.

Achillea millefolium: Colonizes dry, infertile sites on free draining soils, Flowers are now available in various pastel shades.
Anthyllis vulneraria: Deep rooted species, with many colour forms and ecotypes, some exceptionally tolerant of heat and drought.
Bellis perennis: Ubiquitous shallow rooted species, spreads rapidly by seed to colonise gaps on damp, poorly drained sites.
Festuca ovina: An excellent, drought tolerant grass, providing a good base for matrix formations with other plants.
Festuca rubra: Low growing, very fine-leaved perennial grass, available in various forms for different situations.
Helianthemum nummularium: This and other spp. and cvs. thrive in sunlit sites on dry soils thinly covering calcareous rocks.
Hieracium pilosella: Many hawkweeds and cat's ears are excellent colonists of thin grass swards on well drained soils.
Koeleria cristata: A tough, rather stiff little grass forms open swards that associate well with herbs on dry, base rich soils.
Linum catharticum: A slender annual self-sowing amongst grasses in open swards on well drained, infertile soils.
Lotus corniculatus: Colourful, vigorous leguminous plant able to establish and reproduce itself even in competitive situations.
Medicago lupulina: Very tolerant of close mowing and able to colonise moderate swards on dry, well drained sites.
Plantago media: Spreading rosettes of leaves establish readily from seed in open or thin swards on well-drained sites
Polygala vulgaris: Several species and cultivars maintain themselves successfully amongst grasses on dry, sunlit sites
Poterium sanguisorba: Deep rooted, drought resistant plant for hot sunny slopes amongst fine-leaved grasses.
Primula veris: Easily established on fertile, base rich meadows and open swards on thin soils above calcareous rocks
Prunella grandiflora: Adaptable species growing in semi shaded and sunlit sites in mixed communities of grasses and herbs.
Thymus serpyllum: Forms intimate mixtures with fine leaved grasses on exceptionally well drained, sunlit sites
Trifolium pratense: Variable and adaptable species associated with grasses in rich, moist meadows on thin soils
Trifolium repens: Drought resistant species, very tolerant of close cutting and adaptable to a wide range of conditions.
Viola hirta: Able to grow with other broad leaved plants amongst open grass swards in sunny well drained situations.

Lawns on well-drained soils – whether acid or alkaline – are almost impossible to maintain in dry weather without constant watering. Often they are remarkable during droughts for the green patches of deep-rooted clovers which survive assaults by most lawn weedkillers and stand out amongst the shrivelled remnants of grasses burnt crisp by sun and dry weather. Such settings are ideally suited for garden versions of downland or heathland communities of grasses and wildflowers, which can be encouraged to develop by abandoning herbicides applied in futile attempts to maintain grass-only swards, and forgetting about the standards by which good lawns are judged. Then worms become allies, because their casts are places in which seeds germinate, and can be deliberately seeded with suitable wildflower mixtures; regular applications of lime can be used on already neutral or slightly alkaline soils to accentuate the conditions many downland plants need to compete successfully with grasses. The blades of the mower can be adjusted to raise the cut a little higher than a purist would approve, and in early summer the interval between cuts can be extended to allow more opportunities for flowers to appear.

Plants for floral lawns on sandy or acid soils.

Plants suitable for floral lawns in acid conditions, may form more open, less stable matrices than those on calcareous soils. Most depend on very good drainage to do well, and top dressings of sand and peat – laced with seeds of suitable species – encourage their development.

Acaena inermis: Several others amongst the smaller, less invasive acaenas are suitable – but their burrs may cause problems

Agrostis alba: An attractive, small grass, spreading by underground stems to form colonies – drought resistant

Arctotheca calendulacea*: Cape weed, only for frost-free areas, is strongly drought resistant, and floriferous over a long period.

Blechnum penna-marina: A small fern, tolerant of many situations, will establish and run gently amongst grasses

Calluna vulgaris: Good mixer on dryish or wet, acid sands. Forms a dense ground hugging sward when mown

Campanula rotundifolia: Several forms available. Also sometimes successful are forms of *C. carpatica*.

Dianthus deltoides: Several named forms – mostly with flowers in shades of magenta, or white – available

Erigeron philadelphicus: This and *E. karvinskianus* will form spreading colonies – the latter in drier conditions than the former

Festuca ovina ssp.glauca: Low growing, tufted grass with glaucous foliage. Numerous horticultural forms have been selected.

Geranium molle: An annual with tiny, fugitive flowers, but the main attraction is its soft textured, round lobed foliage.

Hieracium pratense: Invaluable for its small yellow 'dandelions' from mid to late summer.

Houstonia caerulea: Bluetts form scattered, low, tufted clumps of usually pale blue, occasionally white flowers, in early spring.

Leptinella perpusilla: Mat-forming perennial

with rounded flower heads, and fern-like grey, sometimes brown, leaves.

Oxalis purpurea*: Large purple, pink or white flowers carried low amongst grasses above typical lobed foliage; withstands moving.

Pratia (Lobelia) angulata: Several horticultural forms and natural selections are available – also *PP. pedunculata* and *perpusilla*.

Primula vulgaris: Old-fashioned, unimproved forms are much more likely to establish successfully than modern strains.

Soleirolia soleirolii: Can be extremely invasive, but can also form superb luxuriant swards in damp, shaded, mild situations.

Tunica saxifraga: Also needs open, well drained conditions to do well – particularly suitable for sunny banks.

Veronica filiformis: An invasive, but very beautiful, speedwell that can form colonies over extensive areas; withstands moving.

Viola tricolor: Very variable flower colours and forms ranging from pale yellow to deep purple – likely to establish better on acid soils.

Meadows

Intractably heavy land used to be permanent pasture before tractors provided overwhelming horsepower. This avoided the problems of teams of horses stuck in the mud in wet weather, and brick-like surfaces impossible to cultivate in summer droughts. Annual crops of hay, followed by grazing, made full use of the great reserves of fertility possessed by many clays, supplemented by deep-rooted herbs which tapped minerals from the lower levels. Dense mats of grass roots close to the surface maintained the structure and natural profiles of the soils, conserved their fertility, and perpetuated drainage channels which disposed of surplus water.

Gardeners faced with the problems of coping with heavy, poorly-drained soils replete with clay and silt might look towards these meadows for a solution to their problems. But amongst other things old meadows: (a)contain a community of plants that have become precisely adapted to the conditions in which they are growing over a long period; (b) have achieved a balanced distribution of the resources available, particularly nutrients, which have often been depleted by the annual removal of grass (as hay) over many years; (c) possess an established soil structure and well-developed soil profile appropriate to the composition of the soil and the situation.

These qualities come only with maturity, and newly-sown meadows possess so little of the self-sustaining balance of established grassland communities that they can scarcely be described as meadows at all. Well-endowed garden soils do not provide easy conditions for meadow-making. Like fertile beds and borders that distort developing matrices by favouring vigorous plants to the exclusion of all others, such places provide a living that is too favourable for take-over bids by coarse grasses and vigorous, weedy wildflowers. Balanced mixtures of grasses and attractive wildflowers are much more easily established where water or

fertility, or a combination of the two, are seasonally, or even perpetually, limiting.

Plants for fertile relatively moist meadows

Satisfactory meadow communities are more difficult to set up on fertile, normally moist soils, because the vigorous growth of the grasses, in the early years dominates the matrix and overwhelms other plants. It is essential to match the vigour of broad leaved plants and grasses.

Achillea ptarmica: Rhizomatous growth enables it to infiltrate grasses, and hold its own, even amongst dense growth.
Aster novae-angliae: A tall daisy with numerous small pale purple flowers spreading amongst grasses by surface rhizomes.
Camassia cusickii: One of several camassias that contribute little to a matrix, but are valuable for their spikes of flowers.
Cardamine pratensis: Short-lived, but regeneration from leaf bases makes this an excellent gap filler in moist situations.
Cimicifuga simplex: Does well in very wet situations even amongst strong-growing grasses.

31A

31B

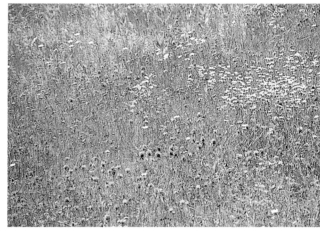

31C

31A, B & C. Meadows are delicately-balanced communities which take many years to develop. The rich community of grasses and wildflowers in the natural meadow (top left) is based on an undisturbed matrix formed by the roots of the grasses just below the surface. The fritillaries (bottom right) grow in water meadows in which the natural fertility of the land has been moderated by cutting and removing hay for centuries, and the wildflowers and grasses (right) have developed spontaneously on old agricultural land over a period of several decades. Near Verkniy Pereval, Bikin, Ussuriland, Far Eastern Region, Russia. Town Meadow, Cricklade, Wiltshire, England. Green Mountains near Wilmington, Vermont, USA.

Cynosurus cristatus: A moderately vigorous grass that associates well with broad-leaved plants.

Deschampsia caespitosa: A very attractive clump forming grass that does not overwhelm neighbouring plants.

Eupatorium maculatum: A strong grower that can maintain itself amongst vigorous grasses in wet situations.

Festuca pratensis: Another moderately vigorous grass that occupies ground without suppressing neighbouring plants.

Filipendula ulmaria: Vigorous, persistent plant that can hold its own in the wettest meadows with strong grasses.

Fritillaria meleagris: Spring flowering bulb, that grows best in regularly mown swards that are not too vigorous.

Geranium pratense: Clump forming, long-lived perennial, spreading slowly by short rhizomes.

Helenium autumnale: Late summer, autumn flowering yellow/orange daisies able to grow in strong matrices in wet meadows

Heracleum sphondylium: Vigorous umbellifer,with white or pale crimson flower heads, excellent matrix former.

Liatris pycnostachya: One of several blazing stars that establish well amongst herbs and grasses in moist situations.

Lychnis flos-cuculi: Best in wet conditions in old, well balanced meadows in which competition from grasses is not too great.

Polygonum bistorta: Will grow in moist to wet situations in established meadows, but vulnerable to competitive grasses.

Ranunculus acris: Another typical established meadow species, able to self-sow in established swards.

Rumex acetosa: A characteristic plant of old damp meadow matrices, with a wide tolerance for different situations.

Sanguisorba tenuifolia var. purpurea: One of several sanguisorbas capable of competing with vigorous grasses, chosen for its deep crimson flowers.

Plants for dry meadows.

Numerous, often very colourful perennials, grow well in matrices dominated by grasses. Fashion suggests we should use native plants in wildflower meadows, but suitable species from similar habitats anywhere in the world are candidates for these situations.

Anthoxanthum odoratum: A tufted perennial grass that associates well with other plants. Smells of new mown hay.

Asclepias tuberosa: Produces bright orange flowers, highly attractive to butterflies, from mid to late summer.

Asphodeline lutea: Suitable for very dry situations – e.g. banks – in association with thin grass swards.

Aster amellus: An aster with open growth and pale purple daisy flowers on 1 m (3 ft) tall stems for an exceptionally long season.

Cichorium intybus: Deep rooted, self-sowing perennial with large bright blue flowers produced over a long period.

Cimicifuga dahurica: Stately plant that grows well in association with rough grasses and shrubs in well-drained situations.

Dianthus carthusianorum: Bright crimson flowers on strong, spiky stems – does best in very well drained situations in thin swards.

Dipsacus fullonum: Deep rooted, Self-sowing biennial forming a broad, weed-suppressing rosette the first year.

Hieracium aurantiacum: A rapid spreader; best in dry, competitive situations that reduce its rate of movement.

Hordeum jubatum: Attractive, short-lived perennial grass that does best in open swards in which seedlings can germinate.

Lathyrus pratensis: One of a number of *Lathyrus* and *Vicia* spp. able to grow amongst grasses in open situations.

Leucanthemum vulgare: The ox-eye daisy a good matrix former – spreads slowly amongst grasses by surface rhizomes.

Lotus corniculatus: Low growing, persistent legume associates well with a variety of grasses and other plants.

Lupinus polyphyllus: A deep rooted perennial, best in neutral to acid soils in very well drained situations. short-lived but self-seeds.

Phleum pratense: Widely cultivated, moderately vigorous grass; good matrix former in mixed meadows.

Plantago lanceolata: Easily grown species that

32A

is tolerant of a wide range of conditions.

Poa pratensis: Another excellent, persistent matrix forming grass that associates well with other plants.

Scabiosa ochroleuca: A plant for very well-drained, dry situations – elsewhere it can grow too vigorously.

Solidago speciosa: One of many golden rods that produce meadow colour in late summer and autumn.

Trifolium pratense: Red clover is a widespread, tolerant plant that associates well with grasses and other herbs.

32B

32C

Lawns sometimes turn themselves into meadows when the mower breaks down and sits idly in the tool shed while the grass grows long – that would probably have happened with my grandfather's 'neglected' lawns. But apart from notably dry or infertile situations, it is better practice to kill existing swards by spraying with glyphosate, and sow or plant the colonists which will eventually combine to form the meadow into the remains of the dead turf.

Control by mower – which makes the maintenance of a lawn the favourite occupation of many a tidy-minded gardener – is largely replaced by control from within the community of plants itself, supplemented by mowing. This change of emphasis leaves the gardener with

much less power to dictate what goes on. The composition of the community and the relative success of different members depends on factors like the timing, frequency and height of successive cuts, and the use or non-use of fertilizers of one kind or another. A matrix of some sort will develop on any bit of ground left or left to itself and mown from time to time, and the gardener's part is to channel these developments, as far as possible, in a direction

32A, B & C. Garden meadows establish most easily in sunlit situations on dry, relatively infertile and well-drained soils, like the dry bank covered by gloriosa daisies (top left), or the meadow in Victoria (lower right) where ixias spring up amongst the rough grasses in spring, or on well-drained, gravelly soils where mulleins (upper right) grow with other drought-tolerant, broad-leaved plants. Botanic Garden, Khabarovsk, Ussuriland, Far Eastern Region, Russia. Ton ter Linden's Garden, Ruinen, Drenthe, Holland. Cloudehill Garden, Oolinda, Dandenongs, Melbourne, Victoria, Australia.

which produces an attractive mix of species. Everything possible should be done to:
a) Select species whose requirements match the physical and climatic conditions of the site.
b) Combine those which appear likely to be compatible, in terms of vigour, with one another.
c) Blend together species whose various growth forms provide the essential components of a matrix. This includes a mixture of grasses, bulbs and broad-leaved herbs; a variety of flowering seasons and periods of growth; and ability to occupy ground or to infiltrate and occupy spaces as they become available.

No meadow has the in-depth matrix of woodland, nevertheless they present formidable obstacles to the successful establishment of invading plants, and only those well adapted to cope with the conditions are likely to gain entry or persist. Apart from gaps produced by mole and ant hills, and damage to the sward by the feet of large animals, the matrix of an established grassland can be nearly impenetrable for much of the year. It may appear to be ragged and open to invasion after winter weather and storms, but seedlings germinating in the spring face immediate competition from established grasses and perennials whose well-developed roots and reserves of storage compounds give them an immense advantage. After the grasses and meadow plants have gone to seed, their growth is much less vigorous, and this, combined with the effects of drought, often produces gaps in the matrix which provide opportunities for colonists. Attempts to introduce new species into established meadows, whether by scattering seed or setting out plants from containers, are likely to be more successful in late summer and autumn – provided conditions are not too dry – than in the spring.

Broad leaved plants growing amongst grasses adopt one of two strategies: either they hold their ground year by year, putting down deep roots that tap nutrients and water at lower levels than the grasses, eventually developing into large, well-defined individuals; or they infiltrate the grasses, producing crowns horizontally, at or just below ground level, with short, annually-renewed roots, that extend continuously into new ground. Deep tap-rooted meadow herbs

like chicory, hellebores, meadow clary and pasque flower are examples of the former. Meadow composites like erigerons, heleniums, hawkweeds, and moondaisies represent the latter and move amongst the grasses, sometimes spreading extensively.

Seed mixtures composed to suit different situations are now widely available, and are likely to be the first choice of most people trying to form a meadow. But these mixtures have limitations:

a) Many attractive and desirable plants do not germinate or establish readily from broadcast seed.
b) In some mixtures, quite high proportions of the seed will be cornfield weeds rather than meadow wildflowers. These germinate quickly and reliably and produce attractive flowering plants rapidly, but will not establish themselves, and will disappear within a year or two.
c) The species represented are most likely to be those that are native to the country concerned – although the seeds will not necessarily be collected from native populations – and many gardeners might prefer to use a broader range drawn from similar habitats in other parts of the world.
d) Seedlings that emerge do so in direct competition with the on-site population of weeds – closely adapted to the actual prevailing conditions – and may not be able to compete successfully with them.

It may be necessary to propagate stocks of some plants under protected conditions, planting them out in the meadow later as young plants from containers or a nursery bed. This can be done immediately prior to oversowing with a meadow mixture.

However comprehensive and well-chosen the seed mixture may be, it will be diluted by the presence of seeds already in the soil.

On dry, infertile soils, plants from seed mixtures usually establish themselves successfully in spite of competition from native species, and the two very often complement each other and develop together into a more complex and interesting community. In moister, more fertile conditions, a few vigorous species are likely to take over unless precautions are taken to prevent this. The most effective measures include those that reduce the levels of available nutrients: either by mowing closely or scything three or four times a year for several years, removing the cuttings each time, or more radically, and often preferably, stripping 5–15 cm (2–6 in) of topsoil off the surface before attempting to form the meadow. This sounds drastic, but should be no problem now that earth-moving equipment is readily available to tackle any scale of operation from a few square metres to several hectares. The topsoil removed is valuable material that can be used to increase the depth of soil in other situations, and the arrival of a digger is very likely to stimulate ideas about excavating hollows that could be filled with water, transforming a simple ambition to make a meadow into a much more satisfying garden landscape, following the classical recipe of grass, wildflowers and water.

Gardening with Tussocks

In dry situations, tussock grasses can be used to form a striking and characteristic gardenscape based on the repetitive patterns of the spaced-out grasses. Wide spacing is essential to give each one room to develop, and the size and vigour of the species used must be carefully matched to the situation – ranging from the compact tussocks of the glaucous-leaved festucas, which can be used effectively in the smallest gardens, to the vast, space-consuming mounds of pampas grasses.

Spaces between the grasses can be occupied by other plants, using carpeters like lamiums, acaenas, duchesnias and thymes or, especially in situations where seasonal droughts occur regularly, with temporary occupants like annuals and bulbs.

Tussock (or bunch) Grasses for Gardens

Some tussock grasses produce powerful, but often seasonally open, matrices formed by the often strikingly regularly spaced 'citadels' of the grasses between which bulbous and broad-leaved plants grow at seasons when sufficient rainfall is available to provide for their needs

Andropogon gerardii: This and other species eg *A. ternarius* and *virginicus,* are effective in groups or as individuals in borders.
Arundo donax*: Extremely tall, broad-leaved species. Most effective as a specimen – especially var. *versicolor.*
Carex buchananii: Bright copper bronze foliage and tight tussock form make this ideal for spaced planting with bulbs etc.
Chionochloa conspicua: A large, strikingly handsome tussock for an imposing specimen, or a sensational community effect.
Chionochloa rubra: Russet red foliage provides contrasting tones when groups are interplanted with bulbs and flowers.
Cortaderia selloana: Pampas grasses make very imposing specimens. Even more impressive in colonies, where space allows.
Dactylis glomerata: A tussock that grows naturally as individual clumps forming part of the matrix of fertile meadows.
Deschampsia cespitosa: Numerous named forms available; best planted in groups, or interplanted with bulbs and ground cover.
Elegia capensis*: One of many restios with strikingly architectural inflorescences, and narrow, upright reed-like stems.
Festuca amethystina: This and *FF. glauca* and *cinerea* are represented by numerous small, glaucous-leaved cultivars.
Helictotrichon sempervirens: Excellent as a specimen or in groups, in well-drained, cool situations. Not in hot, humid conditions.
Luzula nivea: Dense clump-forming grass for semi-shaded situations – seeds freely to occupy spare spaces.
Miscanthus sinensis: Giant grasses, best in moist situations with long growing seasons. Numerous cultivars are available.
Molinia caerulea: Excellent in groups interplanted with bulbs and ground cover, but small plants take time to establish.
Pennisetum alopecuroides: Excellent in small groups, or massed for effect. Good ground holding, associates well with other plants.
Poa labillardierei: Dense, weed resistant hummocks are effective in groups interplanted with bulbs etc.
Sorghastrum nutans: Strikingly effective grass from early summer to late winter, individually or in interplanted groups.

33A

33B

33C

33D

33A, B, C & D. Gardeners habitually use tussock grasses as accent plants in borders in contrast with broad-leaved plants (top left and right, and bottom left). Only occasionally do we find them grouped as they grow naturally (bottom left).

Arboretum, North Carolina State University, Raleigh, North Carolina. USA. Slot De Nisse, The Netherlands. De Kempenhof, Domburg, The Netherlands. Speight Gardens, Arrowtown, Queenstown, New Zealand.

Stipa gigantea: A tall and strikingly handsome grass. Most effective planted as a specimen or in widely spaced groups.

Themada rubra*: Rufous foliage, graceful inflorescences and tight tussock form provide a fine setting for interplanted bulbs and flowers.

Open matrix communities

Open communities, in which grasses play minor parts and broad leaved plants are more prominent, occur in some situations. Traditional gardeners, regarding these as deplorable examples of neglected, threadbare lawns, would set about remedying their problems with top dressings of marl, peat and any other materials they could lay their hands on to build up the soil and enable it to retain the water and fertilizers on which well-maintained swards depend. But it is a model that can be applied in the garden – directly when soils are thin, stony or gravelly, and indirectly, even on heavy clays, in poorly-drained situations where lawns remain so saturated with water during the winter and wet spells that they are almost unapproachable. As they stand, these are totally unsuitable for this kind of planting, but covered with a layer of gravel up to 30 cm (1 ft) deep , the problems of the clays are buried with them, and they lie forgotten but not gone – out of sight, but still within reach of roots that can tap their reservoirs of water and nutrients.

Plants for Open Matrix Communities

An open matrix is vulnerable to invasion by weeds – unless climatic or other conditions on site prevent their establishment. Seasonal drought or free-draining substrates such as gravel, scree or small stones are usually essential prerequisites for success with these communities. They can be particularly effective when interplanted with upright tussocks of small grasses especially those with glaucous, rufous or copper foliage.

Acaena novae-zelandiae: Several suitable spp. and cvs. produce dense mats of foliage. Vigour must be matched with space available.

Alchemilla erythropoda: Compact ground-holding Lady's mantle, that contrasts effectively with grasses, and prostrate neighbours.

Campanula cochlearifolia: Infiltrates by underground rhizomes to occupy spare spaces, but is not vigorous enough to be a threat.

Crocus chrysanthus: Numerous small bulbs are invaluable for their spring colour, but contribute little to the matrix.

Cyclamen cilicium: This and *CC. coum* and *hederifolium* are as valuable for their attractive and ground holding foliage in winter, as their flowers.

Globularia bellidifolia: Tenacious, long-lived, creeping perennials that gradually build up mats of evergreen foliage.

Hebe odora var. *prostrata*: Forms spreading, weed excluding evergreen mats, with attractive glossy leaves.

Iris pumila: Excellent for seasonally dry settings, but contributes little to the matrix in competitive situations.

Laurentia (Isotoma) fluviatilis: Builds up into dense, ground hugging mats of tiny green leaves studded with blue or white flowers.

Mazus reptans: Requires perennial moisture in a gravel garden, where its woody stems and large flowers are effective.

Phlox hoodii: Also cvs. of species like *PP. douglasii* and *mesoleuca* – that are drought tolerant and not invasive.

Pimelea prostrata*: Naturally moulds itself over rocky outcrops – good prostrate forms make excellent ground holding mats.

Polygonatum hookeri: A tiny Solomon's seal, that spreads underground as an infiller and modest colonizer.

Pratia (Lobelia) pedunculata: More vigorous than *P. angulata* (for smaller areas) – but its wider ranging mats suit large spaces better.

Raoulia hookeri: This and several other species are mainstays of the scabweed communities that provide models for gardens.

Saxifraga 'Whitehills': Many saxifrages, including encrusteds, make good ground-holding dot plants in non-competitive settings.

Sempervivum arachnoideum: This and other spp. and cvs. are excellent ground holders, especially in seasonally dry situations.

Thymus citriodorus: Numerous prostrate thymes are mat formers that produce effective

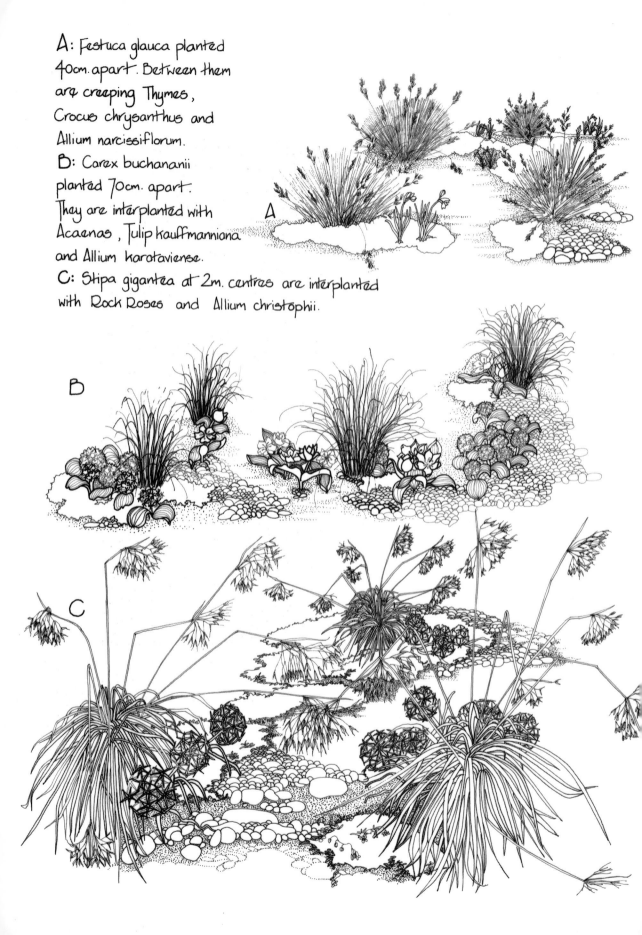

A: Festuca glauca planted
40cm. apart. Between them
are creeping Thymes,
Crocus chrysanthus and
Allium narcissiflorum.
B: Carex buchananii
planted 70cm. apart.
They are interplanted with
Acaenas, Tulip kauffmanniana
and Allium karotaviense.
C: Stipa gigantea at 2m. centres are interplanted
with Rock Roses and Allium christophii.

matrices in well drained situations.

Veronica prostrata: Forms dense, compact mats of evergreen foliage; occupies space without being invasive.

Viola hederacea: Vigorous mat former for perennially moist situations. Other montane spp. more suitable for gravel gardens.

The gardens

Bowing to the inevitable

The owner's grandfather planted many of the trees in this 1.5 hectare (4 acre) garden in the English Midlands, and the last planned changes had been made by his parents in the 1930s, when two gardeners, an odd-job man and a garden boy were employed to keep the place immaculate. More recently, the owner, with the help of a retired farm worker, struggled vainly to arrest progressive dereliction, amongst which once broad and neatly gravelled paths wound between misshapen Lawson cypresses looming amongst a scattering of peplows (senile and potentially dangerous trees – see Chapter 9). Bindweed threatened to envelop shrubberies surrounding broad, moth-eaten lawns, and overgrown hedges encroached on flower beds full of ground elder. The farm worker died shortly before the owner retired from his practice as a solicitor in Derby, forcing serious thoughts about the future.

The solicitor is an active, physically strong man for his age, who enjoys being in the open air, and has played and worked in the garden since childhood. He has never married, and friends have repeatedly urged him to move to a smaller, more manageable place, but he loves it, and

34A

34B

34C

Fig 6. Tussock grasses on gravel.
Tussock grasses should be carefully chosen according to the space available. These three drawings show different tussocks set out at appropriate spacings and interplanted with broad-leaved plants and bulbs.

34A, B & C. Fragile matrices of mosses, lichens, grasses and broad-leaved wildflowers grow in extreme conditions, where they form single, interlocking layers like pieces of a jigsaw (top and centre). Such communities are very vulnerable to invasion by more vigorous plants in the relatively benign conditions of most gardens. Success depends on setting up free-draining (but not dry), infertile conditions which do not encourage weeds to take over – gravel gardens (bottom) are one way to do this.

Tasman Glacier moraine, Mount Cook National Park, South Island, New Zealand.
c.1,400 m (4,600 ft), above Whakapapa. Tongariro. North Island., New Zealand.
John Treasure's Garden, Burford House, Tenbury Wells, Worcestershire, England.

hates the idea of changing its comfortable familiarity, let alone moving out altogether. Eventually, he had to accept the fact that something drastic had to be done if he wanted to continue living there.

Review

A This garden, designed when labour was cheap and plentiful, could only be adapted to today's circumstances by fundamental, often distressingly destructive changes. The only way to make these acceptable was as part of constructive improvements which captured the interest of the owner.
B He had long grown so familiar with the place that he found it difficult to imagine it in any other guise, and quite impossible to visualize changes radical enough to solve his problems.
C The main assets were a number of fine specimen trees; some good-quality stone in the tumble-down walls of the kitchen garden, and a generally well-structured, easily-worked, now rather impoverished, light, sandy loam soil.
D He was finally persuaded that one increasingly elderly man could look after a garden of this size only by following the principles of matrix planting, and paying a contractor occasionally to do the heavier, more laborious tasks.

Outcome

A & B

Operations started with a survey of the garden, and an assessment of the condition of the trees. Following this, a plan, visual impressions of parts of the new garden, and detailed notes about the proposals were presented to the owner; after discussions and some modifications, these formed the basis for work on a radically different lay-out.
Dead, decaying and redundant trees were removed; broken-down walls were demolished, or in a few cases rebuilt; almost all the hedges were grubbed out, and most of the paths were eliminated.

C

The patchwork of old paths, lawns and flower beds was dealt with by removing all unwanted plants, filling in the paths and spraying the lawns with glyphosate to kill the turf. The whole area was then graded and scarified to produce a continuous surface. A small area on a terrace constructed close to the house was sown with lawn grass seed. The rest was turned into meadows with mown paths through them, no wider than could be cut by two passes of the mower.

The finer existing specimen trees were used as focal points, and supplemented by new introductions. The latter included native and exotic species, chosen for their ability to grow with minimal attention, and planted to frame the garden.

Stone from the walls was used to make a terrace in front of the house, to provide a view over the garden.

D

The outstanding innovation was the formation of two small lakes set amongst the meadows and trees to form the centrepiece of the garden, with grass and meadows in the foreground, and trees on a raised bank, made from the excavated topsoil, in the background. The subsoil was used to raise the level of the terrace.

The plants

The soil, well-structured, free-draining and rather impoverished, proved to be an ideal foundation on which to set up meadows. Numerous bulbs were planted, with an emphasis on the relatively small hybrid species daffodils and crocuses, and an attractive balance of grasses and wildflowers was produced by planting selected species individually from plugs, oversown with meadow seed mixtures.

The raised bank behind the lakes was planted moderately densely with a screen of trees, chosen for their diverse shapes, foliage and autumn colours and affinity with water, such as *Alnus cordata* and *A. glutinosa* 'Pyramidalis', *Populus alba* 'Richardii', *P. lasiocarpa* and *P. tremula* 'Pendula', *Salix alba* 'Britzensis' and var. *vitellina*, and *Taxodium distichum*. Few wildflowers, apart from *Primula vulgaris*, *Anemone sylvestris*, *Viola riviniana*, *V. odorata* and *Galium odoratum*, were planted amongst the grasses in this area, since it would soon become heavily shaded, but bulbs including *Narcissus* 'Little Witch', 'Jack Snipe'. 'Liberty Bells', 'March Sunshine' and 'Thalia' were planted in large drifts amongst the trees.

A variety of wildflowers and grasses were

planted or sown in the more sunlit meadows, amongst the specimen trees between the house and the lakes. Amongst these were *Galium verum, Lotus corniculatus, Daucus carota, Ranunculus arvensis, Silene alba, Primula veris, Leucanthemum vulgare, Centaurea scabiosa, Prunella vulgaris, Plantago lanceolata, Geranium pratense, Scabiosa columbaria, Rumex acetosa, Vicia cracca, Lathyrus pratensis, Trifolium campestre* and *Achillea millefolium*. Expanses of the large Dutch crocuses and several patches of *Fritillaria meleagris* were planted in these meadows, but no daffodils, since the owner, sensitive to hay fever, insisted on mowing just before the grasses came into flower, before daffodil foliage would have died down.

Kiwi antique dealer's blessed plot

The owner runs an antiques and applied arts business from the ground floor of a fashionable timber house on The Terrace in Wellington, New Zealand. He has had a new house built for himself and his mother on a stony, well-drained, dry section of bush south of Blenheim, to which he commutes at weekends, and often nips home for a day or two in the middle of the week too.

Formerly covered with bush, it had been a sheep run before being abandoned some years earlier, and colonized by manuka and gorse, with occasional tree ferns in the damper hollows. A few ancient cabbage trees are the only remnants of the original forest. The Marlborough rock daisy (*Pachystegia insignis*) grows in a small, abandoned quarry in the garden and is a source of great pride. He tells everybody that it grows nowhere else in the world.

The owner's previous perceptions of gardening, derived from wet and windy walks in the Botanic Gardens in Wellington, left him with a decidedly cold attitude towards its attractions. His new acquisition has fired a passion for it, and now he not only spends all the time he can spare gardening, but ropes his boyfriends in to help at the weekends.

Review

A
Grass covering much of the site maintained a moderately good but fragile soil structure, due to the low levels of humus. The soil is very free

draining, and bad management had wasted such small reserves of potash and phosphates as it ever possessed.
B
Despite the owner's enthusiasm for his new-found recreation, the section is too large for all of it to be gardened intensively, or for any attempt at rapid overall soil improvement.
C
He expressed an aversion to the only form of extensive gardening he knew: the stilted arrangements of specimen trees and shrubs set out in grass in the Botanic Garden.
D
Annual rainfall is not as deficient as the desiccated appearance of the vegetation during spring and early summer droughts suggests. Water conservation measures, combined with the use of suitably drought-resistant plants, enabled him to make a very attractive garden.

Outcome

A
No attempts were made to dig, plough or cultivate the ground – actions which would have destroyed the fragile structure and profile of the soil.
Intensive planting and management was confined to a small area centred on the house, and radiating from it to form vistas flanked by more extensively treated settings. One or two of the damper spots, where tree ferns were growing, were also picked out for intensive planting.
In these areas, the soil was covered with mulches to reduce surface evaporation and provide a source of humus to boost its water-holding capacity.
Top dressings of a general fertilizer were applied on top of the mulches before planting, and repeated annually until a complete cover of plants had developed.
B
Elsewhere, invading gorse was sprayed with weedkiller and grubbed out, and broad paths were cut between thickets of manuka to form a pattern of clumps separated by more open areas.
C
Much of this was planted as 'garden bush', centred on the clumps of manuka. These areas were not mulched or fertilized, apart from

individual trees and some of the larger shrubs, which were given a generous mulch of pea haulm and fed with a balanced artificial fertilizer for the first three years after planting. 'Garden bush' consisted of mixtures of native and exotic trees and shrubs, planted to form matrices based mainly on canopy and shrub layers above a patchwork ground cover, including numerous bulbs.
D
An area on the steeper slopes round the quarry to one side of the house was landscaped with tussock grasses interplanted with bulbs, perennials and shrubs.

The plants

Overall, the planting will eventually establish dense, self-maintaining groups of trees and shrubs separated from one another by winding paths – broad in places and narrower in others – to form a pattern of interconnected glades, and providing permanent shade and shelter over much of the garden. The main exception, apart from the 'gardened' areas close to the house, will be the sunlit slope occupied by tussock grasses.

A number of trees, including a proportion of the pea family, chosen for their drought-tolerance and ability to fix nitrogen, were planted in the early stages. Amongst them were *Albizzia julibrissin* 'Rosea', *Callistemon citrinus*, *Cornus capitata* and *C. controversa* 'Variegata' (as a pair of specimens flanking a vista from the house), *Dodonea viscosa* and 'Purpurea', *Gleditsia triacanthos* 'Sunburst', several American hybrids of *Lagerstroemia indica* and *L. fauriei* (including the low-growing 'Victor' and the taller 'Acomo' and 'Tonto'), *Leucadendron argenteum* (chosen more in hope than expectation for its gleaming silver foliage), *Pittosporum crassifolium*, *P. eugenioides* and *P. ralphii* (used for rapid matrix development), *Quercus ilex*, *Sophora japonica*, numerous *S. tetraptera* (to attract tuis).

In the areas of 'garden bush', trees were underplanted with a variety of tough, self-maintaining, drought resistant shrubs, including *Artemisia arborescens* and *Atriplex halimus* for their silver foliage, *Brachyglottis repanda* 'Purpurea' and clumps of hybrid *Dunedin brachyglottis*: several cultivars of *Callistemon* with scarlet or mauve bottle brushes, *Carmichaelia odorata* and *C. williamsii*, *Colutea arborescens*,

Corynocarpus laevigatus and its cultivar 'Picturata' to attract pigeons, *Euphorbia characias* subsp. *wulfenii* (which seeded itself freely), *Euryops pectinatus*; *Grevillea juniperina* 'Sulphurea' and *G. rosmarinifolia*; *Hebe* X *franciscana*, *hulkeana* and *speciosa*,. *Indigofera heterantha* and *I. potanini*, amongst other nitrogen-fixing members of the pea family, *Olearia albida* and *O. traversii*, *Pachystegia insignis*, *Phlomis fruticosa* and *P. italica*, *Pomaderris kumeraho* (tried despite misgivings about its hardiness) and *Pseudopanax ferox*.

The tussock grass community was based predominantly on *Chionochloa rubra*, supplemented with *Carex buchananii*, *C. flagellifera* and *C. lucida* (the latter planted in patches as ground cover, rather than as tussocks) and with *Chionochloa flavicans* and *Cortaderia richardii*, individually or in small groups, emerging boldly above the general level. A number of perennials were set out amongst the tussocks, including *Acanthus mollis* and *A. spinosa*, *Astelia nervosa*, *Eremurus bungei* (*stenophyllus* subsp. *stenophyllus*) and Shelford hybrids, *Eryngium agavifolium* and *E. proteiflorum*, and *Phlomis russelliana* to provide contrasting foliage textures and forms, or bright splashes of flower, and along one margin large groups of phormium cultivars complemented the grasses and formed a link with the 'garden bush'.

Spaces between the tussocks were planted with bulbs, including *Crocosmia* 'Firebird', 'Spitfire' and 'Vulcan', cultivars of *Nerine bowdenii* and *N. undulata*, *Brodiaea* 'Queen Fabiola' and a variety of ixias, sparaxis and tigridias.

Here, and also amongst the 'garden bush', several transients, including *Digitalis* X *mertonensis*, *Foeniculum vulgare* 'Purpureum', *Salvia sclarea* var. *turkestanica* and *Silybum marianum* were introduced in the hope that they would seed themselves and occupy spare spaces within the developing matrices.

Working magic in Essex

The garden belongs to a cottage surrounded by an old orchard and meadows in a village near Billericay in Essex. It is owned by a free-lance dubbing mixer, who is single, approaching thirty, and works from home, and part-time in a production company in Grays on the Thames estuary.

The garden is exposed on one side to east winds, but otherwise lies in a sheltered position with exceptionally low rainfall. Her predecessor had grown vegetables on most of its 0.1 hectares (quarter of an acre), apart from the far end, where heavier soil borders a ditch, which he had used as a hen run.

The owner enjoys her garden, but for weeks or even months is too busy to spend much time in it. Neighbours regard her as an eccentric, arty person with an incomprehensible job. They make knowing comments about her knowledge of herbs and poisonous plants – one or two have nicknamed her 'the witch'. They are nonplused by her contention that lawns and conifers are out of place in a country cottage garden.

Review

A
The owner's strong affinities with the rural setting of the garden made her averse to 'gardenesque' approaches which would set it apart from its surroundings. She preferred an informal design which would also make fewer demands on her time.

B
Previous owners had neglected the soil in their pursuit of vegetables, reducing it to an infertile, stony state, apart from the site of the chicken run on a heavier clay loam.

C
The infertility of the soil near the house, combined with low rainfall, thwarted initial attempts to make a cottage garden with masses of plants crammed into borders. The soil of the old chicken run encouraged plants to grow lushly and grossly in the spring, before collapsing as the soil cracked open at the first hint of summer drought.

D
Different plants, and different management, were necessary to make the most of variations from one part of the garden to another.

Outcome

A
Taking a cue from the orchard over the hedge, the owner decided on a simple design of grass and fruit trees for the whole garden. The only path was a 1 m (3 ft) wide strip of mown grass winding between the trees and returning in a broad loop to the house.

Tests showed that the ground did not need liming, and since the meadow would be easier to establish without it, she decided not to apply a general fertilizer. Instead, when planting trees, she mixed soil removed from the holes in which they were planted with a few good handfuls of blood, fish and bone before replacing it over their roots.

Trees were planted early in the winter, almost a year before the first meadow plants, and surrounded by circular sheets of black polythene 1 m (3 ft) in diameter, to preserve a weed-free space round each.

B
Half-standard apple and pear trees were planted towards the house, with plums on the old chicken run – set out as an open, irregular orchard, and left unstaked to allow the stems to adopt natural, balanced postures as they developed.

During the first summer, the ground between the trees was sprayed twice with glyphosate to destroy weeds – mainly couch grass in the old vegetable patch, and stinging nettles in the hen run.

C
Seeds of meadow species sown in containers in a cold frame in January germinated during the spring, and seedlings were potted into small pots. They were planted out around the trees during the late summer; a few weeks later, bulbs were put in amongst them.

She also set out small plants of a number of species obtained in plugs and rootrainers from the British Trust for Conservation Volunteers, as well as exotic meadow plants bought from nurseries and garden centres.

Meadow seed mixtures were broadcast over the whole area the following spring, and gently raked in amongst the plants and bulbs.

A

B

C

D

The meadow overlying the old vegetable garden, was scythed twice a year, in late June, and again in early September to tidy up for the winter, leaving the cuttings where they fell, to recycle nutrients and as a source of humus. (Scything was adopted because the owner found it did her a lot more good than inhaling fumes from noisy mowers or strimmers, and was much kinder to frogs and other wildlife.)

The meadow established on the site of the chicken run was scythed monthly from the end of April to late June, and again in October each year, removing the mowings to reduce excess nutrients inherited from the chickens.

The plants

The owner was astonished to discover the range of fruit trees obtainable from a local nursery, many completely unfamiliar to her, and eventually chose the apples 'D'Arcy Spice' (for its local associations), 'Ellison's Orange', 'Arthur Turner' (as much for its beautiful flowers as for its fruits) and 'Orleans Reinette'. Plums included 'Cambridge Gage', 'Early Transparent' and 'Goldfinch', and pears 'Beth', 'Louise Bonne of Jersey' and 'Beurre Hardy'.

Plants adapted to relatively heavy, fertile soils were planted in the old chicken run, particularly species that flower during mid- to late summer and into the autumn. Grasses used as the basis of the matrix included *Agrostis stolonifera*, *Alopecurus pratensis*, *Briza media*, *Hordeum secalinum* and *Poa pratensis*. A mixture of native and exotic wildflowers planted or sown amongst these included: *Astrantia maxima*, *Achillea ptarmica*, *Leucanthemum vulgare*, *Lotus corniculatus* and *L. uliginosus*, *Medicago lupulina*, *Primula vulgaris* (using an 'old-fashioned'

perennial strain), *Campanula glomerata*, *Prunella vulgaris* (in several colour forms), *Aster amellus*, *A. divaricatus* and *A. laterifolius*, *Persicaria bistorta* 'Superba', *Gentiana cruciata*, *Geranium sylvaticum* and *G. endressii*, *Centaurea scabiosa*, *Filipendula vulgaris*, *Sanguisorba officinalis* and *Ranunculus repens*. *Cyclamen coum*, *Galanthus nivalis* 'Flore Plena' and *Erythronium dens-canis* were planted for winter colour.

On the site of the vegetable garden, most of the grasses and plants used grow naturally on well-drained, calcareous grasslands. The grasses included: *Briza maxima*, *Cynosurus cristatus*, several fine-leaved *Festuca* cvs, *Koeleria cristata* and *Phleum pratense*. Wildflowers included *Anthyllis vulneraria*, *Galium verum*, *Hippocrepis comosa*, *Cichorium intybus*, *Eryngium planum*, *Plantago media*, *Primula veris* (including copper coloured forms), *Veronica chamaedrys*, several cultivars and colour forms of *Achillea millefolium*, *Aquilegia atrata* and *A. vulgaris* (which promptly hybridized), *Dianthus carthusianorum*, *Geranium pratense*, *Hieracium aurantiacum* and *H. pilosella*, *Ranunculus bulbosus* and *Tragopogon pratensis* (for its vast, globular 'dandelion' seed heads).

Numerous bulbs were also planted in this section, including cultivars of *Colchicum autumnale*, *Crocus speciosus* and *C. zonatus* (the autumn crocuses), *Galanthus elwesii*, several *Narcissus* hybrids such as 'Rip van Winkle' 'Jumblie', 'Bambie' and 'Tête à Tête' (for its early and prolonged flowering period), several fosteriana tulips, like 'Madame Lefeber' and 'Yellow Purissima' (chosen for their flamboyant flowers and ability to persist amongst grasses for many years), *Ornithogalum umbellatum* and a few clumps of *Camassia cusickii*

Fig 7. Working magic in Essex
'A' Couch grass, nettles and other tenacious weeds are sprayed with glyphosate as soon as they have developed a good cover of growth. The fruit trees had been planted during the Christmas holidays. They have been deliberately left unstaked, and planted in groups to achieve an informal effect. 'B' In late summer, after a repeat spray to destroy any surviving weeds, meadow herbaceous plants are set out in

the clean ground.
'C' In the autumn bulbs are planted in groups and drifts after marking out the areas to be planted with canes and string, and making several adjustments by eye before deciding on the final layout. Very early the following spring a meadow seed mixture was broadcast over the whole area and lightly raked into the surface amongst the perennials and bulbs.

Chapter seven

Garden pools and wetlands

My first water garden was disappointing. I had grasped the principle that a pond is a hole in the ground filled with water, inhabited by interesting creatures, so I dug a hole, poured in a couple of cans of water to fill it to the brim, and colonized it with a dozen tadpoles out of a jam jar. I was more than disgruntled the next morning to discover that my expectations of a band of happy tadpoles disporting in a limpid pool, had turned into a muddy hole dotted with the dead hopes of future frogs.

My naive belief that a pond is simply a hole in the ground filled with water is shared by many people, including those who sell us bath tub-sized pond formers made of fibreglass. Ponds are not simple. They are amongst the most complex and dynamic of all natural environments, and like meadows, they remove gardeners from a world where control can be enforced with spade, fork or hoe, and confront them with one where they must depend on their skills at matching the needs and aptitudes of different plants with the nature and demands of different situations.

In nature, ponds are:

constantly evolving – filling up with mud and debris so that eventually they become swamps, that turn into wet lands and end up as meadows;
repeatedly changing – through the seasons, and even day by day, as water levels, nutrient availability and temperatures rise and fall;
intensely competitive – due to the unlimited availability of water, the constant renewal of nutrients, and exposure to abundant sunlight;
prone to excess – changing conditions allied to ready availability of water, nutrients and sunlight lead to periodic flushes of algal growth, excessive proliferation of water plants and

marginals, and other events which temporary disturb the balance of aquatic ecosystems.

Ponds that are large – usually known as 'lakes' by proud owners – seldom cause problems, but the majority of garden pools are far smaller than most natural ponds, often scarcely more than puddles. They experience large and rapid variations in temperature, and high ratios of decaying plant material in proportion to their volume, producing conditions seldom found naturally except during the final stages in the evolution of a pond to a bog. Not surprisingly, small ponds raise fears and doubts about their state of health and suffer from well-meant

35A

35B

35A & B. Large expanses of water (upper right) are easier to manage than the ornamental pools found in most gardens. Small volumes of shallow water suffer from variations in temperature and evaporation, and the need to top them up produces undesirably high levels of nutrients. A policy of leaving them alone to achieve their own balance, accompanied by skilful and varied planting (lower right), is the best recipe for success.
Stourhead, Mere, Wiltshire, England. Stourton House, Mere, Wiltshire, England.

36A

36B

good; anything which depletes it is bad.

Siting

Sunlight drives photosynthesis, producing sugars that plants need from carbon dioxide and water, and just as importantly, oxygen which is released into the water. So a pond should be sunlit. But small, shallow ponds exposed to the unremitting force of the sun become airless, tepid baths in which their inhabitants gasp and die. Shading of some kind must be provided – by arranging for the surface to become partially covered by foliage, and/or by plants or structures around the edge.

Aquatics with leaves that float on the surface, including water lilies and water hawthorns, provide ideal shade – at its densest in summer, decreasing to nothing in the winter. Cultivars of water lilies can be found to fit almost any size of pond, from expansive lakes to a puddle in a tub, and choosing these is just a matter of taking care and taking advice. The subtropical water hawthorn survives frost in cold climates, provided it is planted 60 cm (2 ft) deep or so, and its vigour is restricted in these cold conditions. In warmer situations, it is likely to grow too vigorously for a small pool.

Plants can be positioned close to the edge of a pond to provide shade for any part of the day – on the east, during the morning; on the west, during the afternoon, etc. But if quantities of falling leaves blow into the pond, bacteria may

attempts to 'balance' them. The commonest error is to condemn as stagnant, water that turns green, followed by its removal, vigorous cleansing activity and replenishment with fresh water. But green water is healthy water, taking its colour from the photosynthesizing algae that maintain its supply of life-giving oxygen. From the gardener's point of view, plants rather than algae perform this service more decoratively, and the route to success lies in installing carefully-selected mixtures of plants to mop up the nutrients and light on which algae depend. Meanwhile, it is much better to leave well alone than indulge in catastrophic clearances and renewals that set back the processes through which well-sited, well-designed and well-planted ponds manage themselves.

Siting, design and planting of ponds

Oxygen is the vital force that enables water to support life, and successful management of any pond – but most critically small ones – depends on ensuring a supply of dissolved oxygen in the water. Anything which adds to this supply is

36A & B. Ponds should be sunlit – yet at least part of their surface should be shaded! This contradiction is resolved by a combination of water lilies, whose pads cover the surface, and plants with broad, spreading leaves on the banks (left). Very shallow ponds (right) are safer for children, but have even more need of shade to reduce rapid fluctuations in water temperature. Rapaura Water Garden, Tapu, Coromandel. New Zealand. Rapaura Water Garden, Tapu, Coromandel. New Zealand.

37A

37B

than small ones may bring little comfort to owners of small gardens in search of a *water feature*. Nevertheless, a great many ponds are made unnecessarily puny: a measly couple of square feet gracing the rock garden; a trivial, ditch-like moat dividing the patio from the lawn; a dank, dark hole like a dinosaur's lost kidney in the corner of a flower bed. Ponds, like lawns, provide horizontal spaces that interact with the vertical planting around them. In design terms, they can substitute for, or complement, a lawn, and they do so most effectively when bold enough to make an impression. Ponds as major features in gardens – rather than secondary attributes of something else – are easier to look after, and more effective too.

Still waters proverbially run deep, and depth is a desirable attribute in a pond, however small, though it is seldom necessary to exceed 60 cm (2 ft) in a small pond, and 2 m (6 ft 6 in) in a large one. But the sound and play of moving water is an attractive part of any pond, and also helps boost its oxygen supply. Fountains come to mind, and can lead on to grandiose dreams of vast water works, or memories of the simple jets playing into a long canal that relieve the heat of the gardens of the Generalife in Granada.

Fountain-makers, on whatever scale, invariably contend with problems of water supply and blocked jets. At a modest level, in a small pond, water supply is not usually a problem, and pumps of all sizes can be bought to drive any fountains your imaginations can devise. But blocked jets remain a problem, caused mainly by the long strands of filamentous algae, one of nature's most effective essays in devising a material guaranteed to clog small holes. An attempted solution to the problem can be seen at Longwood Gardens, where a clear bourn of chlorinated water floods over the lip of the impressive spring known as the Eye of the World, and cascades down a gorge into the pond below – a model which becomes less appealing at close quarters, where the air is filled with the stench of chlorine. An

consume all the oxygen during their decomposition, producing the black lifeless brew that is truly stagnant water. Trees and deciduous shrubs whose leaves blow in the wind make bad neighbours for small ponds, and should be used sparingly; plants whose spent leaves can be removed more easily – such as bamboos, phormiums, palms and large perennials such as rheums, rodgersias and ligularias – pose fewer hazards. Structures like bridges, summer houses and decking can be used to provide shade decoratively, effectively and precisely, with no problems from fallen leaves, while making the water more accessible and available for enjoyment.

Design

The fact that large ponds are easier to manage

37A & B. Moving water, from fountains (top) or a rill (bottom), adds immeasurably to the atmosphere of a water garden. Fountains and water lilies are incompatible, and problems with blocked jets and the wayward dispersal of water by wind cause frustrations too. Rills offer attractive, relatively problem-free alternatives. Gardens of the Generalife, Granada, Andalucia, Spain. Rapaura Water Garden, Tapu, Coromandel. New Zealand.

alternative is to install a filter system to remove algae and other debris from the water before they reach the pump, and if this fails, you might do better to avoid fountains in favour of less ambitious situations. The simplest is some form of rill through which water flowing (or pumped) into a basin at a higher level than the pond itself drops over an edge into the pool below. This creates movement and sound, and oxygen is absorbed from the air by the disturbance of the falling water. It also makes it possible to grow water lilies, whose leaves provide such valuable shade in pools of any size, but are averse to the pitter-patter of drops of water from a fountain onto their horizontal pads.

Ponds often exist naturally as part of a system that includes wet land as well as open water. This extends the volume of water, and helps to buffer the system as a whole so that it is less subject to sudden, short-term changes in temperature, nutrients and water level. But the impermeable membranes of plastic, fibreglass or concrete that contain small ponds in gardens all too often act as abrupt – and most unnatural – boundaries between the pond and the dry land beyond it. The flexibility of plastic liners make it relatively easy to combine clear water with neighbouring areas of bog or wetland by excavating well beyond the actual area intended to be open water. The use of fertile garden soil in these situations can cause problems when nutrients leach out into the pool, increasing algal and other undesirable growth. This can be avoided by substituting gravel, or mixtures of gravel and soil in the proportions of three to one as the substrate.

Plants capable of growing in wetland conditions.

Perennially saturated soil around ponds and in marshy situations supports vigorous communities of plants that form strong matrices, resistant to invasion. Only well adapted, robust species can compete and establish themselves successfully in such conditions.

Aster novi-belgii: Forms persistent, spreading colonies through rhizomes which infiltrate and mix well with grasses.

Astilbe hybrids: Numerous cvs. & spp. available – grow well in light shade provided soil is constantly moist in summer.

Bupthalmum salicifolium: A useful, long-lived plant for moist, sunny situations, producing a long succession of yellow daisies.

Calamagrostis arundinacea: Cvs. include variegated forms: a compact grass that does well in moist conditions and some shade.

Carex pendula: Sedges are naturally at home in these situations, and form persistent matrices with grasses and herbs.

Equisetum robustum: Horsetails spread vigorously by underground rhizomes and are suitable only for large areas.

Filipendula rubra 'Venusta': Flowering in late summer, these Asiatic meadow sweets associate well with strong growing grasses.

Glyceria maxima 'Variegata': A vigorously spreading but attractive grass, useful where space, and competition from neighbours allows.

*Hibiscus moscheutos** hybrids*: Numerous cvs. available. Do best in moist, boggy conditions, high summer humidity & temperatures.

Iris sibirica: Upright clumps of narrow foliage combine well with grasses; contrasting with broad leaved plants.

Matteucia struthiopteris: A fern that spreads by underground rhizomes, and provides attractive contrasts to other foliage forms.

Osmunda cinnamomea: A vigorous persistent, ground-holding fern forming strong upright clumps of leaves.

Panicum virgatum: Tolerant of varied conditions:forms persistent cover that produces a strong matrix with associated plants.

Patrinia scabiosifolia: Tall branching perennial, best when emerging from a ground cover of lower growing plants.

Phormium tenax: A very wide choice of garden forms is available in different sizes, forms and foliage colours.

Primula helodoxa: Several candelabra primulas do well, if neighbours are not too competitive. Appreciate some shade.

Rubus speciosus: Infiltrates well amongst grasses and herbs producing spreading colonies of upright stems.

Spartina pectinata 'Aureomarginata': Spreads moderately by rhizomes and needs to be restrained by strong local competition

Thelypteris palustris: A fern that forms

a

b

g

f

e

d

c

A

B

C

A

B

C

moderately by rhizomes and needs to be restrained by strong local competition
Thelypteris palustris. A fern that forms excellent spreading ground cover, amongst perennials and grasses.

The varying depths of natural ponds increase the variety of plants that grow in them. But shallow and deep ends, or broadly-defined areas, are more satisfactory than the narrow shelves that appear in so many diagrammatic illustrations of pond construction. These shelves may impart interestingly craggy profiles to take-away pools of fibreglass, but plants lodged on them tend to slide gently off their narrow perches into the depths below.

In the recent past, most ponds were made with concrete, and almost inevitably this led to designs intended to maintain a constant water level throughout the year. Plastic and butyl rubber sheets allow more flexible approaches, but an unchanging water level remains a standard aim of pond construction and management, and the idea of deliberately allowing changes in water level from one season to another may seem strange. But this opens the way to different effects at different times of the year; it avoids the need to top up falling water levels in summer with fresh water from the tap, disturbing the balance and adding undesirable doses of nitrates and phosphates; and because it mimics natural events, it makes it possible to grow plants that do not thrive when levels remain constant.

Pools that dry up for a time are widespread in places where summers are warm and relatively dry. Many plants are adapted to survive these conditions, and even do better in them because of the elimination of competition from more vigorous, truly aquatic plants and algae. Similarly, amphibians, particularly frogs and toads, with lifecycles adapted to seasonally dry pools benefit from the elimination of fish that prey on their tadpoles.

Plants suitable for inclusion amongst communities growing in and around ponds that dry out in summer.

It is natural, in some areas, for the water levels of ponds to fall during the summer, and many marginal aquatics adapted to this occurrence are widely grown in gardens.

Asclepias incarnata. An upright, perennial, grown mainly for its bright flowers that contrasts well with low growing plants.
Bulbinella latifolia*. Forms dense weed-excluding colonies on the margins of seasonally water-filled depressions.
Caltha palustris. A vigorous, ground occupying perennial. Several forms, varying in vigour, colour and flower form are available.
Gladiolus tristis*. Suitable for use amongst low-growing plants, e.g. grasses – in situations subject to winter flooding.
Gunnera manicata. Forms a gigantic, weed excluding mono-matrix. Requires constantly moist soil throughout the summer.
Iris pseudacorus. Spreading rhizomes occupy ground effectively to form a robust matrix with other equally vigorous plants.
Lysichiton americanus. Forms colonies of plants whose large leaves shade the space between them, and inhibit growth of intruders.
Mimulus moschatus. A useful herbaceous perennial growing rapidly in early summer, to

---

Fig 8. Pool and associated wetland
'A' The maximum depth of the pool shown here is 1.5 m (5 ft). The hole excavated to accommodate the pool and its associated areas of wetland is encased with a plastic liner. The open water provides the water lilly zone.
'B' The area of shallow water was formed by careful shaping during excavation – back-filling with a mixture of gravel and topsoil 3/1 to provide a basin filled with saturated soil 15 cm (6 in) deep. 'C' The wetland area was also back-filled with the gravel/topsoil mix and separated from, but kept in contact with, the pool by an earth bank formed from turves. This was planted with perennials whose interlacing roots will hold the

bank in place, but allow water to seep through to maintain bog conditions in the wetland throughout the year.
Key to upper diagram:
a – header pool with small fountain.
b – stepped rill – formed to hold water continuously whether the pump is running or not.
c – inlet to overflow.
d – return pipe from pool to tank containing the filter and pump.
e – filter unit and pump.
f – feeder pipe for fountain and header pool.
g – fountain jet.

38A

38B

38C

combine with other marginal plants.

Monochoria korsakowii: This and the related *Pontederia cordata* contribute effectively to matrices formed by marginal plants.

Myosotis scorpioides: Very effective, early spring flowerer that produces a dense growth of short stems and foliage.

Osmunda regalis: An exceptionally retentive ground-holding fern that associates well with other vigorous plants.

Ottelia alismoides*: A fragile but attractive plant that seeds itself freely to occupy spaces in the matrix.

Ranunculus ophioglossifolius: A rarely grown annual buttercup. More common and effective are the very vigorous *RR. lingua* and *flammula*.

***Salix alba* 'Britzensis'**: In most situations best cut back every year or two, to emphasise the scarlet bark of the young shoots.

Schizostylis coccinea* 'Major': Numerous cvs. are available, needs mild, frost-free autumns for the flowers to develop.

Spiraea douglasii: Forms dense, weed excluding thickets – amongst which few other plants grow well.

Typha laxmannii: One of the smaller, less invasive cat's tails. Others may be too robust for most situations.

Veronica beccabunga: Forms dense, weed excluding masses of stems and glossy foliage in shallow water and wet ground.

Viburnum opulus: An upright water-tolerant shrub, excellent for the upper canopy of a matrix in very wet conditions.

Zantedeschia aethiopica*: Grows well covered with water in the winter – benefiting from frost protection in cold areas.

In Britain and other parts of the world where winters are relatively mild and wet, we take it for granted that pools are flush with water in winter. But many of the marginal aquatics that we grow – or would like to grow – come from the summer rainfall regions of the Natal Drakensberg, places with temperate, monsoonal climates like Ussuriland, areas with intensely cold winters such as Alaska or Canada, or from high altitudes where rainfall is low or water is immobilized in ice and snow during the winter.

38A, B & C. Wetlands associated with pools modify violent fluctuations in temperature and water level, and the luxuriant growth of the plants (top left) mops up excess nutrients. Even narrow, stream-like watercourses, like the one photographed in spring (top right), and at the height of plant growth in high summer (bottom left), can be combined effectively and beneficially with wetland. Bev McConnell's Garden, Ayrlies, Whitford, Auckland, New Zealand. John Treasure's Garden, Burford House, Tenbury Wells, Worcestershire, England.

Marginal aquatic plants in such places grow in ground that is saturated with water in summer but comparatively dry in winter. These conditions are hard to replicate in Britain, the mid-Atlantic states of the USA or New Zealand except by deliberately constructing ponds in which water levels are designed to fall in the winter.

Plants suitable for inclusion in communities of plants around ponds where water levels fall in winter

Many gardeners would not associate most of the plants on this list with water – though they would be aware of their sensitivity to drought. Only a few of the following grow in water; the remainder depend on saturated or near-saturated soil to support growth and flowering throughout their growing seasons – but are often intolerant of excessive wet in winter.

Acer ginnala: An upright shrub, or small tree, useful as a low canopy former in wet, but free-draining situations.

Agapanthus campanulatus*: Spreads by short rhizomes to form extensive clumps of congested, weed excluding crowns.

Cornus alba 'Sibirica': This and other forms of *C. alba* associates well with low growing weaving perennials.

Dierama dracomontanum: This and other species are arching perennials than combine well with low growing perennials.

Eupatorium coelestinum: Very late emergence in spring provides good ground cover for bulbs, flowers late summer till autumn.

Filipendula palmatum: Vigorous perennials in rich, moist soils capable of forming persistent matrices with other plants.

Iris ensata: A plant that prefers to be just below water level in summer, but benefits from dryer conditions in winter.

Kniphofia uvaria: This and several other species will grow in shallow water – preferably circulating – in summer.

Leucanthemella serotina: Strongly competitive, late-flowering ox-eye daisy forms a robust matrix with other vigorous perennials.

Ligularia dentata: Numerous garden forms exist – all have very high water requirements during the growing season.

Lilium canadense: Produces wide-ranging underground rhizomes through which extensive colonies of bulbs develop.

Lobelia cardinalis: This and *LL. syphilitica* and *vedrariensis* grow in water or saturated soil in summer, preferably drier in winter.

Lysimachia clethroides: Short rhizomes form compact weed-excluding clumps – providing the ground remains moist in summer.

Miscanthus sinensis var purpurascens: This and cvs of the species need constantly moist rich soils to achieve maximum growth and development.

Monarda didyma: Easily grown from seed, this attractive perennial is a useful member of damp community matrices.

Primula rosea: Like other wetland primulas from high altitudes requires saturated conditions in summer to do well.

Rheum palmatum: A massive ground occupying plant that combines well with other plants provided copious water is available.

Sorbaria sorbifolia: A small shrub with a long-flowering season; a useful member of mixed communities in damp conditions.

Spiraea salicifolia: Will grow in standing water through the summer, but requires drier conditions in winter.

Vaccinium corymbosum: Another shrub that is a useful member of mixed shrub/perennial communities in wet conditions.

Planting

Ponds and the areas around them in gardens provide all kinds of opportunities for varied and attractive planting, provided we understand the needs of the plants we use, and match them closely with the conditions in the places where we plant them. This matching depends on recognizing the ways one habitat differs from another, and some of those that occur under natural conditions are listed below. All can be adapted to garden settings with attractive results provided their problems are taken into account.

Constantly available water, high levels of sunlight in open, unshaded situations and – increasingly frequently – high levels of nutrients

39A

39B

in the water supply favour very vigorous plant growth, and the edges of ponds and the ground around them are battlegrounds in which one plant competes vigorously with another for rootholds and space for leaves and stems to develop. The matrices formed are extremely dense and persistent, made up of vigorous, long-lived, robust perennials. Annuals are rare and play little part in these communities.

Wet meadows

These are often found on heavy loams containing high proportions of clay and silt, or peat. The soil may be waterlogged in winter, and even in high summer never dries out completely. Matrices are composed of vigorous perennials and grasses, many of which flower in late summer or autumn – a valuable attribute in gardens. Areas of wet meadows around ponds maintain a reservoir of water; their soils remain cool beneath the blanket of foliage above them, and the vigorous growth of the plants removes and retains surplus nutrients – all this contributes to the stability and well-being of water in adjacent pools.

The impermeable plastic or rubber membranes widely used to retain water in garden ponds can be used very effectively to extend water-holding areas in order to form a high water table around the pond itself, with similar benefits to those that occur naturally. The intractable soils typical of natural situations

can be replaced by gravels or coarse grits – with or without additions of soil – to make them easier to manage.

When such areas are formed, planting should follow natural patterns, and aim to establish a dense, impermeable and permanent plant cover as soon as possible. Unoccupied spaces will be rapidly filled by vigorous weeds that are very tenacious, so rapid establishment of the initial planting and careful removal of unwanted intruders in the early stages is very important. Later on, glyphosate or ammonium sulphamate can be used as spot treatments to control weeds.

The natural communities of plants in wet meadows and bogs are dominated by grasses and sedges, and these provide strong contrasts to plantings elsewhere. Alternatively the proportion of grasses and sedges can be reduced, or they can be omitted altogether in favour of broad-leaved plants and petalloid monocotyledons, provided these are capable of developing the dense, vigorous matrices necessary to exclude intruders from what are, in plant terms, most desirable residential situations.

Swamps

Swamps occur naturally around the inlets and outlets of lakes and ponds, where water lying just above or just below ground level is colonized by reeds, shrubs and trees, including many willows. They may sound less than instantly appealing as a garden setting, but their

39A & B. Vigorous plants with dense, erosion-defying mats of roots can be used to stabilize the edges of a pond. These must be chosen carefully, because once they have become established, misplaced plants cannot be removed without damaging the banks.
Both Longstock Water Gardens, Stockbridge, Hampshire, England.

use as water-purifying systems is now being recognized in the treatment of sewage effluents by willow and reed beds, and this service can be extended effectively and attractively to the maintenance of the balanced conditions that contribute to the well-being of the water in ponds and lakes. They are often rich in wildlife, acting, amongst other things, as nurseries in which young fish and other creatures find cover and readily available food.

Swamps large enough to contain willow trees fit only into large-scale water works, but garden variations by an ornamental pool can be reduced to small areas of reeds or water-loving shrubs, including *Cornus alba*, *Spiraea salicifolia* and *S. douglasii* or *Sorbaria sorbifolia*, and perennials, amongst them the brilliant *Lobelia cardinalis*.

Water's edge

The point where water and land meet is a critical boundary, where the ground must be stabilized so that it is not continually eroded by water, or by the dabblings and fritterings of ducks, fishes and other creatures. Concrete or plastic/rubber sheets do this effectively but unattractively; stones or wooden piles more aesthetically. Alternatively, the dense mats of fibrous roots produced by plants in these situations may serve this purpose. Those who doubt the extent and resilience of such root systems should spend an hour or two digging up a well-established plant of gypsy wort or royal fern. These water's-edge plants produce formidable matrices of roots and rhizomes which are the basis of defence against erosion from water and once in place can scarcely be removed without extensive breaches to the defences.

Bank formers for ponds

Pond edges are subject to erosion and breakdown – particularly if exposed to weathering. Tenacious, soil-binding plants which prevent exposure and hold the soil together is one way to keep them together. Many of the

40A

40B

40A & B. Numerous plants like reeds, bulrushes, and lotus (upper), some extremely invasive, grow in shallow water. These are unable to spread into the deeper parts of a pond, and occupy a clearly-defined band along the margins (lower). Their invasion of areas closer to the centre is a sure sign that a pond is silting up. Near Lesozavodsk, Ussuriland, Far Eastern Region, Russia. Lake Khanka, near Gayvoran, Far Eastern Region, Russia.

plants in the previous list will also fulfil this role. Some of the following are tall, exceptionally vigorous plants suitable for large ponds. It is important to match plant vigour with the intended affect.

Acorus gramineus: Also a dwarf form – 'Pusillus' and several other cvs. available – all are grass-like and quite low growing.

Astilbe taquetii 'Superba': A tall, clump-forming, vigorously retentive plant with attractive foliage and flowers.

Athyrium filix-femina – Victoriae group: The dense rhizomes of this and other forms of the lady fern, are good stabilisers for shaded locations.

Carex elata (stricta) 'Aurea' (Bowles Golden): An excellent small, upright clump former for relatively low cover along the margins of pools.

Cotula coronopifolia*: Masses of stems and flowers protect bank edges and mask shore lines – Submerged shoots survive frost.

Darmera peltata: Vigorous plant with broad densely shading leaves, and thick rhizomes that are excellent ground stabilisers.

Dulichium arundinaceum: Clump-forming sedge with retentive roots and upright stems, provides dense cover on edges of pools.

Eupatorium fistulosum: Garden cvs. of Joe Pye weed are available – including compact forms – provide useful late colour.

Hemerocallis flava: This and other vigorous, rhizomatous species make excellent colonizers in spacious situations.

Hosta ventricosa: Strong clump forming species – a vast range of cvs. and spp. fulfil similar roles. Choice depends on space.

Houttuynia cordata 'Variegata' *: Spreads rapidly by invasive underground rhizomes – infilling amongst other plants.

Iris forrestii: Several species of moderate sized, clump-forming irises provide excellent, non-invasive bank support.

Ligularia przewalskii: This and other spp. and cvs. make excellent vigorous waterside plants with decorative foliage and flowers.

Lycopus americanus: Several species provide plain but extremely solid, almost ineradicable protection from erosion.

Lysimachia nummularia 'Aurea': Excellent for creeping cover, either by itself or infiltrating amongst other plants.

Lythrum salicaria: Also *L. virgatum* and many cvs. Colourful, medium sized to tall, late-flowering plants.

Primula japonica: Many species fulfil the role. Some are short-lived but replace themselves readily by seed.

Rodgersia aesculifolia: Vigorous, large-leaved highly retentive plants that provide excellent, permanent bank support.

Scrophularia aquatica 'Variegata': A tall plant that emerges above lower vegetation – the variegated form provides useful contrast.

Spartina pectinata 'Aureomarginata'*: Upright, moderately tall, clump forming grass with dense mats of soil retaining roots, for large ponds.

Shallow water

The margins of ponds hold a variety of plants, many of which can colonize soil around the water's edge, helping to stabilize the banks. Most do not depend totally on immersion in water, and survive and thrive in pools that dry out in summer, provided moisture remains available below the surface. Unlike the plants of wet meadows and pondside banks, many have exploratory rather than dense root systems, and are comparatively fragile rather than robust, tending to break apart without great difficulty, and some are intolerant of frost, surviving only when covered by water during the winter. Their talent for disintegration, combined with a readiness to produce new roots, enables them to spread easily throughout a water system, and their questing, rhizomatous roots exploit the opportunities of new situations when they reach them. Like all water plants, they live in a world where competition is intense, but do so in situations where opportunities for new entrants and new combinations of plants in the community occur more frequently.

In gardens too, these plants can be used more flexibly than those that stabilize the banks on the water's edge, which cannot be replaced without doing structural damage to the margins of the pond. They are easily propagated and easily established and the disappearance of one or two from a plant matrix – whether intentionally or as a result of unfavourable weather – is equally easily made good by the introduction of replacements.

Many grow rapidly, and in small ponds – and even in larger ones – the choice of species becomes very important, and regular reductions to restrict spread may be necessary. These marginal plants are only partially-adapted aquatics, often capable of growing in the saturated soil close to a pond, but not able to embark on a wholly aquatic lifestyle. Their spread can be restricted to the margins of ponds by increasing the depth of water a short way from the banks – once this exceeds 30 cm (1 ft) or so, the number able to grow falls off rapidly, and very few can tolerate depths greater than 45 cm (1 ft 6 in). Take-overs, even by very vigorous species of *Phragmites*, *Typha* and *Ranunculus*, can be prevented simply by ensuring that areas intended to be clear water are too deep for them to colonize.

The rhizomes of reeds like *Scirpus* and *Phragmites* – and many bamboos too – have sharply pointed tips that puncture sheets of plastic and butyl rubber, and should not be planted round any pond where these are used as liners.

Plants for shallow water round the margins of ponds

These are useful for reducing abrupt contrasts between bank and water, and, form links with wetland communities which wildlife will use to enter and leave the pond. Most are sensitive to the depth of water and will not invade clear water spaces in deeper, central parts of ponds.

Acorus calamus 'Variegatus': A good 'interface' plant, growing equally well in shallow water and wetlands around a pool.
Alisma plantago-aquatica: A vigorous, tuberous self-seeding marginal useful for its ability to fill gaps, in larger ponds.
Butomus umbellatus: Spreads vigorously by rhizomes. Does best in fertile situations with cool summer temperatures.
Calla palustris: An acid loving marginal that increases by floating rhizomes, and will spread into adjacent wetlands.
Colocasia esculenta*: Enormous leaves provide shade and contrast with other plants. Suitable

only for warm water settings.
Hydrocharis morsus-ranae: Needs shallow situations with rapidly warming water in summer. Hardy resting buds sink to mud in winter.
Iris laevigata: Numerous cvs. – all are easily grown, moderately spreading plants that will link with wetland areas.
Juncus effusus 'Spiralis': A shallow water marginal and wetland reed, producing compact clumps of corkscrew foliage.
Nelumbo komarowii*: This and *NN. lutea* and *nucifera* are attractive marginals for ponds large enough to hold them.
Orontium aquaticum: Wetland and marginal plant that spreads by runners – but only winter hardy beneath a covering of water.
Peltandra virginica: Best for shallow marginal water; grows slowly unless summer water temperatures are moderately high
Phragmites australis (communis): Extremely vigorous wetland and shallow water reed – suitable for large areas.
Pontederia cordata: Needs fertile warm water conditions in summer, and frost protection from a covering of water in winter.
Ranunculus lingua 'Grandiflora': Spreads vigorously by runners, excellent for colonising shallow water and adjacent wetland areas.
Sagittaria sagittifolia: Multiplies by bulb-like organs at the ends of the roots – but spreads only moderately in most situations.
Sarracenia flava*: For exceptional situations in bogs or shallow water in warm sites on nutrient poor, acid soils.
Saururus cernuus: Spreads vigorously by runners into adjacent wetland, but only underwater shoots survive cold winters.
Schoenoplectus (Scirpus) lacustris: This and less vigorous spp. colonize shallow water – beware of spike-like root tips that puncture liners.
Trapa natans*: An annual. The nut-like fruits, known as water chestnuts, survive only beneath a covering of water. – prohibited in the USA.
Typha latifolia: All but *T. minima* are suitable only for large ponds. Their needle-like root tips easily puncture liners.

The water lily zone

Species with leaves that float upon the water in the genera *Nuphar, Nymphoides, Aponogeton, Euryale* and *Nelumbo* play such major roles amongst the communities of plants in ponds that it seems entirely appropriate to use their name as a label for the situation where they grow. Not only are their flowers – and very often their foliage – extremely decorative, but they are also ecologically dominant in the communities amongst which they live. Truly aquatic plants, like these, form a small but vitally important minority amongst the communities that live in and around watery habitats. They depend on constantly available water; they grow best at intermediate depths – deep enough to ensure that they are not threatened by periodically falling water levels, but not so deep (up to 2 m [6 ft 6 in] or more) that the stretch between mud and water surface is beyond the reach of their stems.

The roots of water lilies and similar plants are anchored in the mud at the bottom of pools, and their leaves float on the surface. Other aquatics like lemnas and azollas, and fragile-looking *Hydrocharis* species, float freely on the surface, and *Stratiotes saloides* migrates from the mud to the surface, depending on the season. Their floating leaves shade the water beneath them, prevent excessive growth of algae and underwater plants, and restrain undesirable rises in water temperatures.

At least some of these plants are almost indispensable in both large and small ponds, but in the former they need to be very carefully chosen and used. Vigour and ultimate size need to be carefully matched to the size of the pond, and they should be grown in containers from which they can be removed and divided occasionally if they threaten to overwhelm. Vigorous specimens growing freely in the mud at the bottom of larger ponds and lakes become ineradicable without great effort. However extensive the situation, the initial choice of species and cultivars should be very carefully considered, and the most vigorous used only where their colonizing powers not only seem unlikely to cause problems – but offer positive advantages.

The impression of fragility conveyed by some of the free floaters should be treated with suspicion. Even the tiny water ferns *Azolla* and *Salvinia* and the minute pads of duckweeds quickly become all-pervasive, and are exceedingly difficult to eradicate. More vigorous floaters like water lettuces and hyacinths spread so assertively in favourable conditions that they have become internationally recognized pests, outlawed in the few countries, such as New Zealand, where they remain a threat rather than an immediate problem. Like the pads of water lilies, they cover the surface and shade the water below – and often do it very decoratively – but their tendency to escape control makes them dangerous allies for this purpose in comparison with more sedentary alternatives.

Plants for the water lily zone or deep water.

Water lilies are ideal plants away from the margins of ponds, since their floating pads and flowers are decorative and shade the water below. Other species can be used in similar roles, or, as submerged aquatics, to oxygenate the water while leaving the surface clear.

Aponogeton distachyos: A deep water aquatic with narrow floating leaves associates well with water lilies.
Azolla filiculoides (caroliniana): Invasive, but usually harmless, floating fern with attractive foliage – useful for its shading effects.
Eichhornia crassipes*: An invasive floating aquatic. Repeated removal can be a way of reducing excess nutrient content of water.
Elodea canadensis: A vigorous submerged aquatic that proliferates too rapidly for all but large areas of water.
Euryala ferox*: A tropical plant with broad, round leaves able to survive cold winters beneath about 30 cms (1 ft) of water.
Hottonia palustris: Moderate or slow grower in still, acid water in relatively shallow situations.
Lagarosiphon major: Submerged aquatic, grows most rapidly in warm situations, but easy to establish elsewhere.
Lemna gibba: Floating duckweed, invasive, possible use as shade producer while other floating leaved aquatics are developing.
Myriophyllum aquaticum: Submerged plant for deep water – good oxygenator and cover for fish fry etc.
Nuphar japonica: This and *NN. lutea, japonica*

41A

41C

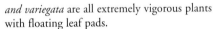

41B

and variegata are all extremely vigorous plants with floating leaf pads.

***Nymphaea capensis* hybrids *:** Produce masses of rounded leaves in warm pools, that shade out algae and submerged aquatics.

***Nymphaea odorata* hybrids:** Important to match vigour of numerous hybrids and cvs inc. *NN. mexicana* and *tetragona*: with space available.

***Nymphaea pygmaea* hybrids:** A race of small water lilies that provide excellent floating pads of foliage in restricted spaces.

***Nymphoides peltata*:** This and *N. aquatica* are floating aquatics filling in between plants with upright stems in shallow water.

***Pistia stratiotes* *:** Invasive floating aquatic in warm pools. Dense shader that can be useful before other plants develop

***Potamogeton crispus*:** Vigorous submerged aquatic – prefers slowly moving water, and may take over restricted situations.

***Ranunculus fluitans*:** Numerous water crowfoots exist; are most likely to grow successfully in flowing, base-rich waters.

***Stratiotes aloides*:** Floating aquatic in summer that submerges for winter – forms dense colonies in moderately shallow water.

***Utricularia inflata*:** Numerous species: produce

41A, B & C. Shade from floating leaves restricts the growth of submerged aquatics, which can otherwise choke the water and upset the balance of a pond when they decay. Water lilies (top left) are the most typical, flexible and beautiful of these plants, but the distinctive pads of **Euryala ferox** (right) and the delicate foliage of water hawthorn (bottom left) are attractive variations on the theme.
Bev McConnell's Garden, Ayrlies, Whitford, Auckland, New Zealand. Near Lesozavodsk, Ussuriland, Far Eastern Region, Russia. Knysna Forrest, Knysna Cape Province, South Africa.

dense growth of submerged leaves and stems with small flowers above the water.
Vallisneria spiralis: Submerged aquatic. Undemanding plants preferring warm water, tolerant of frost when submerged.

Deep water

When the depth of water reaches and exceeds 2 m (6 ft 6 in), constantly cool conditions at root level, and the distance between the surface of the water and the mud below defeat even the most vigorous species of *Nymphaea* and *Nuphar*. In these conditions, submerged aquatics, including species of *Elodea*, *Myriophyllum* and *Potamogeton* (kept under control by the overhead shadow of the floating pads of the water lilies and their allies in shallower water), come into their own. They grow with their roots in the mud, and their stems and foliage reach up through the water towards the light. Free from competition, they can form dense, impenetrable thickets of stems and foliage that choke waterways, increase the rate of silting, and when they die in the autumn, produce masses of dead plant material which overloads the oxygen capacity of the water, leading to lethal conditions for fish and other pond life. *Elodea canadensis* is one of a number of these plants whose range has been extended by unwise – and later, bitterly regretted – introductions; others, including *Egeria densa* from South America, species of *Lagarosiphon* from central and southern parts of Africa: the eel grasses, *Zostera* spp., hornworts, *Ceratophyllum* spp. and the berry-bearing *Hydrilla verticillata* have all proved such effective and adaptable colonizers that their propagation and use in gardens is banned in some countries.

The gardens

Exotic water gardens in Hull

The 200 sq. m (2,200 sq. ft) garden belongs to a house on an estate built by the council on the outskirts of Hull. A few years ago it was bought by its tenant, a car mechanic, who recently

formed a company to buy the garage where he has worked for many years. He and his wife live here with their two teenage children. Both came to Britain with their parents in the 1960s from Uganda, where their families had been long-established members of the Asian community. Hitherto, they have grown a few flowers in the garden, and some of the vegetables which they like but cannot find in the local greengrocers' shops, However, a recent outing to Fountains Abbey introduced them to Studley Royal, and he returned determined to make a water garden. In direct contrast to his former totally practical and utilitarian use of the garden, he dreamed up a series of ponds, one leading to another, almost hidden amongst the sensationally atmospheric, tropical-looking planting that surrounds them.

Review

A
Flights of fancy have been rare on this estate. Until recently, everyone rented their houses from the council, few trees were planted, and little was spent on gardens – a situation that has begun to change since most tenants became property-owning democrats.
B
The place has a utilitarian, even drab, atmosphere, and an overall lack of privacy, due partly to its lay-out, partly to its history. This is a place desperately in need of someone to break the mould and do something imaginative and unusual.
C
The conditions offered few impediments to his ideas. The topsoil is a neutral, light, sandy loam that is easily worked and could be used for almost any purpose.
D
The heavy clay subsoil is almost entirely stone-free, and becomes almost watertight with a little puddling. It makes an excellent base for ponds, using liners to ensure they do not leak.

Outcome

A
Action started one bank holiday weekend, when

Fig 9. Exotic water gardens in Hull
This may be only a small garden but, as the drawing shows, this does not demand that it be filled only with small plants used in a prim fashion. Here water and exuberant planting, making maximum use of contrasting foliage and textures, have created an exciting jungly effect in a very small space.

a neighbour, who owned a contracting and plant hire business, turned up with his Bobcat and said, 'Let's give it a go, VJ.'

B & C

The extended holiday was spent moving the topsoil from one place to another, excavating holes for pools linked by channels, digging out shallow trenches in which to lay paths, and constructing a raised bank at the end of the garden for a screen of shrubs and trees.

Much of it was done impulsively – no plan had been prepared beforehand – and most of the first day's work was reconstructed during the following few days.

However, they took great care not to mix the topsoil with the heavy clay removed during excavation of the pools. Much of this was used to form different levels in the almost flat garden, so that water, circulated by a pump, could drop from one pool to another.

D

Heavy-gauge, nylon-reinforced polythene sheet was used to line the excavations – all of it obtained as offcuts or unaccounted surpluses from the contractor's business. The edges were hidden beneath paving slabs, or extended beneath wetland areas adjacent to the pools and channels and disguised by plants growing above them.

These wetland areas were filled in to about 5 cm (2 in) above the level of the water with a 3:1 mixture of pea gravel and topsoil, in which plants were set out.

The planting was done by plundering local garden centres in a triumphant finale to the operation. They ended with a feeling of having indulged not wisely but too well, and some of their choices may cause problems as they develop.

The plants

In his imagination, VJ's water garden was a chain of dark, mysterious pools, almost lost amongst the surrounding vegetation. In fact, there was little room for trees, and instead height and shadows were obtained by using bamboos like *Phyllostachys aurea* (which died in the first winter), *P. flexuosa* and *Pleioblastus (Arundinaria) auricomus* (not so large, but non-invasive and dramatically beautiful), with *Fargesia (Arundinaria) murieliae*. These were planted with

evergreen shrubs, including *Choisya ternata* and especially *Fatsia japonica* (for the sake of its luxuriant, tropical-looking leaves) and a few upright, deciduous shrubs, notably *Decaisnea fargesii* (whose blue beans he found an irresistible prospect). Phormiums, including 'Dazzler'. 'Maori Maiden', 'Purpureum' and 'Yellow Wave'; were planted in the lower layers of the matrix, and although rather battered by the end of the winter, did well in the shade and shelter of the bamboos and shrubs.

Several cultivars of *Miscanthus sinensis*, including 'Cabaret', 'Gracillimus' , 'Malepartus' and 'Zebrinus', were planted in wetland areas or on the margins of pools, and grew so well that they upstaged the bamboos, and he wished he had used them more. Apart from these, touches of opulence were provided by the large leaves of groups of *Darmera peltata*, *Hosta* cvs, *Ligularia* 'Desdemona' and 'Gregynog Gold' and *Lysichitum americanum*. He was sorely tempted to try *Rheum palmatum* 'Atrosanguineum' as a substitute for the obviously Gulliverian *Gunnera manicata* in his Lilliput, but was persuaded that even this was excessively large. Ferns including *Matteucia struthiopteris*; and several forms of *Osmunda regalis* were used as effective foils to the broad-leaved perennials.

A variety of aquatics were planted in the pools – mostly cultivars of *Nymphaea pygmaea*, with *Acorus calamus* 'Variegatus' *Butomus umbellatus*, *Myosotis scorpioides*, *Myriophyllum aquaticum*, *Orontium aquaticum* and *Ranunculus lingua* 'Grandiflorus' around the edges. He was determined to include the red fairy moss *Azolla filiculoides*, not hardy enough to survive outdoors, but ingeniously kept alive in a bucket of water in the utility room through the winter and reintroduced each spring.

Cold comfort for keen gardeners

This garden of about 0.5 hectares (one and a quarter acres) belongs to a shopkeeper (china, glass and craftware) and his wife, in the country north of Concord, New Hampshire. They bought it impulsively, after a visit late on a summer's day when the whole place was bathed in sunshine and radiated warmth, after selling their previous house close to Moriches Bay on Long Island.

Now that they live here, they have discovered

that their impression of a sheltered, wooded valley with a stream babbling through the garden was misleading. This can be a very cold place. It faces north-west towards the coldest winter winds, which funnel ferociously down the valley, and bring heavy falls of snow in winter. Late frosts in spring and early ones in the autumn are common as cold air from above settles in the valley, and in moments of desperation the owners say their garden might as well be on top of Mount Washington. The soil is a very acidic, poorly-drained sand beneath a surface layer of peat – the remains of a bog that was drained years ago.

The couple run the shop between them and have a fair amount of time to spend at home, when they enjoy being in the garden, but their attempts, based more or less on the things that did well on Long Island, have been less than successful.

Review

A
Cold is a feature of this garden, and north-west winds, lack of sun, and late and early frosts result in short growing seasons that strongly effect the prospects of growing plants successfully. But heavy winter snowfalls protect plants from extreme winter cold, and summers are warm, moist and very favourable for plant growth.

B
Another problem is wet, particularly when snow melts, and water drains from frozen soil in spring. Then pools of water and mud can persist for weeks on end.

C
Many plants fail to grow well due to the acidity of the ground, but there are others which thrive in these conditions and are well adapted to make the most of the alternations between long periods of dormancy in winter and rapid growth and development during spring and summer.

D
The owners were used to styles of gardening based on brightly colourful flower beds and trim lawns and hedges. They were adamant that they 'did not want to go back to nature'!

Outcome

A
Little could be done to protect woody plants from the cold, and only those adapted to do well in spite of it were used.

The protective effect of snow, reinforced by a blanket of mulch in late autumn once the ground had frozen, were put to advantage by concentrating on herbaceous perennials whose tops die down completely in winter.

B
Problems with water were due mainly to the silting up of water channels which had drained the lake before it evolved into a bog.

The first attempts to remedy this by excavating the old lake bed and supplying it with water direct from the stream were satisfactory, until the stream flooded and washed away most of the plants.

They now supply the lake indirectly from the stream, using a weir and monk to control the inlet and outlet so they can regulate the flow and the water level.

Lowering the water level in winter and clearing the bed of the stream and other drainage channels has greatly reduced the problems of excess water in the spring.

C
Beds close to the house were raised and given extra depth by spreading spoil from the dug-out lake over them. Excess acidity in these newly-formed beds was reduced by heavy applications of lime.

D
Discussion of the owners fear 'of going back to nature' revealed that they did not want the garden to look like a wilderness. They agreed to forgo the suburban styles of their Long Island garden in exchange for intensively-gardened, brightly-planted beds of bulbs and perennials close to the house, and more natural plant matrices composed of trees underplanted with drifts of perennials around the lake – provided this conveyed an impression of visual logic and intentional effects.

A proportion of native plants were included for their reliability and affinity with the surroundings, especially around the lake.

Suitably hardy exotics, chosen for their garden impact, were largely confined to areas close to the house.

The plants

Elaeagnus angustifolius and variegated forms of *Acer negundo* were planted near the house to provide light, bright leaf canopies above polyanthus, *Mertensia virginica* and masses of large-flowered daffodils in spring, followed in summer by hybrid delphiniums, border phloxes like 'Bouvardier', the sunset-red 'Charles H. Curtis' and the white 'David', paeonies and 'Karine', 'Kleine Tanzarin', 'Degas' amongst other cultivars of *Papaver orientale* bred by Countess von Zeppelin, with numerous other splendidly colourful herbaceous perennials.

Lakeside plantings away from the house were designed to develop a robust matrix based on native deciduous trees and conifers, several of which were already present, emerging from a well-developed shrub layer, above broad, mixed drifts of a relatively few perennials and ferns, generously underplanted with bulbs.

The trees included *Acer rubrum* and *A. saccharum*, *Amelanchier arborea*, *Prunus serotina*, *Quercus bicolor* and *Q. palustris*, interplanted with *Larix laricina*. *Picea mariana* and *Tsuga canadensis* used as a background and shelter belt.

Shrubs consisted of a mixture of native and exotic kinds, many chosen for their autumn colours, and amongst them were *Amelanchier sanguinea*, *Aronia arbutifolia* 'Brilliant', *Cornus alba* 'Elegantissima' (planted in groups on the edge and into the lake for its enlightening foliage and brilliant winter bark), *Corylopsis pauciflora* and *C. sinensis* (for spring flowers). *Fothergilla gardenii* and *F. major*, *Leucathoe fontanesiana*, *Lindera benzoin*, *Symphoricarpos* X *chenaultii* 'Hancock' (as dense ground cover along the edges) and *Ilex verticillata*, *Viburnum betulifolium* and *V. opulus* 'Xanthocarpum' (planted close to each other for their contrasting scarlet and translucent orange-yellow berries).

The main drifts of perennials were formed from *Aegopodium podagaria* 'Variegata' (to light up areas beneath the trees), *Sanguinaria canadensis* and *Cornus canadensis* (both used in large, ground-hugging patches), *Alchemilla mollis* and drifts of the single paeony 'Dainty' with *Galax urceolata* (for its 'varnished' foliage) interplanted with *Tiarella cordifolia* and *Vancouveria hexandra*. Taller perennials emerging above these and used to supplement flowering at shrub level included: *Aconitum napellus* 'Bicolor', *Aruncus dioicus*, *Cimicifuga racemosa*, cultivars of *Trollius chinensis*,

and the 'Excelsior' hybrids of *Digitalis purpurea* as gap-fillers.

Ferns were freely planted, partly for contrasting affects with broad-leaved plants, partly to create atmosphere. Amongst them were *Adiantum pedatum* (forming flowing drifts), *Gymnocarpium dryopteris*, *Onoclea sensibilis* (especially its red form) and the evergreen *Polystichum acrostichoides*, with *Osmunda cinnamomea* and *Dryopteris goldiana* set out in compact clusters as repeated focal points.

Changing styles in North Carolina

This garden surrounds a small country house south of Raleigh in North Carolina belonging to the owner of a manufacturing business. After years of hard work and stress, the business is running smoothly and profitably, and he has time to spare for other things.

The garden is set in gently undulating countryside on the edge of the Piedmont and the coastal plain, surrounded by old fields, many now reverting to woods dominated by sweet gum, tulip poplars and loblolly pines. A small tributary of the Neuse River runs through the garden, which lies on well-structured clay, sometimes covered by sandy loam.

His wife, who had been almost entirely responsible for the garden, died a while ago. Her 'bible' had been *The Englishwoman's Garden*, and he always admired the garden while it was in her care, and liked the bright combinations of flowers and foliage in the borders, and had made an attempt to take care of it, driven by a feeling that he owed it to her to do his best. This was not very successful, because he knows little about gardening, and as he eventually had to admit, it was not his kind of garden.

Review

A

The garden was too complex and demanding for someone with little knowledge of gardening and only a passing interest in flowers. The hot, humid summers spelt death to the silver-leaved plants so vital to his wife's style of gardening, and he had no idea how to replace them.

B

The site is idyllically set amongst trees, with slight but interesting variations in topography that lent themselves to landscaping.

C

The owner had more spare time than previously, but he has other interests than gardening. He said that he enjoyed mowing the grass, finding it relaxing, with a satisfyingly visible end result.

D

The topography, the water-retentive clay soil, and a source of water in the form of a stream lent themselves to the construction of a pond or two.

Outcome

A & B

The garden was fundamentally changed, completely replacing the original lay-out of borders, hedges and lawns with a more natural, much simpler, landscaped garden.
Structure was provided by a pattern of lawns and trees, arranged as a sheltering, relaxing setting for the house.
Water replaced borders as major features of the garden, in the shape of informal ponds and adjacent wetland areas.

C

Maintenance consisted largely of grass-cutting, employing a local contractor when business took the owner away from home, mowing frequently, and leaving the cuttings where they fell.

D

Three linked, medium-sized ponds were formed, supplied indirectly by water from the stream. They were not lined, but filled with water naturally. The ponds were up to 1.5 m (5 ft) deep over the greater part of their area ,with shelves up to 2 m (6 ft 6 in) wide providing shallow water round their margins. Vertical banks were simply cut out of the clay.
Associated wetland areas were made close to the ponds, in which the soil surface was just above summer water levels.

The plants

Additional trees, planted to provide shade and reinforce the wooded atmosphere, were mostly native species, with a few exotics. Amongst them were *Asimina triloba* (grown as small, multi-stemmed trees), *Cercidiphyllum japonicum* (for its burnt-sugar fragrance and colours in autumn) and *Cladrastis lutea*, *Diospyros virginiana*, *Hamamelis intermedia* 'Arnold Promise', cultivars of *Magnolia grandiflora* (including the tall, columnar 'Main

Street' and 'Galaxy' with crimson flowers), *Nyssa sylvatica*, the fragrant snowball *Styrax obassia*, and *Taxodium distichum*.

Plants with floating leaves planted in the water lily zone included *Nymphaea* hybrids, amongst them 'Marliacea Chromatella', 'Caroliniana Nivea', 'Rosea' and 'Carolina Sunset', *Nymphoides lacunosum* (with variegated, mottled leaves), *N. indicum* (with masses of short-lived white flowers), and *Aponogeton distichum*.

Marginal aquatics in shallow water included *Trapa natans*, *Acorus gramineus* 'Ogon', several cultivars of *Iris laevigata*, *Pontederia cordata* and *Sagittaria latifolia*; but by far the most striking affects were produced by large groups of the pale-sulphur-yellow *Nelumbo lutea* and cultivars of *N. nucifera*, notably the white 'Alba Grandiflora' and deep-rose 'Osiris'. All did well in spite of muskrats' fondness for their tubers.

Wood ducks, black ducks and mallards frequented the ponds, and the banks had to be protected from their feet and dabbling bills by a covering of plants. *Lycopus virginiana* (bugleweed) sowed itself naturally and provided effective protection, but its coarse, unattractive appearance was not appreciated, and in most places it was destroyed with glyphosate and gradually replaced by other plants, including vigorous *Hostas* like 'Piedmont Gold', 'Aurora Borealis', 'Francee', *H. montana* 'Aurea-marginata' and *H.* 'Royal Standard', cultivars of Louisiana iris such as 'Black Gamecock' and 'Gulf Shores', *Iris sibirica* cvs, *Darmera peltata*, *Ligularia stenocephala* 'The Rocket', *Gunnera manicata* and forms of *Osmunda regalis*.

Quite extensive wetland areas – particularly between and beyond the ponds were heavily planted with robust, summer-flowering perennials, mostly in bold clumps, with infiltrators like *Houttuynia cordata*, *Lysimachia nummularia* 'Aurea', *Myosotis scorpioides* 'Pinkie' and 'Sapphire' and *Phalaris arundinacea* 'Feesey's Form' filling the ground between them. The clumps included *Lobelia cardinalis* 'Royal Robe', *L. syphilitica*; *L. gerardii* X 'Vedrariensis', *Sarracenia flava* and some of its hybrids, several species of *Rodgersia*, and *Ligularia* 'Desdemona' and 'Othello'. These were set off by colonies of *Matteucia pennsylvanicum*, and dramatic clumps of *Miscanthus* cvs, especially the boldly-variegated 'Cosmopolitan', 'Gracillimus' and 'Kaskade' with clouds of tinted pink flowers.

Chapter eight

Scrubberies and the 'mixed border'

Daunted by the demands of the herbaceous border and the problems of gardening without help, the twentieth-century gardener sought refuge in the shrubbery. Here was a sturdy breed of permanent plants, less intimidating than trees, less exacting than the sun-loving occupants of herbaceous borders, that seemed ideally suited to a time-and money-saving formula. Gardens were reduced to lawns surrounded by borders packed with shrubs – a light garnish of King Alfred daffodils appeared each spring, and a bed or two of hybrid tea roses near the house provided a summer talking point. The result was mind-numbingly humdrum, but while a pair of shears hung in the shed, and a mower was ready in the garage, the gardener was in command and all was well in the garden.

This mid-century crisis in the life of gardening ended, not because the system does not work – it is still being operated as efficiently and bleakly as ever in unimaginatively managed parks and gardens all over the temperate world – but because it sacrifices everything that makes gardening interesting and exciting. Reacting against the lack of variety, the constant demands of the mower, brief phases of flowering, and the deadening impact of dull, overgrown blocks of twiggy greenery, gardeners turned again to perennial plants for inspiration. Somewhat to their surprise, they discovered life after the herbaceous border. Unsuspected treasures lurked behind the ranks of delphiniums, sidalceas, heleniums, phloxes, and lupins that had damned all these plants as demanding prima donnas. Treasures designed by nature to occupy spaces between other plants. Gradually, the penny dropped as gardeners realised that the key to growing perennials successfully is to grow them amongst the plants they associate with naturally. Practically nowhere in the world are herbaceous perennials dominant members of their communities – they almost always grow amongst trees, shrubs and grasses. Little wonder that herbaceous borders depend constantly on our attention for survival.

Perennials have now been found parts in a trinity of gardening styles – following, though seldom consciously modelled on, natural associations of plants. The most familiar of these are:

meadows – in which perennials and bulbs are combined with long grasses (see Chapter 6);
spinneys – these are less clearly recognizable, but present in one guise or another in almost all gardens, sometimes in the form of a woodland garden, but much more likely to be found as shaded spaces beneath trees, pergolas and other structures;
scrubberies – known more elegantly, but less all-embracingly, as 'mixed borders'.

Shrubs and scrub

Mixed borders have become rather fashionable, and are often proposed as an alternative to the demanding temperament that has put people off exclusive dependence on herbaceous plants. But unless they are skilfully designed with careful attention to the interplay of different plants, they become even more difficult to maintain than herbaceous borders. The plants in a mixed border may have little in common apart from the gardener's whim to place them side by side, with few shared patterns of growth on which to base their maintenance. The natural models for these mixed borders are the communities of plants that form scrub, and it is to these that we should look for guidance when trying to devise similar communities of garden plants.

Scrub grows in more specialized conditions than woods or grasslands, but exists in a great many forms. Shrubs form the heaths that cover exposed, acid and often wet mountain ridges in which the predominant plants may be heathers, but depending on where they grow, may also be rhododendrons, junipers, helichrysums, hebes or any of dozens of other species. Shrubs are the most conspicuous vegetation of patches of gorse, acacia or broom on well-drained, sunny slopes; of the sage brush of semi-desert areas, of protea

42A

savanna in seasonally dry, fireswept grasslands, and the evergreen maquis of the Mediterranean and California. These communities occur on well-drained, seasonally dry, sometimes infertile soils, in situations which experience frequent, often prolonged, periods of drought and/or exposure to wind or low temperatures. The places where scrub develops are often the antithesis of the fertile, sheltered, well-watered situations which have contributed to the success of so many human settlements, and which, in turn, have become the places where most of us make our homes and gardens.

Consequently, those who garden in rather unusual contexts – on sandy soils, in exposed places, in hot, dry situations or other places where water is scarce, either because there is little of it, it drains rapidly out of reach or is frozen solid for long periods – are likely to find that shrubs provide a satisfying and relatively simple solution to the problems of gardening in conditions which many would describe as difficult, while those who garden in kinder conditions struggle to maintain a balance in their mixed borders.

The mixed border

The 'mixed border' is a rather vague term that leaves maximum freedom for imaginative interpretation. But it is impossible to discuss

42B

42C

something with no limits. So perhaps we can define it by a process of elimination. Evidently it is not a border planted with a mixture of herbaceous plants, with or without bulbs, or even with or without annuals – that would be too close to the dear old herbaceous border of

42A, B & C. Scrub grows naturally in situations which are unfavourable for the growth of trees, or infiltration by grasses, but the balance that maintains scrub is often precarious. The communities of proteas, restios and heaths found in fynbos in South Africa (top left) are very vulnerable to invasion by introduced species. Heather (top right) forms tight-knit communities over huge areas, but overgrazing tips the balance in favour of bracken or coarse grasses. Hebes and other evergreen shrubs (bottom right) form dense, single-layered matrices in perpetually wet, cool, sub-alpine situations. Cape of Good Hope Nature Reserve, near Cape Town, South Africa. The Long Mynd, Shropshire, England. Above Stratford Mountain House, Mount Taranaki, New Zealand.

late and seldom lamented memory to merit a new title. Nor should the name be used for a border in which successive layers of trees, shrubs and perennials, with or without bulbs, are grown together – although certainly mixed, that constitutes a garden version of woodland: a spinney. Similarly, borders filled exclusively with mixtures of shrubs are already familiar to us as shrubberies. So we are left with a border containing shrubs (evergreen or deciduous), perennials (including grasses as well as broad-leaved plants), perhaps ferns and even club mosses, bulbs of all sorts and – why not? – annuals and biennials. A community of plants, which, as noted above, when found growing together under natural conditions, is called 'scrub'.

A return to that analogy confronts us once again with the conflict of interests represented by this kind of planting. The natural matrices of shrubs, perennials, grasses, annuals and bulbs that make up scrub depend on precarious balances between soil and climate which prevent grasses from taking over on the one hand, or trees occupying spaces between the shrubs and turning it into woodland on the other. Apparently stable examples of scrub occur in South Africa, where different fynbos communities, all based on proteas, ericas and restios, form long-lived, persistent communities across hundreds of square miles of lowland and mountain countryside – stable, that is, until the arrival of Australian wattles and Mediterranean pines introduced newcomers able to exploit gaps in the matrix and turn fynbos into open woodland. Similarly, the maquis around the eastern Mediterranean has been familiar to holidaymakers and travellers as mixture of evergreen shrubs for years, and accepted as the natural vegetation of the area until the reduction of grazing by goats (because goat-herders can make a better living tending to tourists) allowed the stronger members of this scrub to grow up above the shrubs and form dense, evergreen woodlands of strawberry trees, oaks and pines – the true climax vegetation of the region.

The matrices of the mixed border are similarly under pressure, and success depends on finding ways to prevent these pressures turning the border into something else – in natural terms,

woodland dominated by trees, or savanna with grasses filling the spaces between the shrubs. Unwanted trees are seldom a problem, because even the most tenacious elders, sycamores, kanukas, birches, eucalyptus and wattles invade sporadically, and can be dealt with individually. But grasses, designed to enter and exploit gaps, and very often the natural sub-matrix beneath shrubs within which the broad-leaved plants exist, are much more difficult to control.

Unless our gardens are naturally endowed with the qualities that favour scrub, how do we maintain our mixed borders? Meadows are similar anachorisms in most gardens, vulnerable to infiltration by pioneering shrubs and trees, but those are automatically eliminated when the grass is mown – something that is done naturally by fire or grazing animals. We have no such simple, straightforward panacea when we grow mixtures of shrubs, perennials and bulbs together. We cannot lift them and divide and replant every three years like a herbaceous border. We cannot scythe or mow them like a meadow. We cannot fork over the ground between the plants. We cannot set fire to them (even though fire is one of the ways by which natural scrub is maintained: *Buddleia salvifolia* responds to a good blaze like a reviving tonic, but do not expect *B. davidii* to attract many butterflies after being torched). Nor can we smother plants that grow in sunny or lightly shaded spaces between shrubs with an annual blanket of mulch, unlike the woodland perennials that flourish under a winter covering.

Mixed borders are a gardening wild card – full of promises, but unless we want to spend our days inextricably immersed in sorting out the problems of a hundred different plants with a hundred different needs, we must learn how to play the hand.

Elsewhere, problems of this sort have been resolved by analogy with wildflowers in similar situations. But the relatively precise comparisons possible in Chapter 7 on water gardens and Chapter 9 on shaded situations are not available to us in the open, sunny, fertile situations of borders in the majority of gardens. In these undemanding settings, the habitats in which plants grow naturally become much less relevant. When planting such borders, we think nothing of putting peach-leaved bellflowers, which grow naturally amongst grasses and shrubs on dry banks, beside Siberian irises from marshy meadows, alongside coral bells, an inhabitant of open, deciduous woodland. These three species would not inevitably form a successful matrix, but we can be pretty confident that they would be much more likely to do so in open, sunny, fertile borders than in any of the situations where each individually would find itself at home.

This breadth of choice can be disconcerting. First impressions may suggest that anything goes, leading, when that proves a failure, to bemusement at the complexity of the situation. But, as in any other kind of planting, communities of plants in borders play a variety of roles, occupy different levels in the planting, and perform at different seasons, all of which

43A

43B

43A & B. Spaces between unsociable shrubs are occupied at certain seasons by bulbs or annuals. Dry, or even arid gardens (top) provide much more favourable conditions for this kind of matrix than moist, fertile situations. Gregarious shrubs including roses, lend themselves to attractively-composed versions of scrub (bottom), in which shrubs grow above ground-covering layers of grasses, perennials and ephemerals.
Hester Malan Nature Reserve, Springbok, Namaqualand, South Africa. Clark & Kathleen Abbot's Garden, Three Mile Bush Road, Whangarei, New Zealand.

contribute to the development of a matrix. They are unusual only in the breadth of choice of plants. Instead of basing this choice predominantly on the habitats in which plants grow naturally, we have to pay more attention to the roles of different plants, placing emphasis on those whose forms and seasons of growth complement each other in the formation of a matrix.

Shrubs – Sociable, unsociable and gregarious

Many shrubs grow naturally in intimate associations, their branches growing together, often interlaced or emerging through the lower growth of grasses and herbs, and other pioneer, often spiny, shrubs. Smaller shrubs, perennials and bulbs growing close to them are not deprived of light, water or nutrients by their leaves and roots. Social shrubs are mostly deciduous and are likely to share one or more of the following characteristics:

upright shoots – which tend to become bare towards the base, or are easily pruned to make space at ground level for other plants;
light leaf canopies – formed by open branch structures and small or widely-spaced leaves;
Thongy roots – which draw most of their nutrients and water from the deeper layers of the soil;
late bud break – remaining leafless till well into the spring.

They are mostly shrubs of open woodland and transitional situations, rather than scrub itself, and form complex, multi-tiered matrices in situations where water is seldom severely deficient. They find naturally congenial conditions in gardens in Britain, in all but the Mediterranean, montane and northern parts of Europe, in the mid-Atlantic and Pacific north-west of the USA, and in Japan, New Zealand and south-eastern Australia.

Sociable shrubs

Many have relatively open branch structures beneath which ground covering perennials can grow – at least when the shrubs are leafless – and tolerate close association with other shrubs and climbers, or the overhead canopies of foliage from trees.

Abutilon vitifolium: An upright shrub or small tree for sunlit situations, with an open structure that associates well with perennials beneath it.
Aralia elata 'Variegata': Large, pinnate leaves shade other plants in summer, but bare winter branches favour undercover plants.
Buddleja davidii: Open structure, combined with hard-pruning in spring provide ample light and space for close planted perennials.
Chimonanthus fragrans: A tall shrub, easily pruned to allow space beneath it for perennials and low-growing shrubs.
*Clianthus puniceus**: Low growing, but rather rangy shrub that mixes well with other shrubs, and ground covering perennials.
Cornus florida: Large, broadly spreading but open shrub that combines well with spring flowering perennials in its shade.
Corylopsis pauciflora: Several species available, all do well in open woodland with an undercover of woodland perennials.
Euonymus hians: A tall, spreading shrub adapted to light shade, that can be pruned to provide space for perennials below it.
Fuchsia magellanica: Grows as a tall shrub or small tree in frost free situations, sheltering smaller perennials and ferns. Evergreen only in mild climates.
Hibiscus syriacus: Upright form, and very late bud break provide excellent conditions for other shrubs and perennials.
Indigofera potaninii: Small leaves and an open framework of branches make this a good mixer with other shrubs and perennials.
Lonicera tartarica: A tall shrub, providing protection in winter and spring for evergreen, spring flowering perennials.
Magnolia stellata: Usually grown as an isolated specimen, but combines very well with ground covering perennials in light shade under deciduous trees.

44A

Medicago arborea*: Easily pruned to provide space for low growing plants that benefit from its nitrogen fixing bacteria.

Rhododendron yunnanense: This, and other deciduous species, form attractive associations with low perennials, ferns and bulbs.

Rosa moyesii: Upright sparsely branched forms of shrub roses provide space for perennials and lower shrubs.

Spartium junceum: Stem forming habit provides room at ground level for bulbs, perennials and small shrubs.

Stachyurus praecox: A woodland shrub, thriving in light shade in company with spring flowering perennials.

Viburnum plicatum: Numerous forms available, all grow well in open woodland and with ground covering perennials.

Vitex agnus-castae*: Tall shrub, easily pruned to provide clear space near ground level for perennials and compact shrubs.

Other shrubs are unsociable. A high proportion are evergreen, often with silver or hairy leaves. They grow in compact, humped or dome-shaped forms in which the foliage forms an overlapping canopy like a tiled roof. They seldom form close matrices, but typically, each occupies its own ground, separated from neighbouring shrubs by spaces which may be

44B

44C

44A, B & C. Sociable shrubs like the pinxter (top left) that grow in companionable associations with other plants lend themselves to varied and flexible uses in the garden. Pruning can even be used to convert a vine (top right) into a sprawling shrub growing amongst perennials and bulbs. But gregarious shrubs like heathers (bottom right) are less flexible, and perform better in blocks that maintain a degree of integrity amongst the mixtures of other plants. Dark Hollow Falls by Big Meadows, Shenandoah National Park, Virginia, USA. Godspiece Leaze, Norton St Philip, Somerset, England. Little Norton Mill, Norton sub Hamden, Somerset, England.

filled constantly, but more likely only at certain seasons, with herbs, grasses and bulbs.

This is a common pattern in situations with exceptionally free-draining soils, or recurring seasonal droughts, as well as inhospitable and specialized situations like the high Andes and dry, extreme continental areas of Eurasia and North America. It is also a pattern that formally-inclined gardeners adopt – planting their shrubs as specimens, separated by spaces filled with flowers of one kind and another. This is highly appropriate for gardens on dry, sandy, gravelly or infertile soils, or in places where seasonal droughts are a regular feature and in which unsociable shrubs interplanted with bulbs, and low ground-covering perennials make good use of the conditions.

In settings more amply supplied with water, there is nothing to restrict vigorous growth of the plants between the shrubs. Left to themselves, these quickly fill the spaces before invading or overwhelming the shrubs which are ill-adapted to cope with such aggression. Fairly radical preparations are needed to make this kind of planting practicable, without dependence on frequent maintenance – something which traditional gardeners would take for granted, but which matrix planting would aim to make redundant. One alternative is to make a gravel garden, covering the soil with a layer of gravel at least 15 cm (6 in) and preferably 25 cm (10 in) deep, into which the shrubs and their associates are planted.

Unsociable shrubs

These are very often found growing as individual plants, in small groups or in extended rather open communities in which each plant remains more or less separate. They usually do best in gardens when this inclination to individuality is recognised by providing space for individuals.

Banksia grandis *: A large shrub or small tree with heavy foliage that grows best without competition from ground cover.
Callistemon viminalis **'Little John'** *: Compact shrub with dense needle-like foliage to ground level.
Carmichaelia monroi: Garden forms grow slowly into rounded hummocks, formed by densely crowded branches.
Carpentaria californica *: A spreading broad-leaved evergreen, densely shading the ground beneath it.
Cistus **'Silver Pink':** Numerous spp. and cvs. May associate in dry heaths naturally, but present better in isolation in gardens.
Euryops pectinatus: Dome shaped silver leaved evergreen forming compact ground hugging shrubs.
Halimium ocymoides: Low growing twiggy shrub that can be interplanted with drought adapted perennials and bulbs.
Hebe cupressoides **'Boughton Dome':** Naturally heath forming species that is more likely to be grown individually in gardens.
Laurus nobilis *: Large shrub in cold areas or small tree in mild situations that forms dense, weed excluding cover in its shade.
Lavandula stoechas: Species and cvs of lavenders may grow leggy with age, but can be kept compact with annual shearing.
Lechenaultia biloba *: Grows naturally in seasonally arid conditions – does not associate well with close neighbours in cultivation.
Nerium oleander: Vigorous, drought-adapted, rounded evergreen shrub – broadly tolerant of a wide range of frost-free situations.
Othonna cheirifolia: Low ground covering shrubby plant for fully exposed situations in sunlight.
Phlomis suffruticosa: Drought adapted shrub that grows naturally in spaced communities over wide areas.
Pimelea rosea *: Compact, rounded evergreen – vulnerable to invasion and suppression by other plants in gardens.
Protea scolymocephala *: Low growing, densely foliaged shrub with moderate sized drought adapted leaves.
Rosmarinus officinalis: Upright, spreading shrub – vulnerable to invasion by grasses etc under garden conditions.
Santolina chamaecyparissus: Dense eversilver shrub, responds to annual shearing to maintain compact weed-excluding form.
Sarcopoterium spinosum: Small, rounded, intensely prickly shrub often growing spaced out in dry, semi arid conditions.
Thymus nitidus: Shrub found in dry, stony situations – vulnerable to invasion in garden

Sociable shrubs, on the other hand, are naturally adapted to compete with other species, and hold their own in gardens where water is seldom or never a limiting factor, and where, very often, fertile soils support a great deal of vigorously competitive vegetation. Far from being overwhelmed, such shrubs, left to themselves, form robust matrices that resist infiltration by outsiders and develop into interlacing thickets from which most of the ground flora – apart from plants like ground elder and others whose evergreen or semi-evergreen leaves provide for a winter living – are eliminated. Few intruders can invade such thickets, apart from climbers like clematis brambles, woody nightshade and honeysuckles, and pioneering trees like ashes and sycamores, which eventually grow above the shrubs, shading them out to form a woodland. That scenario may not inspire any creative gardener, but it illustrates the ability of these sociable shrubs to cope with competition, requiring only a dash of imagination to devise more attractive ways to use them.

Roses are amongst the most sociable of all shrubs – many are trail-blazing species that invade meadows in the first stages of its progression to scrub. Their thorns (prickles may be botanically correct, but fails to convey the ferocity that many possess) deter grazing animals, and help them scramble up amongst tall herbs and fellow colonizers, like brambles and thorns; their roots are long, thongy and deeply penetrating, quickly descending below the surface mats of grasses to draw water and nutrients from lower levels of the soil. Yet gardeners prefer to grow their roses apart from other plants, in the belief that they do better without competition – a belief which leads to rose beds being treated with pre-emergence weed-killers as a drastic recourse to keep their surfaces weed-free, even though the sight of rose bushes emerging from beds filled with hardy geraniums, violas, euphorbias, crucianellas, pinks and other perennials is much prettier.

A third type of shrub community forms heaths of one kind or another – often in exposed, cold, wet, acid conditions – where a dense growth of small evergreen shrubs or sub-shrubs grow as a single-layered matrix. Heather (*Calluna vulgaris*) is an extreme example of a species which grows in almost pure stands over enormous areas. These are gregarious, rather than sociable – combining well in flocks of one or a few similarly disposed kinds but are less friendly towards outsiders, and are not good mixers like the sociable shrubs described earlier. Other heath-formers include species of erica; the closed communities of shrubs, including hebes, cassinias and coprosmas above the tree line in New Zealand, or the moorlands covered with dwarf rhododendrons, and other ericaceous shrubs, on the mountain chains across Asia. Each consists of well-matched, often relatively few, species of low-growing evergreen shrubs, growing as a single tier of plants usually less than a metre high. No trees emerge above them, and few perennials, bulbs and grasses are able to survive beneath them – though these may occupy areas clear of the shrubs, such as boggy patches, rocky outcrops and other spaces.

Few of the shrubs that grow in these heath communities are suitable for the mixed border, but gardeners use them in other ways, and their natural inclination to combine in weed-resisting phalanxes of self-supporting ground cover make them well adapted for easy-care plantings in the garden. Gardens made of heathers, often with low-growing conifers, are a widely encountered example of their use in which the polychromatic tones of the foliage of the heathers and conifers combine in long-lasting, often brilliantly colourful effects, at their brightest and best during the winter. In the National Arboretum in Washington, the Punchbowl at Virginia Water, near London and the Olinda Rhododendron Gardens amongst the Dandenong Hills in Melbourne and many other places, extensive areas almost entirely covered by evergreen Kurume azaleas provide 'ooh-ahh' spectacles every spring. Compact species and forms of hebes combine equally effectively as weed-excluding, self-maintaining matrices, though they lack the technicolour effects of heathers and evergreen azaleas.

Some useful gregarious (heath forming) shrubs

Many of these grow naturally in extensive communities – sometimes limited to a very few species – that extend over large areas. Familiar

45A

45B

examples are provided by heaths (*Erica* and *Calluna* spp.) on which heather gardens are modelled.

Astelia nervosa: Several cvs and hybrids with *A. chathamica* – notable for strong, arching broadly grass-like, sometimes silver, foliage. Suitable for acid, wet settings.

Brachyglottis (Senecio) monroi: One of several New Zealand daisies that combine with other compact shrubs in dense heath communities.

Calluna vulgaris: Numerous cvs provide a great variety of flower and foliage tones. Acid soils are essential for success.

Cassiope lycopodioides: Almost prostrate. dense evergreen shrub especially suitable for small scale heaths on acid, peaty soils.

Coprosma repens 'Pink Splendour': Bushy shrub with burnished, variegated leaves. Suitable for dry sandy soils and coastal situations.

Daboecia cantabrica: Many forms & cvs. Also requires acid soils, will do well in comparatively wet conditions.

Dracophyllum recurvum: Grows in mixed communities. Relatively drought tolerant, but may be difficult to establish and grow in some situations.

Erica carnea: This and other *Erica* spp. include social shrubs ranging from lawn-like ground cover to 3–4 m (10–13 ft) high screens.

Euonymus fortunei: Numerous cvs with varied foliage – all are tolerant dense ground dense coverers, even in shade.

Gaultheria (Pernettya) mucronata: Vigorous, medium sized shrubs that form dense communities in damp, cool, acid situations.

Genista hispanica: An exceptionally dense gorse with prickly stems for hot, dry infertile situations.

Hebe ochracea: This and several other compact hebes form dense, weed excluding communities when grouped together.

Helichrysum splendidum: Densely packed, upright silver leaved stems – prefers abundant summer rainfall and good drainage in winter.

Leucathoe keiskei: Low, densely foliaged procumbent shrub that will stand some shade- needs acid, cool conditions.

Microbiota decussata: Densely foliaged, spreading conifer combines with other low, relatively vigorous heath forming shrubs.

Olearia nummularifolia: Small shrub with upright shoots that associates well with other heath community species.

Phylodoce caerulea: Exceptionally hardy low growing shrub that requires acid soils, in cool, lightly shaded settings.

Potentilla fruticosa: Numerous forms exist – extremely tolerant, easily established, long flowering, easily managed shrubs.

Rhododendron fastigiatum: Compact shrub with glaucous foliage that is one of many high altitude, heath forming species.

45C

Vaccinium vitis-idaea: Several forms available, make excellent low, dense ground cover for acid soils in cold, wet situations.

Perennials

Perennials (and in this context, that term emphatically covers grasses) are the vital components of the mixed border. Unlike a shrubbery, where the eventual aim is a complete cover of shrubs, the mixed border aims to maintain – in perpetuity and against all the forces of nature – a patchwork of shrubs and other plants, and the close cover at ground level produced by perennials is the line of defence against intruders, supplemented to a greater or lesser extent by ephemeral annuals and biennials and bulbs. Annual weeds cease to be a problem as the matrices develop, but perennial weeds are adapted to invade communities of perennials and shrubs – dense though they may be – at seasons when their matrices become temporarily less effective.

These invasions can be reduced by skilful planting, but intruders that do appear have to be removed by hand, and during the early stages of the development of the border, that is bound to be a major method of maintaining control. Spaces between the plants can also be covered with weed-suppressing mulches as a stopgap

45D

until the plants in the border knit together. Such matrices depend on mixing together plants with different growth forms – some that grow as ground-occupying fortresses of matted crowns, from which flowering stems ascend into the air, others with low, carpeting foliage that fill the ground between the settlers, and work their way beneath the shrubs; others that are explorers, seeking out and occupying spaces and repairing holes in the matrix as they arise.

Settlers

Many familiar herbaceous plants are clump-forming settlers by nature – the oriental poppies, globe thistles, phloxes and lupins show little inclination to spread sideways, and are moderately resistant to invasion. Others, including heleniums and Michaelmas daisies, produce crowns close to the surface that extend outwards year by year, but as they do, they become separate, leaving spaces open to invasion. The later can only be satisfactorily grown in borders by digging them up from time to time, dividing and replanting them in fresh soil. They are ill-adapted for situations where intervention is undesirable.

45A, B, C & D. Ground-holding, evergreen perennials are an essential part of many weed-excluding matrices. They may be found in modern interpretations of the traditional format of perennial borders (opposite top left), as weed-excluding carpets in sunny, well-drained situations (opposite bottom and top left) or as easily-grown plants like ajugas (top right), able to grow in the shade of taller shrubs and perennials during the summer, and plugging gaps in the matrix in winter after their leaves have fallen. Arboretum, North Carolina State University, Raleigh, North Carolina, USA. Red Lion House, Horderley, Shropshire, England. Netta Statham's Garden, Nr Ellesmere, Shropshire, England. Iford Manor, Bradford on Avon, Wiltshire, England.

Long-lived, clump-forming settlers are a valuable part of the mixed border, rivalling the shrubs in their permanency and visual impact, and greatly extending the season of flowering, the range of textural contrasts and harmonies available, and variety of form. Their impact has been increased in recent years by recognition of the value and increased availability of numerous clump-forming grasses ranging in size from low growing fescues to cultivars of *Miscanthus sinensis* and *Arundo donax*. Herbaceous plants contribute most effectively to the matrix during summer and autumn, when they fill spaces between shrubs, casting dense shade on the ground below them that totally inhibits the development of annuals and most perennial seedlings. After their tops die down, their roots remain in permanent occupation of the ground during the winter, deterring, but not totally preventing, invasion by outsiders, but the spaces between them provide entry points through which seedlings can infiltrate the border.

Long-lived, vigorous, clump-forming perennials

These plants occupy the ground very tenaciously, producing dense crowded roots that exclude most intruders, and expanding relatively slowly over the years:

Acanthus spinosus: Deep rooted, eternally persistent perennial, adapted to sunshine but will cope with dry shade.
Aconitum napellus: Upright stems produced from clustered tubers best in moist soil, in cool, shaded settings.
Amsonia hubrechtii: Numerous upright stems produced from a compact rootstock – with attractive foliage colour in autumn.
Baptisia alba: Long-lived, tenacious legumes – other spp. with yellow or blue flowers – sandy, infertile, dry situations.
Cassia hebecarpa: A perennial with the

appearance of a shrub – nitrogen fixing nodules improve fertility of poor soils.
Cimicifuga racemosa: One of several spp. – all are retentive space holders. Well drained, moist, humus rich soils in light shade.
Dictamnus albus: Gradually develops into a solidly based cluster of stems, in full sun on fertile, well drained soils.
Eremurus x isabellinus Shelford Hybrids: For very well drained soils in full sun, radiating roots require space around the crowns.
Euphorbia characias ssp. *wulfenii:* Shrub-like perennials that renew themselves biennially to form broad weed-excluding 'bushes'.
Gentiana lutea: Very deep rooted, long-lived perennial with spikes of flowers carried on strong upright stems.
Helleborus argutifolius (corsicus): Vigorous and persistent in sun or light shade, hardy in most situations apart from dry cold winters.
Hemerocallis 'Golden Chimes': One amongst innumerable hybrids producing closely clustered stems in early spring from masses of roots.
Iris pallida ssp. *pallida (dalmatica):* Glaucous foliage produced from short, broad rhizomes – best when free from closely planted competition
Libertia formosa*: Best in well drained, fertile soil in cool settings that do not become too dry – sun or light shade.
Paeonia officinalis cvs: With other spp. and cvs. is an exceptionally long lived persistent perennial able to hold ground indefinitely.
Salvia x *superba:* Quickly establishes densely rooted mats with masses of upright stems – vigorous ground holder.
Thalictrum delavayi (dipterocarpum): Gradually grows into a large multi-stemmed plant – in deep, moist humus-rich soil in lightly shaded settings.
Tricyrtis latifolia: Clustered stems above retentive roots – needs cool, preferably lightly shaded settings and rich, moist soil.
Veratrum nigrum: Establishes slowly but a perpetual tenant – shade or sunshine in, humus

Fig. 10. Planting plan for a mixed border
This is a large area of planting, approximately 65 m2 (700 ft2) in all. It introduces a lush woodland atmosphere into a sheltered garden on a rich clay soil. The garden is bounded by woodland with oaks, ashes, hazels and hollies. The heavy leaf fall from these trees is an added bonus as they supplement the

annual mulch from decayed leaves and stems of the garden plants. This annually renewed mulch creates conditions in which the garden thrives. Slugs are not a problem since no pesticides are used and so a healthy population of predators has built up, including frogs, toads, snakes, hedgehogs and birds.

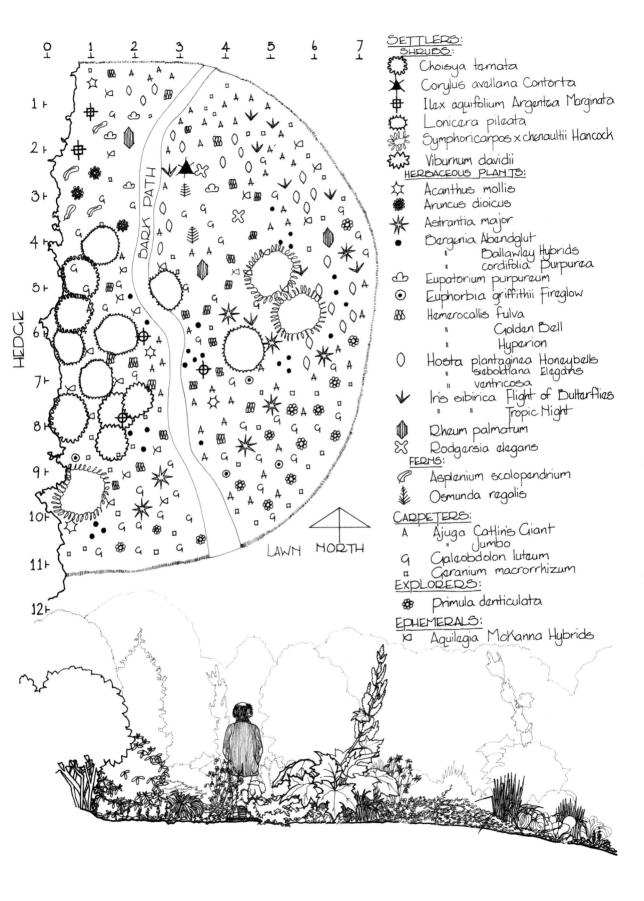

SETTLERS:
SHRUBS:
⬡ Choisya ternata
◆ Corylus avellana Contorta
⊞ Ilex aquifolium Argentea Marginata
⬡ Lonicera pileata
❀ Symphoricarpos × chenaultii Hancock
❁ Viburnum davidii

HERBACEOUS PLANTS:
☆ Acanthus mollis
✸ Aruncus dioicus
✳ Astrantia major
● Bergenia Abendglut
   " Ballawley Hybrids
   " cordifolia Purpurea
☁ Eupatorium purpureum
⊙ Euphorbia griffithii Fireglow
⦚ Hemerocallis fulva
   " Golden Bell
   " Hyperion
◯ Hosta plantaginea Honeybells
   " sieboldiana Elegans
   " ventricosa
⋎ Iris sibirica Flight of Butterflies
   "   "   Tropic Night
▥ Rheum palmatum
✕ Rodgersia elegans

FERNS:
𝒞 Asplenium scolopendrium
🌿 Osmunda regalis

CARPETERS:
A Ajuga Catlin's Giant
   "   Jumbo
g Galeobdolon luteum
▫ Geranium macrorrhizum

EXPLORERS:
❂ Primula denticulata

EPHEMERALS:
⋈ Aquilegia McKanna Hybrids

HEDGE

BARK PATH

LAWN   NORTH

rich moisture retentive soil.

Veronicastrum virginicum: Expands steadily by short rhizomes. Very easy to grow in sunny situations in fertile well-drained soils.

Carpeters

Planting patterns must ensure that seasonal gaps are occupied and overshadowed by foliage. This can be attempted by planting bulbs, but although these make a major contribution to the attractions of the border – particularly when in flower in early spring, before most shrubs or herbaceous plants are doing very much – only a few, such as celandine, winter aconites and the marble-leaved arums, knit together sufficiently closely for their foliage to inhibit weed seed germination effectively; and the usefulness of these few is reduced in many gardens by their inclination to grow too vigorously.

But there are many evergreen or semi-evergreen perennials that grow naturally beneath the shadow of taller perennials and shrubs, carpeting the ground between them, particularly during the late winter and early spring. These not only fill seasonal gaps, but also infiltrate beneath shrubs to occupy the space beneath their shoots, which becomes a vulnerable part of the matrix when the leaves have fallen.

Unlike the settled perennials which grow from year to year, and, hopefully, seldom or never need to be disturbed, these carpeters are flexible plants that can be planted, and removed and replanted if necessary as needs arise. Some like lamiums, persicarias and geraniums can be propagated quickly and easily in great numbers if necessary, and are easily restrained if they wander further than they should.

Interweaving, carpeting and space-filling perennials

These are plants that establish rapidly and spread out to fill spaces between the clump formers. They are vital in the early stages of the development of a matrix, but are necessary to plug gaps later, and weave amongst less mobile ground holding plants. Many are more or less evergreen: some are short-lived self-seeders.

Alchemilla mollis: A long-lived clump forming perennial that fills spaces by self-seeding – sometimes to excess.

Anaphalis triplinervis: Spreads moderately, producing tufts of silver leaves – moisture retentive soils in sun or light shade.

***Anemone sylvestris* 'Macrantha':** For light, humus-rich soil, which does not become too dry amongst well spaced perennials or shrubs.

***Anthriscus sylvestris* 'Ravenwing':** Short-lived, crimson leaved perennial, that fills gaps by self-sowing. Pull out green seedlings.

Asarum canadense: One of several spp., all make excellent evergreen ground cover beneath taller herbaceous perennials, tolerant of deep shade.

Astrantia maxima: Spreads moderately by underground rhizomes, and integrates well with neighbouring plants.

Campanula latiloba: Tolerant of drought in sun or shade, but does better in kinder conditions interplanted with other perennials.

Dicentra formosa: This and other spp. and cvs. make excellent dense ground cover between clumps of perennials and shrubs.

Digitalis grandiflora: A moderately long-lived perennial – seeds freely and seedlings occupy spaces between other plants.

Duchesnea indica: Vigorously runnering perennial for locating and filling spaces in moist, lightly shaded settings.

Eryngium planum: Short-lived perennial that seeds itself freely amongst other plants on light ground in sunny situations.

***Fragaria vesca* 'Multiplex':** Excellent mat-forming ground cover; confines itself to spaces and does not invade established plants.

Geranium macrorrhizum: Invaluable moderately pervasive, evergreen infiltrator amongst clump formers in sun or shade – tolerates drought.

Lamium maculatum: Numerous cvs. provide vigorous, easily controlled ground cover – especially useful during early stages.

Persicaria affinis: Well behaved spreader that occupies ground very effectively amongst taller plants and front of border.

***Phlox stolonifera* 'Blue Ridge':** Vigorous and very attractive infiltrator on moist, humus-rich, preferably acid, soils in light shade.

Phuopsis stylosa: Mat former, responds well to autumn cut backs, Good infiller between more upright plants and shrubs.

***Sedum spurium*:** Numerous forms valuable as space fillers between clump-forming plants at front of dry sunny borders.

***Viola cornuta*:** Hybrids spread seasonally between and into more compact plants – easily cut back to base in autumn.

***Waldsteinia ternata*:** Good ground-holding but not invasive evergreen perennial that fills spaces exceptionally well.

Explorers

Plants with vigorously intrusive rhizomes are prominent members of natural plant communities, either as colonizers – when they may play a preparatory part in the development of a community by stabilizing shifting soils – or later, when they are the means of filling gaps rapidly and effectively. Marram grass, fireweed, stinging nettles and creeping thistle may be useful members of the communities in which they live naturally, but few gardeners appreciate their virtues, and most are justifiably suspicious of plants that spread, vigorously by means of underground runners.

Irrepressible, spreading rhizomatous perennials

Many of these need to be used with great care, matching their potential against space available and the vigour of their companions. Several make excellent rapid colonizers when large spaces have to be filled.

***Acanthus mollis*:** Forms steadily spreading, eventually extensive and extremely retentive colonies, in sun and on dry soils.

***Aegopodium podagraria* 'Variegatum':** Spreads inexorably by underground rhizomes. Light shade in humus-rich, soil that never becomes too dry.

***Alstroemeria aurantiaca*:** Established plants make very vigorous deep seated colonizers – best in moist soils in light shade.

***Anemone japonica* 'Queen Charlotte':** With other spp. and cvs. forms moderately spreading colonies. Very tolerant of shade and poor soils and extremely long lived.

***Campanula poscharskyana*:** Low growing, vigorous evergreen that colonises enthusiastically amongst stones in sun or light shade.

***Centaurea hypoleuca* 'John Coutts':** Good foliage and a long flowering period combine with a not too invasive nature.to make a fine plant.

***Convallaria majalis*:** Spreads vigorously by rhizomes – very tolerant of drought and shade and an attractive infiller.

***Euphorbia cyparissus*:** Low growing, rapidly increasing perennial with good foliage, company for other vigorous ground occupiers.

***Helianthus atrorubens* 'The Monarch'*:** Vigorous spreader and space occupier, more tender, but with better flowers than most others of the genus.

***Heliopsis scabra*:** Usually not more than moderately spreading, yellow daisy for dry, sandy soils.

***Hemerocallis fulva*:** Vigorous spreader that quickly occupies large areas of ground, especially on humus rich woodland soils.

***Lysimachia punctata*:** Extremely vigorous, tolerant and retentive spreader – rapidly forms colonies in moist conditions.

***Macleaya microcarpa*:** Fine plant with excellent foliage that will take all the space it needs in sun on well-drained, fertile soils.

***Persicaria campanulatum*:** A moderately vigorous spreader for moist, shaded situations amongst shrubs and tall perennials.

***Physalis alkekengii*:** A vigorous colonizer tolerant of most soils and situations best amongst large shrubs.

***Podophyllum peltatum*:** Spreads vigorously to form large colonies, particularly amongst grass in partial shade.

***Romneya coulteri*:** Once established spreads vigorously in hot sunny positions on fertile, free-draining soils.

***Solidago* 'Golden Wings':** One of a number of vigorous spp. and cvs. capable of taking over considerable areas.

***Tanacetum vulgare*:** Spreads by dense mats of vigorous roots in sunny situations on any but sodden soils.

***Thalictrum minus adiantifolium*:** Forms dense, extremely retentive growth of short stems covered with attractive foliage.

46A

46B

Ephemerals

Annuals, biennials and short-lived perennials also have roles to play, either deliberately planted out or sown *in situ*. These vary greatly in their aggression and vigour, but all are relatively easily controlled by pulling them out or dead heading to prevent or reduce seed production. Plants that self seed may do so too enthusiastically while gaps are spacious and need a little curbing. However, at later stages of development, they take on the role of explorers, finding and filling incidental spaces in the matrix, and at that stage of development the unplanned appearances of love-in-the-mist, foxgloves, rose campion and other annuals and short-lived perennials provide easy, safe and colourful ways to maintain the matrix and add extra colour and spontaneity to the planting.

Space-filling ephemerals and short-lived perennials

Many of these perform a useful – and decorative – function during the early stages of matrix formation. As the matrix takes shape they are likely to be replaced by perennials, but in some situations will continue to play a part by filling occasional or seasonal gaps. Self-seeding depends on a close match between the nature of the site and the plant.

Ajuga reptans: Numerous cvs exist of this mobile perennial. Seldom stays put but spreads erratically by short runners.
Angelica archangelica: Imposing biennial for fertile, moderately dry, sunny situations self-seeding where there is space.
Aquilegia atrata: A moderately long-lived light woodland perennial that like several other spp. self seeds readily.
Commelina coelestis*: An annual in cold areas that regenerates from seed each spring on moist soils in sun or light shade.

46A & B. Few summer-flowering bulbs contribute materially to the strength of a matrix, but because they compete minimally with other plants, they can be used liberally for their decorative impact without prejudicing the success of their neighbours. Many alliums (top) lose their leaves before the flowers open, and associate well with plants that are intolerant of shade and competition. Lilies (bottom) growing above lower-growing perennials provide brilliant – if rather short-lived – displays without overshadowing the plants beneath them. Elizabeth Kerfoot's garden, North Saanich, Vancouver island, Canada. Little Norton Mill, Norton sub Hamden, Somerset, England.

Dianthus plumarius: Short-lived perennial for dry, sunny, well drained situations in which it will produce occasional seedlings.

Digitalis purpurea: Colourful biennial for light shade or sun on moist, humus-rich soils. Freely self seeding on acid soils.

Eryngium giganteum: Biennial for free-draining, fertile soils, regenerates from seed even amongst established perennials.

Foeniculum vulgare **'Purpureum':** Large short-lived perennial and a very free self-seeder in hot, dry, sunny situations.

Glaucium corniculatum: Unreliable but sometimes moderately long-lived perennial – self-seeds in dry, very stony situations.

Hesperis matronalis: Short-lived perennial freely self-sowing in light shade or sunny situations with moisture retaining soils.

Lunaria annua: Several forms of honesty, including variegated, seed themselves reliable in many garden situations- may need thinning.

Malva moschata **'Alba':** Short-lived perennial – often maintains itself from seed that germinates in gaps in sunny borders.

Meconopsis cambrica: Freely self-seeding species in some situations – but not always easy to establish in a garden.

Myosotis sylvatica: Self-seeds in gaps in light woodland but seldom continues beyond the early stages of matrix formation.

Oenothera glaziouana (lamarkiana): Biennial that regularly self-seeds in sunny, open situations on free-draining, base-rich soils.

Onopordum arabicum: Large and formidable biennial that comes up year by year from seed – often in unexpected places.

Papaver rupifragum **'Flore Pleno':** Freely self-seeding short-lived perennial for dry, sunny banks and other well-drained situations.

Salvia sclarea var turkestanica: Biennial producing self-sown seedlings in gardens – particularly on fertile, free-draining, base rich soils.

Silybum marianum: Biennial thistle broadly tolerant of a wide range of light to medium, well drained or humus rich soils.

Verbascum olympicum: Short lived perennial that is free seeding on warm dry, sandy or base rich soils in sunny situations.

Bulbs

We know they are there, but seldom think about them. Gardeners become so carried away by the attractions of the stems, foliage and flowers of trees, shrubs and perennials that they remain forgetful of their roots. But try to plant beneath established trees and you will soon discover what a formidable deterrent the subterranean parts of plants can be to the entry of newcomers, and what a critical part of the matrix they are. Alliances with roots are an important part of matrix management and some of the most attractive of these allies are those plants that retreat into resting organs below the ground for part of each year. Bulbs, tubers, corms and rhizomes are all refuges against adversity, from which the plant can sally out when drought or cold or shade or whatever other danger threatens has passed, and more agreeable growing conditions return.

This ability to survive difficult conditions makes it possible for bulbs to thrive in situations where other plants would struggle. The woods in the river valleys where I live are filled with snowdrops in February when little else is stirring. Later, the dense canopy of the trees produces so much shade that the ground is almost bare. In other, hotter, parts of the world, alliums flower on naked stems after summer drought has withered their leaves and the colours of the spring display of most bulbs and annuals has faded away. Bulbous plants add to the variety and interest of plant communities by occupying space above ground when other plants are leafless By far the best time to plant them is before or at the same time as other permanent plants are being put in position.

The gardens
Brigadier in seaside retreat
This is a 300 sq. m (3,3000 sq. ft) back garden of a Georgian house in the south coast seaside town of Sidmouth in Devonshire. Most winters are mild, with few nights when temperatures fall below -5°C (23 °F), and it is far enough from the sea to escape serious effects of salt sprays, but westerly gales may buffet it at any time of the year. In common with many long-

established gardens in towns, the soil is almost black, free-draining and easy to work.

The owner, a retired brigadier who never married, is an assistant bursar at a local boarding school, and his part-time duties leave him plenty of time for the garden. He is a pedantic, rather pernickety man with strong convictions about the value of appearances, fretting at the least hint of untidiness. He is immensely proud of his garden, and takes great pleasure in showing it off to his friends. He does not pretend to be knowledgeable about plants, and is a stalwart supporter of 'good old-fashioned flowers', being particularly cool towards those known only by their Latin names.

Review

A
The Brigadier is not as active as he used to be, and the time was ripe for changes that would ensure his garden would not make too many demands, while still offering scope for him to continue to enjoy working in it.

B
The dark, easily-managed soil was less fertile than it looked, and needed a nutrient boost, and treatment to enhance its water-holding capacity and structure.

C
Plants – and weeds – grew more vigorously as a result, and would have added to his problems if changes in planting styles had not been adopted.

D
Over the last few years, the owner's pleasure in sitting out in the garden had decreased as his blood thins, and he feels the effects of the sea breezes and gales more keenly – increased shelter was a high priority.

Outcome

A
A path of paviors was laid from the house along one side of the lawn to make a safer all-weather route through the garden.

Grass paths were dug out, the spoil being spread on adjacent beds, and replaced by gravel, kept weed-free by annual applications of Pathclear (containing diquat, paraquat and amitrole) for immediate effects, plus simazine as a pre-emergence weedkiller.

B
Borders were regularly top dressed in late winter with a proprietary garden fertilizer (NPK 7:7:7) at the rate of 100 g/sq. m.

An annual early-winter mulch of mushroom compost or spent hops was spread under the trees and shrubs, more or less covering the perennials beneath them.

He was finally persuaded that it was better to scatter mowings from the lawn in a thin layer at the back of the borders than dump them at the end of the garden where they had formed a putrid, greasy pile.

C
His regimented parade of well-spaced plants isolated from one another by bare earth was abandoned in favour of less-defined groupings in which shrubs and perennials grew under trees to form a weed-excluding matrix.

This cost very little as, apart from trees, he obtained most of the plants he needed by propagating from those already in the garden, or by buying one or two from garden centres as stock plants for cuttings.

D
The matrices of trees and shrubs around the lawn not only reduced work, but provided shelter that made the garden much more enjoyable for work or relaxation.

A tall hedge along one boundary that he clipped precariously from rickety wooden steps was removed, and replaced by a stout trelliswork fence. This provided more interesting and effective shelter, and was safer for him to look after. It was covered with climbing roses, honeysuckles, clematis and ivies, etc.

A small greenhouse made a warm, sheltered

Fig. 11. Brigadier in seaside retreat
The brigadier insists on an orderly garden, but the necessity of reducing work has introduced him to style and method of planting that he would never have previously considered. Somewhat to his surprise, he is delighted by the effects following his use of matrix planting, and his beds now look much more lively for longer periods than before. The garden is more sheltered in the winter and also more interesting – the groups of new trees are attractive in themselves and provide shelter not only for neighbouring plants but also for numerous birds that were seldom seen before.

place to work, where he could grow plants from seeds and cuttings, including regular replacements of the tender perennials that make such a bright display during the summer.

The plants

The only trees planted were seedling birches and acers, including *Betula albosinensis* and *B. utilis*, and *Acer rufinerve*, *A. davidii* and *A. grosseri* var. *hersii*. Two to four of each were grouped in clusters to emphasize the effects of the stems. A trio of *Cupressus macrocarpa* 'Goldcrest' was planted in an exposed corner as a quick-growing windbreak.

The sheltering effects of the trees were reinforced by underplanting with evergreen shrubs, concentrated towards the boundaries as a background for deciduous shrubs and perennials. Amongst them were dense bushes of *Ceanothus* 'Delight' and 'Italian Skies', groups of solid cover from *Hebe* 'La Seduisante', 'Marjorie' and 'Watson's Pink', with the bright, glossy foliage of *Pittosporum tenuifolium* 'Irene Paterson' and 'Wharnham Gold' like shafts of sunlight, also *Rhododendron* 'Praecox' and the Brigadier's favourite, 'Pink Pearl'.

Other shrubs planted around the lawn and alongside the paths included *Abelia grandiflora* and the tall, fragrant *A. triphylla*, *Cestrum parquii*, *Coronilla valentina* subsp. *glauca* in sunlit places, *Kerria japonica* 'Golden Guinea' (because 'Bachelor's Buttons' was the first shrub he ever knew), *Fuchsia magellanica* var. *molinae (alba)*, var. *gracilis* and 'Dollar Princess' (which grew into large shrubs in the mild conditions), *Hydrangea* 'Generale Vicomtesse de Vibraye' and 'Madame Emile Mouillere', with *Hypericum* 'Rowallane' for late summer colour, and the easily-controlled *Weigela florida* 'Foliis purpureis'.

The Brigadier insisted on numerous roses – 'not those dreadful, blowsy old-fashioned things', but kinds like 'Alec's Red', 'Arthur Bell', 'Peace' and 'Silver Jubilee', which were kept apart from the trees and shrubs in beds underplanted with low-growing perennials like *Geranium macrorrhizum* and *G. renardii*, *Viola cornuta* hybrids, *Lamium* 'Beacon Silver' and *Acaena* 'Blue Haze' and 'Copper Carpet'.

Other perennials, planted amongst the trees and shrubs in the less accessible places, were

encouraged to grow into a complete, weed-excluding ground cover. Closer to the lawn and along the paths, spaces were kept for annual replenishment with bedding plants and tender perennials grown in his greenhouse by the Brigadier, including osteospermums and marguerites, snapdragons, Canterbury bells, Coltness hybrid dahlias, nemesias, petunias and scarlet salvias.

Gardening editor's crisis of confidence

The owners of this garden, at the back of an old house in Saffron Walden in East Anglia, are the editor of a gardening magazine and his wife. High walls on three sides make it a sheltered, warm and tranquil place.

The editor's appointment was a commercial decision, and does not reflect a deep interest in gardening or knowledge of plants. He prefers to spend his spare time sailing, but is not averse to a little fair-weather gardening, cruising, glass in hand, showing it off to colleagues and friends. A pleasure rather spoilt on several recent occasions by the aroma from the neighbour's barbecue drifting over the wall.

His wife loathes cold water, hates sailing and loves gardening. The garden owes everything to her work and imagination, and she looks on it as hers – a view resisted by her husband, whose barbed comments to guests about her efforts grow snider under the influence of the party spirit. He is uneasy about the garden, feeling it falls short of the well-groomed statement he would like to make as editor of a well-known gardening magazine. From time to time, he affronts and enrages his wife by launching into a weekend of frantic tidying and pruning.

Review

A

This garden, enclosed by walls in the centre of a town, would seem to many people, as indeed it does to the editor, an automatic choice for a formal lay-out. His wife's decision to treat it informally was at the root of his ambiguous attitude towards it.

B

The site is a very favoured one. The pH of the soil is too high for rhododendrons to grow well, but otherwise imposes few restrictions on the choice of plants. In other respects the soil is in good condition, with a well-maintained structure, adequate fertility and reasonable water-holding capacity.

C

His appetite for gardening was entirely sated by his job, and he would have been the first to object if called upon to commit himself to any prolonged creative or consistent effort in the garden.

Outcome

A

The informal lay-out provides a relaxing contrast to the hard lines of neighbouring buildings, and the noise and bustle in the surrounding streets.

In particular, it sets the scene for an abundant, free style of growth which has created shelter, shade and privacy in a variety of places, and provides attractively secluded 'hide-outs' at different times of the day.

B

There is no lawn, but a gravel garden forms an open, irregularly-shaped sunny area in the centre, with plenty of space to walk. This was made with a ground layer of about 7 cm (3 in) of broken bricks and mortar, covered with about 20 cm (8 in) of Cerney gravel, consisting of flat, rounded fragments of limestone that are comfortable to walk on.

The warm, sheltered site, and especially the walls, has been used for an interesting collection of shrubs, predominantly roses (there are only a few trees), with a wide variety of perennials beneath them.

C

Recently, the garden featured in a chic homes and gardens glossy magazine with flattering photographs and appreciative comments on its originality and style. He now feels less defensive about the impression it creates, is less given to criticism, but more inclined to claim it as his own.

The plants

Trees were carefully grouped to provide shade and seclusion, leaving an open space in the centre of the garden. Most were naturally small, or could be kept small by judicious pruning,

choosing several with pinnate leaves for their light and airy effects, including *Acacia pravissima*, planted against a wall, *Albizzia julibrissin* 'Rosea' and *Gleditsia triacanthos* 'Ruby Lace'. Also planted were *Magnolia* 'Iolanthe' (a Felix Jury hybrid that flowers freely when young), *Parrotia persica*; *Sorbus aria* 'Chrysophylla'and *Xanthoceras sorbifolium*.

The sunshine and warmth in the centre of the garden were accentuated by the very well-drained, alkaline gravel garden, ideally suited to many of the plants with fragrant foliage that grow on limestone in Mediterranean areas. The planting formed an open matrix of shrubs and woody perennials, amongst which were *Ballota pseudodictamnus*, *Caryopteris clandonensis* 'Kew Blue', with *Indigofera potaninii* and *Perowskia atriplicifolia* for later colour; several of the smaller *Cistus*, including 'Paladin', 'Peggy Sammons' and *C.* X *skanbergii*, *Convolvulus cneorum*, *Daphne cneorum* 'Eximia', *Genista hispanica*, *G. lydia* and *Hyssopus officinalis*. Several cultivars of *Lavandula angustifolia* included 'Loddon Pink' and 'Munstead', with the woolly-leaved *L. lanata*. There were *Phlomis chrysophylla* and *P. italica*, and several cultivars of *Rosmarinus officinalis*, including the tender *R. repens* ('Prostratus' group), *Ruta graveolens* 'Jackman's Blue' and 'Variegata', *Santolina pinnata* 'Neapolitana' and 'Edward Bowles'.

Perennials amongst the shrubs were planted to form mats overlying bulbs, capable of resisting a little foot wear, including *Antennaria dioica* 'Nyewoods Variety', *Aethionema* 'Warley Rose', several colour forms of *Campanula carpatica* and *C. cochlearifolia*, *Dianthus crinitus*, *D. gratianopolitanus* and 'La Bourboule', *Erysimum* 'Jacob's Jacket' and 'Moonlight', *Euphorbia myrsinites*, several different colour forms of *Geranium cinereum*, and a variety of low-growing thymes. More upright, spiky contrasts were provide by *Asphodeline lutea*, *Iris pallida pallida (dalmatica)* and 'Florentina', supported by grasses including *Chondrosum (Bouteloua) gracilis*, *Carex* 'Frosted Curls', the bronze form of *Carex comans*, and *Festuca amethystina*, *F. glauca* 'Elijah Blue' and 'Blue Fox', with background affects from clumps of the tall, mobile *Stipa gigantea*.

Flower arranger's garden showpiece

The managing director of a company selling cars in Folkestone in south-east England is the owner of this garden of nearly a hectare (two and a half acres). It faces north-east at the foot of a chalk hillside a mile or two inland, exposed to cold winds. The soil is an alkaline, putty-coloured boulder clay heavily laced with flints – intractably sticky in winter, dry as a brick and riven by cracks in summer. The rainfall is quite low.

The owner took over the business on the death of her husband, and has since come into her own, both financially and personally, developing into a powerful personality with a taste for getting her own way. She has a reputation as a perfectionist who spares neither effort nor expense in keeping the place looking like a showpiece. The founder and president of a local flower arranging group, she is an outspoken participant in NAFAS, opening her gardens to groups of flower arrangers for visits and meetings several times each year. She employs a full-time gardener but does a great deal of gardening herself. Her previous gardener departed rapidly after a worldly-wise member of a visiting NAFAS group recognized an unfamiliar row of plants amongst the vegetables as Cannabis.

Review

A

The unattractive appearance of the soil is misleading. In spite of physical problems which make it intractable and difficult to work, it is much more fertile than it looks, and plants grow well on it.

B

In the early years the main problems in the garden were its cold position on a north-east slope, accentuated by exposure to cold winds.

C

Employing a gardener to mow lawns, trim hedges and edges, and cultivate vegetables, gave the owner time and energy to think creatively about her gardening, and to try out new ideas – something she does with great verve, and little compunction about dismantling last year's grand scheme.

D

The garden is used imaginatively as a source of material for flower arranging, and this is an important function of the planting – generously deployed to satisfy her friends' needs as well as her own.

Outcome

A

The best way to enhance the appearance of this soil, and make it easier to work, would have been to cover it with a mulch, but the owner considers mulches untidy. First attempts to persuade her to give the idea a try using Forest Bio-mulch, chosen for its appearance, came to nothing when Melcourt Industries, its suppliers, failed to arrange delivery. She continued to insist on regular applications of compost or farmyard manure, dug in or forked between established plants, and timely use of the hoe.

Recently, she was persuaded to invest in a shredding machine, and its practicality and economy have begun to persuade her to use its products directly as a mulch, rather than composting material.

B

Parts of the garden have been terraced with walls of flint and brick, to convert cold northeast slopes into level surfaces, which warm up more rapidly in spring and provide good drainage during the winter.

Yew hedges, planted years ago for shelter, had grown excessively broad, and a programme of drastic reduction was necessary. The first year, every branch on one side was cut back to the main stems, followed by similar treatment to the other side the next.

C

Terraces and hedges formed sheltered compartments, planted to create different effects. The owner spurned the contemporary fashion of narrowly-defined colour theming, and eschewed 'white' or 'crimson' borders in favour of effects obtained by thoughtful compositions of foliage and texture, reinforced by well-co-ordinated repetition, following the flower arranger's precept of 'repetition makes rhythm'.

D

A flair for arrangement made it natural for her to combine plants of different kinds in the multi-tiered fashion of matrix planting, but she had little inclination to surrender control of any kind to the plants.

The result was a highly dynamic, constantly changing version of matrix planting, which produced extremely attractive and varied compositions of flowers and foliage, beautifully graded from the ground upwards, but which never had a chance to develop into a self-sustaining community before being replaced by yet another idea.

The plants

Hybrid tea and floribunda roses are grown mainly in the cutting borders alongside the kitchen garden, and she relies almost entirely on shrub roses for garden use. These include numerous 'old-fashioned' gallicas, albas and hybrid perpetuals, but she has become a convert to David Austin's English roses and every year tries a few out – keeping some and quickly rejecting others. She likes the drooping, glowing, crimson heads of 'the Squire' for arrangements, and amongst others also grows the yellow 'Graham Thomas', 'Abraham Darby' and 'Leander', and has high hopes for 'Brother Cadfael', a modern version of the classic, bowl-shaped, pink rose.

The roses are grown in intricately mixed borders, with shrubs, perennials, bulbs and annuals – the latter are varied year by year and play a major part in the appearance of the border, where they are planted wherever there is space to hold them, between roses, paeonies, hard-pruned *Hydrangea grandiflora* 'Praecox' and 'Grandiflora', *Syringa persica* and its white form 'Alba', *Ligustrum ovalifolium* 'Argenteum' and 'Aureum', cut back hard each spring, *Philadelphus* 'Avalanche' and 'Beauclerk', and other shrubs.

Some of the annuals and other transients tried recently include the tall florist's forms of ageratums and snapdragons, *Ammobium alatum* 'Grandiflorum', *Beta dracaenaefolia*, the bright oranges and yellows of *Calendula* 'Early Nakayasu', 'Orange Shaggy' and 'Radar', the special Matsumoto florist's forms of the China aster and *Celosia* 'Fire Chief', 'Stock Flowered' and 'Imperial' larkspurs, *Euphorbia marginata* for the bright contrast of its variegated leaves, *Helichrysum orientale*, *Helianthemum* 'Taiyo' and other small, branching sunflowers, *Helipterum manglesii*, *H. roseum*, *Limonium sinuatum*,

Molucella laevis (having discovered how to germinate its seeds), *Papaver nudicaule*, *Rudbeckia* 'Gloriosa' hybrids, *Tithonia speciosa*, *Xeranthemum annuum* and *Zinnia elegans* hybrids (especially strains with green or white flowers). Apart from perennial grasses, she also grows annuals, including the hanging lanterns of *Briza maxima*, *Coix lachryma-christii* (which seldom flowers, but is grown for its hummocks of broad leaves), *Hordeum jubatum*, the fluffy tufts of *Lagurus ovatus*, and several very large, broad-leaved grasses which contrast strikingly with other plants, like *Sorghum bicolor* and *S. dochna* var. *technicum*, broom corn growing to nearly 3 m (10 ft) in a good year, with clumps of *Zea mays* 'Harlequin' and 'Quadricolor'.

Bulbs – especially daffodils and tulips – play a major part in the border in spring, and are thickly planted amongst the perennials and shrubs. The former are lifted and divided every third or fourth year, the latter every year. Later, alliums like *A. christophii* and *A. giganteum* are grown for their dried heads, and *Crocosmia* X *crocosmiflora* 'Citronella', 'Jackanapes' 'Norwich Canary' and 'Firebird' for their bright colours after midsummer. She is also very fond of *Galtonia candicans*, with conspicuous white spires that make it invaluable for effective, repetitive use, and *G. viridis* for its silken, light olive-green tubular bells.

Chapter nine

Counting the blessings of shade

Recently, the local newspaper contained a plea from a householder for permission to cut down a large beech tree – headlined as a 'Forest Giant' – in his garden. The tree was healthy and protected by a preservation order, but it was close to his house, and he felt threatened by it. Trees are great assets, but these giant vegetables are not always welcome in gardens, and that householder's fear and distrust was not unusual. Torn between admiration and apprehension, we miss opportunities to use them and the spaces beneath them creatively, and their shade becomes part of our problem. Instead of pruning them constructively, we lop and mutilate them in half-baked attempts to keep them within bounds.

Most gardeners today compose their gardens with mixtures of bulbs, perennials and shrubs. These are the natural associates of trees, whose presence should simplify, not complicate, management. There is an attitude problem here that seems to be a particularly British affliction. Elsewhere, more relaxed attitudes to trees prevail – particularly in parts of New England and Western Canada, but in Holland, Germany and France too – where trees are more likely to be prized for their shelter, and valued for the ways their upright stems and spreading tops provide settings for houses.

The forest in the garden

Few people make gardens in the setting of a natural wood – more often, trees are less obviously at home. Newly-planted trees make little impact. Badly-managed mature trees in older gardens create deserts of dry shade in which few plants are comfortable. Gardens of all kinds contain ornamental trees, chosen on an assurance that they will not grow too big, whose stems, barely 2 m (6 ft 6 in) high, are crowned by densely-foliaged, rounded tops that interrupt every vista and deprive plants that grow beneath them of light. These are situations where

muddled thinking leads to problems, but good management limits the unfavourable aspects of trees, and makes use instead of the benefits they offer by:

Maintaining and, if possible, increasing levels of organic matter beneath the trees – Fallen leaves should not be removed; heavy dressings of organic mulches should be applied before planting, and repeated annually as long as possible. Perennials that grow naturally beneath trees can be covered in early winter with mulches, through which they will emerge the following spring.

Reducing shading effects while maintaining shelter – The height of the canopy is a critical part of the system, and in most situations, the higher the better. Stems occupy little space at ground level, and a long, clear reach to the lower branches raises the canopy high enough to allow light to reach plants growing below.

Making full use of the woodland edge effect – The margins of forests and the perimeter of established trees are sheltered areas, in which numerous wildflowers, shrubs and climbers grow naturally. Most gardens contain examples of a 'woodland edge' – every isolated, or spaced out tree provides them, but they also appear beneath pergolas, along hedges, around the edges of large shrubs in mixed borders, and in the shadow of buildings.

Choosing suitable trees – Shrubs and plants combine much more easily with trees with open foliage and deeply-penetrating roots than with densely-foliaged, surface-rooting kinds. Apples, thorns, plums, many cherries and other popular ornamental trees are not true canopy-formers in forests, but occupants of lesser positions in woodland savanna (where trees grow widely spaced), or scrub. Their low, densely twiggy and heavily-foliaged, rounded crowns lack the long, clear stems that allow light to reach plants beneath them, and provide views through the garden.

Applying appropriate forms of pruning – Trees that become noticeable (an inevitable destiny in

47A

47B

47C

most gardens) too often suffer from unskilful, unthinking pruning. They are drastically lopped to reduce their spread (carried out sometimes to extremes when enthusiastic ignorance replaces skill). This 'short back and sides' treatment does not curb exuberance. It stimulates vigorous, renewed growth below the cuts, and a reversion, within a few years, to an even more densely twiggy and heavily-foliaged version of the original problem. It is almost always better practice to lift the crown by removing lower branches, and thin out rather than cut back the upper branches.

Planting in appropriate ways – Isolated trees suffer from exposure, but planted in groups and thinned out as they develop, benefit from the mutual shelter they are accustomed to under natural conditions. The repetitive, vertical accents of trees with conspicuous bark such as acers and birches is particularly effective when these are planted in groups. Even trees intended to develop as specimens grow best amongst sheltering, faster-growing kinds which are progressively removed to make space. This provides woodland effects with all their benefits early on, and encourages the formation of long, clear stems on those that are left.

Some Deciduous Trees Suitable for Small Gardens

Many more trees are suitable for small gardens than the ubiquitously offered cherries, crab apples, thorns, magnolias and rowans. Many kinds grow naturally as small trees, others frequently thought of as large shrubs can easily be trained into a tree form.

***Acer palmatum*:** Numerous cvs. are widely planted and often preferred to the original green

47A, B & C. The strongest matrices are multi-layered associations of large and small trees, shrubs and perennials (top left). The inclusion of evergreen species (top right) maintains matrices in winter, and shelters spring-flowering bulbs and perennials. The bird's-eye view of birch trees planted amongst heathers (lower right) illustrates the multi-tiered construction of a matrix, and emphasizes the small amount of space occupied by the stems of the trees at ground level. George Tyndall Memorial Garden, Ferny Creek, Dandenongs, Melbourne, Victoria, Australia. Achnacloich Garden, Taynuilt, Argyllshire, Scotland. Royal Botanic Gardens, Kew, London., England.

form, but this makes an excellent, characterful small tree

Aesculus parviflora: A large shrub that can readily be pruned to form a graceful small tree, usually with several stems.

Amelanchier asiatica: This and *A. canadensis* form attractive flowering and fruiting trees – often with multiple stems.

Asimina triloba: More likely to be successful in the USA than in the UK, needs hot summers and moist, fertile, acid soils.

Broussonetia papyrifera: Quick and easy to establish. Can be repeatedly cut back to base to keep within bounds in small gardens.

Cercis canadensis: Others include *C. siliquastrum*. Are excellent small trees for moist well drained, fertile soils in full sun.

Chionanthus virginicus: Large shrub-like form developing into a tree with maturity. Needs moist, acid soils in sun or light shade.

Clerodendron trichotomum var. fargesii: Usually grown as a large shrub, easily trained into a characterful, often multistemmed small tree.

Cornus kousa var chinensis: Needs a sunny position on fertile loam soil. This variety is able to grow on moderately basic soils.

Diospyros kaki: This and other species of persimmon need rich loam soils to do well, in situations with warm summers.

Elaeagnus angustifolia var. *caspica*: A very hardy, olive-like tree suitable for cold and exposed situations provided they are sunny.

Fuchsia excorticata*: Excellent tree in frost free situations combining well with plants and shrubs in its shelter.

Lagerstroemia fauriei*: This and hybrids with *L. indica* need hot summers to thrive – humus-rich, fertile soils in full sun.

Morus rubra: Requires hotter summers to do well than *MM. nigra or alba*. All need fertile loamy soils in warm situations.

Ptelea trifoliata: Low often rather spreading tree, for warm sunny situations on well drained fertile soils.

Rhus typhina 'Laciniata': Extremely beautiful tree with large pinnate leaves. Damage to roots leads to prolific sucker production.

Sophora tetraptera*: Upright open canopied tree with deep roots that associates well with plants set out beneath it.

Staphylea colchica: Very hardy, characterful tree with fine foliage and flowers followed by bladder like fruits.

Syringa reticulata: Hardy densely foliaged small tree with fragrant creamy white flowers for sunny situations. Most large lilacs can be pruned to form small trees.

Tree management

Instructions for choosing trees almost invariably start with an injunction to be careful to match the anticipated size of the mature tree with the space available. That is an obvious precaution when trees are intended to grow to maturity, but that day may be so far away that it is often irrelevant. It is more rewarding to plant for the foreseeable future, and to manage the trees in ways which foresters employ as a matter of course but gardeners largely ignore. Foresters thin trees out, and gardeners, too, should be less reluctant to take them out before they become derelict hulks, taking advantage of the rapid growth of some, and the youthful beauties of others, in situations where full-grown specimens would be out of place. Many broad-leaved trees – and a few conifers – can be coppiced before they become too large by cutting them off at ground level and letting them shoot again. Others can be pollarded (eucalyptus, ashes and willows respond particularly well), cutting their main stems several feet above ground level and establishing a head of strong branches, which can be repeatedly cut back over the years.

These restrictive practices are particularly useful in small gardens, where there is little space for specimen trees to spread their branches, and for which a stereotyped range of offerings are repeatedly suggested that bears little relation to the enormous variety actually available.

Problems with peplows

Mature trees can cause problems. Ancient peplows (a general term for a decrepit, senile tree, likely to be in dangerous condition, derived from an estate in Shropshire where neglected trees were plentiful) can be a hazard that responsible people should take seriously. Senile trees that collapse on cars or drop limbs on people's heads cause more than embarrassment,

48A

48B

48C

and can lead to expensive litigation and claims for damages. It is important to be sure that trees intended to play major parts in the design of a garden have a future. Fortunately, most trees display evidence of problems before these cause extreme structural frailty, and those that are mature or beyond maturity should always be examined from time to time to check their health.

Signs that all may not be well include:

a) rotten wood underlying flaking bark on the trunk or major limbs;
b) badly-healed wounds showing signs of decay after large limbs have broken or been pruned back;
c) thin canopies carrying sparse foliage, and the presence of numerous dead twigs and small

48A, B & C. Trees provide shade and shelter for woodland perennials that benefit from humid conditions, such as hostas (top left). Trees in groups (top right), display the attractions of their bark, shelter one another, and grow up with long, clear stems. As they mature, the lower limbs can be progressively removed (bottom right) to provide uninterrupted views across the garden, and to reduce the shading affects of their canopies. Gordon & Annette Collier's Garden, Titoki Point, Taihape, New Zealand. Newby Hall, Ripon, Yorkshire, England. Mary Ann & Frederick McGourty's Garden, Hillside, Norfolk, Connecticut, USA.

branches;
d) the emergence of bracket fungi on main stems, or cankers girdling major limbs;
e) pockets of water in the angles where stems divide, leading to fungal infections and splits;
f) cavities and rotting wood between the root buttresses close to ground level;
g) damaged roots due to excavations such as trench-cutting close to the tree;
h) cracks in the soil and other signs of instability caused by movement of the roots.

Any of these justify calling in expert help. Sometimes tree surgery will give a new lease of life. Sometimes what you see is due to deep-seated problems, with poor prospects for survival and a high risk of catastrophic collapse, making felling the only responsible and economic course of action. Sad though the loss of a large and characterful tree may be, its departure from the scene opens the way for new developments that often turn out to be even more interesting and enjoyable than the presence of the tree itself.

Using woodland plants in gardens

An earlier chapter described how trees and other plants share out resources between them to establish a balance. The matrices that these woodland communities form are exceptionally robust due to their tiered construction, in which trees, shrubs, climbers, perennials, ferns, mosses and bulbs not only exist as successive layers, but often form secondary tiers within themselves. Young trees grow up amongst older ones, evergreens may reinforce the seasonal matrices of deciduous species, Solomon's seal may arch over dicentras, which in their turn grow above violets.

The diverse, colourful matrices of deciduous woodlands provide attractive models for our gardens, and in many parts of the world these grow in company with evergreen trees and shrubs that reinforce the matrix when deciduous plants are leafless. In gardens, especially in mild areas, their foliage, and often flowers, add

interest in winter, and in their turn provide more sheltered conditions for lesser plants at ground level.

Evergreen trees and shrubs may appear to be so well able to endure frost and snow that they do not need to drop their leaves before the onset of winter – an impression that appears to be confirmed by the great northern forests of Siberia and Canada, in which conifers that endure the coldest winters are prominent. But these hardy spruces and pines are exceptional; much more typical are the evergreen species in the forests of New Zealand, southern Chile, and the maquis vegetation of the Mediterranean, Western Australia and California, and the synbos of South Africa. These are places where photosynthesis can continue right through the winter due to moderate winter temperatures, and many of the most interesting and attractive evergreens are not very hardy – as evidenced by the liberal sprinkling of asterisks in the following list.

Evergreen Trees Suitable for Shelter and Shade

Most of those listed grow as small trees in gardens to limit views, and increase the density of plantings especially in winter. Evergreen trees grow naturally in both hot, often arid, situations, or in wet locations with cool winters and summers. The diametrically opposed requirements of the two groups – imply very different roles in gardens.
Acacia dealbata*: Deep rooted, fast growing tree with light overhead canopy – for well drained soils in warm situations.
Agonis flexuosa*: Fast growing, deep rooting, drought resistant shade tree with trailing branches, for warm situations.
Arbutus unedo: Densely foliaged, slow growing tree, eventually developing extremely characterful form.
Cordyline australis*: Several cvs available. Striking contrasts of form with broad-leaved plants. Tolerant and easily grown.
Embothrium coccineum*: Fast growing pioneer species for moist acid soils in humid, high

Fig. 12. Illustration of a 'peplow'
Trees are too large and heavy to take risks with, so it is important to watch out for signs of instability and decay in elderly peplows and take action promptly if necessary. Symptoms of possible danger are illustrated here.

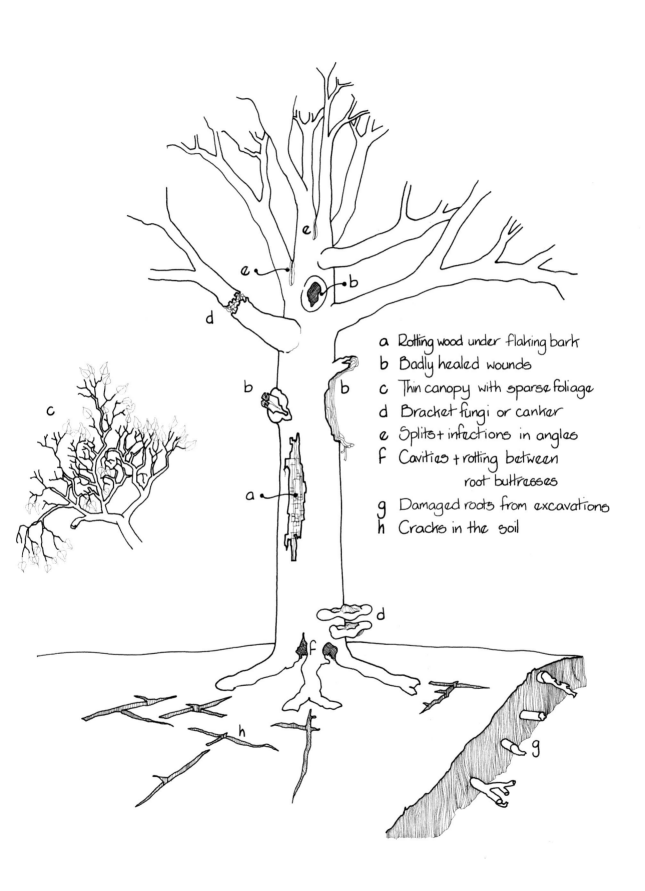

a Rotting wood under flaking bark
b Badly healed wounds
c Thin canopy with sparse foliage
d Bracket fungi or canker
e Splits + infections in angles
f Cavities + rotting between
        root buttresses
g Damaged roots from excavations
h Cracks in the soil

rainfall locations. Wind resistant.

Eucalyptus caesia **'Silver Princess'** *: A weeping, silver leaved tree, suitable for the direst and hottest situations, deep rooted with a light canopy.

Feijoa sellowiana *: Densely foliaged round headed, small, fruiting tree that needs a warm, humid site on moist fertile soils.

Fremontodendron **'California Glory'** *: Very showy, upright tree for hot sunny, sheltered positions on well-drained soils.

Genista aetnensis: Hardy small tree, developing from shrubby form. Light canopy and deep roots favour underplanting.

Ilex aquifolium: Numerous cvs and spp. vary in vigour. Deep, fertile, moisture retentive soils in sun to moderate shade.

Laurus nobilis *: In frost-free conditions develops into a small tree with a clear stem and heavy canopy of broad leaves.

Lomatia ferruginea *: Attractive fern-like evergreen leaves – needs mild, humid conditions and moist, humus rich soils.

Luma (Myrtus) apiculata (luma) *: Notable for cinnamon bark. Sheltered moist, humid conditions and humus rich, acid soils.

Nothofagus dombeyi: Fast growing, large tree for any good garden soil – preferably with shelter for the first few years.

Olea europaea *: Upright tree developing great character with age. Hot summers and deep free-draining soils.

Pittosporum eugenioides *: A broad-leaved fast growing species for mild humid situations, on moist soils in shelter of other trees.

Pseudopanax ferox *: Upright tree slowly developing a dense rounded head – sheltered by other trees on moisture retentive soils.

Quercus coccifera *: A slow growing shrub gradually forming a tree in hot, dry , stony situations – very drought tolerant.

Rhododendron arboreum *: Large shrub developing into a broadly rounded tree on acid, moisture retentive soils in sheltered sites.

Forests of evergreens can be so dense that scarcely anything grows at ground level, and the close spacing of trees in conifer plantations is a forbidding model few gardeners would want to emulate. But as they mature, conifers and broad-leaved evergreens develop long, clear stems – often with compact, rounded canopies. The intimate contact between trees is lost, and light penetrates the spaces between them, providing sheltered, humus-rich, humid and more or less brightly-lit conditions in which a great variety of plants, especially ferns, evergreen shrubs and perennials, thrive.

Climbing shrubs and vines

These can be the most difficult of all the members of the woodland community to use in gardens in the ways they grow naturally. Roses scrambling through ancient apple trees have become something of a garden cliché (and, provided the tree does not collapse too soon, and the vigour of the rose has been accurately judged, can be very effective). But visitors confronted at Kiftsgate by the archetypal rose of that name learn a salutary lesson about the vigour and ferocity with which a powerful climber can infest even full-sized trees, let alone ancient apples. Climbers are naturally adapted to climb, and climb they do – hydrangeas in Chile almost overwhelm evergreen laurels 30 m (100 ft) high, and bridge the gaps between the trees to form dense, light-excluding tangles. Creepers thicker and more sinewy than forearms hang from trees in the Appalachians and the Sikhote Alin mountains overlooking the sea of Japan, the shoots of the vines they sustain lost from sight amongst the tops of 50 m (160 ft) high tulip trees and Korean pines. In gardens, wisterias, *Clematis montana* and *Vitis coignettiae* (not to mention *Chusquea quila*, should anyone be foolhardy enough to plant it) can infiltrate, infest and overpower trees, defying all efforts, short of outright destuction, to control them.

Nevertheless, climbers are invaluable in even the smallest garden. Unlike many woodland shrubs and perennials, these are not shade-tolerant – they climb to reach the sun, and when planted over trellises and pergolas or over arches and arbours in gardens, form fast-growing screens and suppliers of shade – adopting the role of flexible trees. They reproduce the effects of a forest canopy that trees would take years to produce, in a form and

49A

49B

growth and development. The latter can be cut back year by year, removing the greater part of the previous year's growth, and are easily kept within the bounds of small, lightly-built structures.

Vines and Climbers for Pergolas and Trellises

Climbing plants trained over structures of various kinds can be used to provide easily manageable, quickly available shade in gardens. Many combine well with other climbers and can be planted close together to produce a broad spectrum of flowering times, and foliage effects – including evergreens for winter cover.

Actinidia deliciosa (chinensis) **'Hayward'** & **'Tomuri':** Very vigorous dioecious climber – male and female forms needed for fruit. Sunny, sheltered situation.
Aristolochia durior: Vigorous large-leaved climber for partial shade or sun on fertile, humus rich, moist soils.
Celastrus scandens **'Indian Brave'** & **'Indian Maiden':** Vigorous dioecious climber on any fertile soil, in full sun. Males and females should be planted together.
Clematis cirrhosa **var.** *balearica* *: Innumerable spp. and cvs of clematis exist. Vigour and other qualities should be matched to situation.
Eccremocarpus scaber *: Short lived, colourful, moderately vigorous plant – useful for rapid affects in newly planted gardens
Gelsemium sempervirens *: Twining, moderately vigorous evergreen with deep yellow flowers – open sunny situation or light shade.
Hardenbergia violacea **'Happy Wanderer'** *: Moderately vigorous evergreen climber for warm situations on well drained soils.

at a level that can be maintained by pruning within pre-defined limits.

Some, like wisteria, flower on their older wood, which often becomes increasingly floriferous with the passing years; others produce flowers on the current season's growth, like the hybrids of *Clematis viticella*. The former must be grown as a permanent, or at least semi-permanent, framework of branches, which grows ever heavier and more extensive, requiring the support of large and robustly-built structures, unless very severely pruned to restrict

49A & B. Vigorous climbers and vines like *Vitis coignettiae* (top) can envelope the tallest trees. They are more controllable in gardens when grown over trellises, pergolas (bottom) and other structures. Used like this, they rapidly and effectively provide the shade and shelter that a woodland canopy would take years to develop. Savile Gardens, Windsor Great Park, Berkshire, England Hestercombe, Taunton, Somerset, England.

Hedera helix: Numerous cvs. & spp. Vigour and leaf size should be matched to situation. Excellent in heavily shaded sites.

Humulus lupulus 'Aurea': Vigorous, herbaceous climber that establishes rapidly and is useful during early stages of a planting.

Jasminum nudiflorum: Evergreen winter flowering climber. Very tolerant of shade from other plants or buildings.

*Kennedia coccinea**: Moderately vigorous evergreen climber for warm situations on well-drained soils in light shade or sun.

Lapageria rosea: Moderately vigorous evergreen for humid, shaded situations on water retentive, free draining soils.

Lonicera sempervirens 'Cedar Lane': Evergreen honeysuckle for lightly shaded or sunny situations, associates well with other climbers.

*Passiflora caerulea**: One of many species of varying hardiness. Needs warm site in sun and shelter from cold winds.

Rosa 'Zephirine Drouhin': Innumerable climbing and rambler roses available. Absence of thorns makes this one easy to handle.

Schizophragma integrifolia: Vigorous, self-clinging climber suitable for spacious situations – rich loam soils and ample moisture.

Solanum jasminoides 'Album' *: Moderately vigorous climber with a long-flowering period. Ideal for trellises and screens.

*Trachelospermum jasminoides**: With the hardier *T. asiaticum* , the star jasmines are twining evergreens for light shade in summer, sun in winter.

Vitis vinifera 'Purpurea': Hardy moderately vigorous vine, easily controlled by pruning, for sunny situations on any well-drained soil.

Wisteria frutescens: Less vigorous, more controllable than *W. W. floribunda* or *sinensis*: full sun on well drained, fertile soils.

Perennials

The crucial role of perennials in the matrices of the mixed border has already been described. These plants are just as important in woodland settings, where the success of matrices is equally dependent on the way they are used to occupy ground. Some woodland perennials are

evergreen, others produce leaves precociously early – both take advantage of the protection of the trees, and make full use of the period when they are leafless. Dense shade in summer reduces prospects of making a living at ground level, and woodland perennials like dicentras and aconites lose their leaves and retreat below ground; others, including pulmonarias and primroses, retain their leaves but merely tick over, scarcely growing at all. The seasons when leaves play an active part in matrices are less closely synchronized than is the case with plants from more open situations, and become even more varied when bulbs are included in a planting. These variations can be used to create communities in which different kinds of plants play active roles at different seasons to ensure as complete a a cover as possible at ground level throughout the year.

Dry shade beneath mature trees must be one of the most frequently-cited garden problems. Often, it is a problem only because the wrong species have been used, and little has been done to improve the soil or make it easier for young plants to establish themselves. But trees like sycamores, beeches, griselinias and horse chestnuts, with dense canopies and vigorous surface roots, create conditions in which very few flowering plants can thrive, even when the crowns have been raised to let in light, and copious amounts of organic matter have been spread to make the soil more receptive. Then mosses may be the only answer, supplemented perhaps by some of the tougher, more drought-resistant ferns, including forms of *Dryopteris filix-mas Polystichum aculeatum* and *Polypodium* spp.

Evergreen and herbaceous shrubs and perennials beneath trees

Many of the following grow naturally on the woodland floor, beneath deciduous trees or in open evergreen forest. They are invaluable in gardens for any shaded sites, whether beneath trees or structures, or in the shadow of buildings. Many are evergreen or partially evergreen and flower in late winter or spring when the trees are bare of leaves.

Asarum europaeum: Capable of growing as ground covering layer in deep shade beneath deciduous perennials on moist soils.

Aster divaricatus: Light to moderate shade on humus rich soils in open woodland floor communities.

Chasmanthium latifolium: One of comparatively few grasses that thrives in woodland, contrasting well with hostas, tellimas etc.

Clivia miniata*: Excellent for warm deeply shaded situations on moist soils,where it is tolerant of seasonal drought.

Cornus canadensis: Early flowering stoloniferous perennial forming low growing colonies on cool moist, humus rich soils

Desfontainea spinosa: Fine evergreen, sociable shrub for humid locations on persistently moist, preferably acid soils.

Elatostema rugosa*: Vigorous, ground covering rhizomatous perennial with rough leaves, for moist soils in warm, shaded sites.

Epimedium perralderianum: Numerous spp. & cvs: Form dense, steadily expanding clumps of evergreen shoots over matted rhizomes.

Galax urceolata (aphylla): Hardy evergreen with brightly burnished leaves, for cool, moist humus rich acid soils.

Geranium nodosum: Long flowering, vigorously self-seeding perennial capable of thriving on dry soils in heavy shade.

Heuchera americana: Numerous forms all with attractive leaves, good ground covering clump forming species for heavy shade.

Kirengeshoma palmata: Steadily expanding clump former with many stems – acid, moist soils. Very susceptible to spring frosts.

Lamium galeobdolon **'Florentina'**: Potentially smotheringly vigorous runnering perennial. Should be planted amongst competitive neighbours.

Mertensia virginica: Leaves decline in mid summer. Spring flowering perennial for cool, humus rich lightly shaded sites.

Milium effusum **'Aureum'** (Bowle's Golden Grass): Golden-leaved grass for moderate shade on moist humus rich soils. Will self seed freely.

Mitraria coccinea*: Sprawling shrub, growing amongst thick cover in humid situations on constantly moist, humus rich soils.

Pachysandra procumbens: Attractively mottled leaves, combined with the ability to grow in moderately deep shade in humus-rich woodland.

Rhododendron praecox: Many early flowering rhododendrons make good use of light shade beneath deciduous trees on acid soils.

Sanguinaria canadensis: Precociously early in spring – strong, horizontal rootstocks hold ground well on damp humus rich soils

Tiarella cordifolia **'Echo Red Heart'**: One of several forms of the foam flower – all are equally useful as effective space occupiers in shade.

The woodland edge

The borders between forest and scrub, or woodland and meadow, are unusually complex, changeable and competitive. They are partially shaded, partially sunlit, and plants must be able to cope with both conditions. Temperatures, light intensity, susceptibility to drought and exposure to wind all vary intricately over very short distances, and plants need to be tolerant and adaptable to make the most of the opportunities on offer. Conditions change constantly as the trees thrive or decline, and grasses or shrubs infiltrate or are excluded, so that plants not only have to hold their own in competitive situations, but must be equipped to move on and establish themselves in new locations.

Perennials and shrubs of the woodland edge

These communities include plants that are naturally adapted to play a part in shifting, unstable matrices in which opportunities and problems vary continuously. They are very significant in gardens too in semi-shaded situations close to buildings, along fences, beside trees and under shrubs.

Arthropodium cirrhatum*: Develops moderately dense colonies in warm sites in light shade on moisture retentive, free draining soils.

Aruncus dioicus: Splendid plant as a specimen or in bold groups. Widely tolerant of soils and situations, repays good treatment.

Camellia x *williamsii* **'Donation'**:

Camellia x *williamsii* **'Donation':**
Upright, floriferous, broadly tolerant evergreen
shrub for cool, moist situations on humus-rich
soils.

Daphne mezereum: Excellent, early flowering
shrub for lightly shaded positions on humus-
rich, free draining base rich soils.

Gaultheria shallon: Shrub, forms dense
thickets of low evergreen shoots in mild, humid
locations on moist acid soils.

Geranium x *magnificum:* Robust clump
forming perennial for intermittently shaded
settings. Tolerant of most soils.

Helleborus orientalis: Very long-lived persistent
perennial, forming dense mats of roots on heavy
moisture retentive soils.

Itea virginica: Hardy deciduous shrub with
lamb's tails of fragrant creamy white flowers.
Fertile, moist soils.

Lamium maculatum: Numerous cvs. all fill
spaces well with attractive evergreen foliage in
early stages of matrix formation.

Lunaria rediviva: Perennial form of Honesty.
Long-lived in intermittently shaded situations
on fertile soils.

Lychnis coronaria: Short-lived, silver-leaved
perennial. Self sows freely in light shade
amongst other perennials and shrubs.

Macropiper excelsa*: Dense, evergreen shrub
thriving in light to moderate shade in humid
situations on moist soils.

Ruscus hypoglossum: Low growing, prickly
shrub, tolerant of dry shade and extremely
persistant once established.

Sarcococca hookeriana **var.** *digyna:* A hardier
form than the type for deep or moderate shade
on most fertile, not waterlogged soils.

Skimmia japonica: Compact evergreen shrub
tolerant of summer drought in lightly shaded
situations on fertile soils.

Spiraea **'Gold Flame':** Easily propagated, small
domed shrub, excellent bright infiller for
temporary or continued use, in sunlit sites.

Tolmiea menziesii **'Taff's Gold':** Spreads
methodically from plantlets on the ends of
the petioles – drought tolerant but better on
moist soils.

Tradescantia virginiana: Persistent clump
forming perennial for sun or light shade close to
trees. Broadly tolerant of soils.

Vancouveria hexandra: Forms densely
clustered stems above short, creeping rhizomes.
Very hardy and shade tolerant.

Vinca major: With *V. minor,* evergreen more or
less vigorously trailing shrubs: fine ground cover
if space allows.

Analogies between the woodland edge and
semi-shaded, semi-sunlit settings in gardens
have been drawn previously. But more general
comparisons with the complex plantings of
trees, shrubs and perennials typical of many
gardens, and gardening techniques involving
repeated disturbance of the status quo, like
lifting, dividing and transplanting, are also
applicable. Not surprisingly, plants of the
woodland edge tend to be easily-grown, tolerant
and amenable under garden conditions. The
combination of persistence and mobility
possessed by many of them, makes them
particularly useful as space-fillers during the
early stages of matrix formation, and pluggers of
gaps as matrices develop. Evergreen forms, in
particular, like bugles, strawberries (including
Duchesnea) and self-heals can often be used to
provide a carpet of foliage in winter beneath
taller perennials and shrubs.

Bulbous perennials, particularly those that
appear during the winter or spring, are another
group that can be used to fill in gaps in a
matrix. These survive total submersion beneath
the shadow of the densest matrices while at rest
below the ground, and in that state occupy no
space at all. The upright, narrow leaves of some,
including daffodils, push through overlying,
ground-carpeting plants, but their foliage
contributes relatively little to the density of the
aerial matrix. Others produce broad leaves that
spread above the ground and hold space
effectively at times of the year when most
perennials and all deciduous trees and shrubs are
leafless.

Bulbous plants for shaded and semi-shaded situations

Some of these are valuable for their contribution
to matrices, particularly in winter when other
plants lose their leaves. The foliage of others
may make little contribution to the matrix,

50A

50B

50C

though their roots may hold ground effectively below the surface and their flowers add considerably to the interest and attractions of the garden.

Allium triquetrum: In light shade amongst deciduous trees and shrubs, an irrepressible coloniser in many mild moist sites.

Alstroemeria aurea: persistent, almost ineradicable coloniser for lightly shaded situations amongst shrubs and vigorously competitive perennials.

Anemone apenina: With *A.A. blanda* and *nemorosa* can provide good infilling leaf cover before foliage of other perennials develops.

Arisarum proboscideum: Forms steadily expanding colonies in shaded, moist situations with broad leaves close to the ground.

***Arum italicum* 'Marmoratum':** Excellent plant for winter ground cover, spreading, sometimes vigorously, clumps of dense broad leaves.

Cardiocrinum giganteum: Unpredictable, usually temporary matrix former. Broad leaves may be significant in mild, wet locations.

Clintonia borealis: Develops as moderately ground holding, mats of roots and short leaves in moist, cool, acid soils.

Cyclamen hederifolium: Can develop very significant winter ground cover. Tolerates deep summer shade under deciduous plants.

50A, B & C. Deciduous woodlands naturally support a rich growth of perennials at ground level, especially in spring (top left). The easiest situations are those that are fertile and moist, (lower left) in which a great many different woodland perennials and ferns will thrive. Drier spaces beneath conifers (right) can cause more problems, but even these can be filled most attractively provided the planting is kept simple and confined to plants that are naturally adapted to such situations. Oaks Overlook, Shenandoah National Park, Virginia, USA. Gordon & Annette Collier's Garden, Titoki Point, Taihape, New Zealand. Mary Ann & Frederick McGourty's Garden, Hillside, Norfolk, Connecticut, USA.

flowers and foliage provides early ground cover in spaces between woody plants.

Erythronium dens canis: Foliage of spp. and cvs. provides early, nearly rabbit proof cover in sites that are later deeply shaded.

Galanthus nivalis: Can develop into large colonies in clusters dotted over the ground but narrow foliage forms a weak matrix.

Hyacinthoides non-scripta: With *H. hispanica* can form dense colonies that take over ground between woody plants until midsummer.

***Iris foetidissima* 'Citrina'**: Excellent plant for dry, deeply shaded sites, broad evergreen leaves form persistent, retentive clumps.

Lilium martagon: Colonizes well in light shade amongst grasses and herbs where it can contribute to matrix formation.

Narcissus pseudonarcissus: This and other spp. and cvs. are outstanding spring flowers, but not great contributors to matrices.

Nectaroscordum siculum* ssp. *bulgaricum: Will colonize moderately in light shade on well-drained soils. Plays little part in matrix formation.

Oxalis pes-caprae*: Like some other species, inclined to excess, but in competitive situations can provide useful early cover.

Ranunculus ficaria: A useful matrix former amongst dense planting. Too possessive for fertile non-competitive situations.

Sandersonia aurantiaca*: A colourful plant for lightly shaded woodland margins of free draining soils.

Scilla bifolia: Forms widespread colonies below deciduous woody plants as a minor contributor to spring matrices.

Trillium grandiflorum: The broad foliage of trilliums is a useful part of the woodland floor matrix before trees develop leaves.

Ferns

Optimistic assertions in articles in gardening magazines have been telling us for years that 'ferns are coming back'. Perhaps so, but judging by what I see in gardens, and on visits to garden centres, the tide comes in excessively slowly. It is exceptional to find these plants given any prominence, and hard to find nurseries that supply more than a handful.

Ferns are remarkable plants – the possessors of primitive sexual procedures superseded aeons ago by the development of flowers. This apparent improvement should have led to the rapid extinction of the ferns, but never did. Their alternative lifestyle, with its alternating generations, and fragile dependence at critical stages on delicate tissues and freely-available water, appears to be laborious, chancy and inefficient, but it is combined with extraordinary tenacity. Once established, ferns tend to be long-lived, self-maintaining, self-sustaining plants that are distinctly disinclined to surrender their space.

Ferns evolved in wetter and warmer conditions than those generally found in temperate parts of the world today, and although many have adapted to cope with cold, the consummation of their sexual routines still depends on saturated atmospheres and freely-available water. They grow most abundantly in the forests of wetter and warmer parts of the world, where they flourish on levels of nutrients and light which would be starvation rations for more active, more evolved and more demanding, higher plants.

In gardens, too, few ferns can compete with flowering plants in the feather-bedded conditions of the mixed border or the luxuriantly competitive battlefield of a rich meadow, but beneath trees, in damp, dank corners amongst buildings, in cool, wet upland gardens, and even in crevices of walls, ferns can answer any gardener's need, unless that need specifies flowers as an essential and 'colour' a prerequisite. Ferns produce no flowers and are almost always green. The grace of form and texture of their foliage compensates for lack of flowers, and makes an entirely individual and irreplaceable contribution to a garden. They are colourless only to those whose prejudices blind them to tones of green, which are the most important part of a garden's spectrum – not because they cannot see green, but because it is so abundant they have become accustomed to ignoring it.

Hopefully, the predictions that ferns are coming back will prove to be accurate, and we can look forward to seeing these beautiful plants play a more conspicuous role in our gardens. There is even a possibility of a return of the

51A

51B

There is even a possibility of a return of the ferns on a scale that would transform the garden landscapes of Britain and the more oceanic parts of Europe and North America wherever winter temperatures do not fall too low. Gardening is most vigorously pursued in many places where winters are too cold for tree ferns to survive, but frequently by a margin of only a degree or two. If predictions that our planet is warming turn out to be accurate, one of the first effects could be the possibility of introducing these plants to gardens where they cannot be grown today. That would be a notable event since their distinctive form has no equivalent at present. An event made all the more dramatic because similar increases in temperature would allow us to to grow, amongst other plants, cycads, agaves, cordylines and some of the hardier palms. Very small increases in minimum winter temperatures would allow millions of gardeners on mainland Britain, the oceanic borders of Europe and many cool temperate parts of the United States to play variations on gardening themes which have never before been possible in these places.

Ferns for lightly and deeply shaded situations in gardens

The great majority of ferns grow naturally in the shade of trees, other plants or rocks, and do well in similar situations in gardens. Few thrive in consistently dry soils, or in fertile sunlit borders amongst other plants, but in the right settings they make reliable, easily grown garden plants.

Adiantum pedatum: A hardy and graceful maidenhair, dense rhizomes and wiry stems form steadily expanding clumps.

Asplenium bulbiferum*: Broad, arching ground shading fronds – for wet, humid, mild conditions in light or moderate shade.

Athyrium filix-femina: Numerous forms available – for light shade on moist, free draining acid or neutral soils.

Blechnum capense*: Spreads vigorously by surface rhizomes – even in situations with thin soils, provided they remain moist.

Blechnum discolor*: Clump forming fern, spreading by rhizomes in moist to wet conditions in light to moderate shade.

Blechnum spicant: Hardy, enduring fern, broadly tolerant of a range of conditions – but always in shade on humus-rich soils.

Cyathea dealbata*: A tree fern for mild, humid situations on generally moist soils – has a measure of drought tolerance.

Dicksonia antartica*: A relatively hardy tree fern for mild, humid sites – preferably in light or intermittent shade.

Dryopteris wallichiana: Numerous spp. and forms are mostly broadly tolerant and capable of thriving even in relatively dry sites.

Gleichenia cunninghamia: Branching, creeping rhizomes colonize thin soils and rocks, produce

51A & B. Mosses planted as a dense, ground-covering mat beneath acers and azaleas feature in this version of a Japanese garden (left). Elsewhere, especially in naturally humid settings (right), they and ferns can be used – with evocatively atmospheric effects – to carpet the ground beneath trees. Tatton Park, Knutsford, Cheshire, England. Bloedel Gardens, Bainbridge Island, nr Seattle, Washington, USA

an umbrella of shading fronds.

*Marattia salicina**: An extremely large ground fern that thrives even in deep shade, in warm humid situations on wet soils.

Matteucia struthiopteris: Spreading rhizomes produce separate clusters of fronds in sun or light shade, on wet, humus-rich soils.

Onoclea sensibilis: A hardy woodland fern – producing masses of upright fronds from spreading rhizomes in shaded, moist sites.

Osmunda claytoniana: Fronds produced in clusters from spreading rhizomes in light shade on humus-rich, moist well-drained soils.

Phegopteris connectilis: Slim underground rhizomes produce numerous separate fronds – on humus-rich, moist acid soils.

*Phymatosorus diversifolia**: Leathery, very broad fronds produced from creeping rhizomes provide excellent ground cover in shade.

Polypodium vulgare: Rhizomes able to colonize thin soils, rocks and tree branches – tolerant of periodic seasonal drought.

Polystichum aculeatum: Vigorous fern for lightly shaded, well drained sites – established plants tolerant of periodic drought.

Polystichum munitum: Evergreen species for humid situations in shade on moist, acid soils.

Polystichum setiferum: Semi-evergreen, numerous forms available – tolerant of infertile, heavily shaded situations.

Mosses

The dry sterility beneath mature beech trees that is so discouraging to plants – and gardeners too – has already been mentioned. But even the most extreme of these places are not lost causes. Flowers may fail; ferns find them too spartan but mosses can cope, and free from competition at ground level, thrive. The possibilities of mosses are barely explored by Western gardeners, who know them only as intruders to be raked from lawns, and as disturbing indicators of damp on roofs and paths. We hear of their use, and see pictures of the results in gardens in Japan. We see them used in Japanese gardens constructed in the West, and almost invariably move on to think about other things.

But mosses play a part in many matrices formed by communities of wildflowers. That is why they move into our lawns and can be so difficult to expel – especially in poorly-aerated, badly-drained swards, when they can grow more luxuriantly and abundantly than the grasses. They, and their distant two-dimensional cousins, the liverworts, are often conspicuous amongst ferns and woodland plants in damp woods, and even in dry shade, where they have little competition.

Anyone who uses paraquat or glyphosate to kill weeds on shaded paths or between shrubs in borders discovers that mosses colonize the bare surfaces, often making them as green as they would be if covered with more familiar plants. This opens the way to gardening with mosses without the expertise, patience and attention that we associate with their culture in Japanese gardens. Mosses can be grown simply. All we need do to encourage them is destroy other plants by spraying them with weed-killers; and the first place where this knowledge can be put to good use is in the dry shade beneath mature trees.

We should look more closely at mosses and their place in matrices of plants growing in other places, too, such as those that are wet and cold – moorlands and mountains perhaps, or as part of the vegetation of the forest floor – and often the trees too, in damp forests, and beside springs and streams. Mosses, liverworts, filmy ferns, lichens and club mosses, comprising between them a very large part of the plant kingdom, possess forms and textures all their own, and many thrive in places that gardeners despairingly label 'difficult'. Yet we have scarcely begun to consider the possibilities they offer when we plan and plant, and in our role as casting directors, provide practically no parts for them to play in our gardens.

The gardens
A new life on Vancouver Island

This garden, by a sheltered sea inlet, surrounds a recently-built house near Victoria on Vancouver Island in Canada. The well-structured, neutral loam soil, adequate rainfall (the greater part during the winter) and temperate conditions are very favourable for gardening – most of the time. The area is old Douglas fir/western hemlock forest, with some

52A

52B

big-leaf maples and a few madrones. Trees left standing in the garden rather intimidated the owners, and they had to learn how to garden beneath them.

They lived previously near Regina in Saskatchewan, and had little experience of trees or gardening. Now, in a kinder climate and with the children at school during the day, the wife spends much of her spare time gardening. She regularly buys *The Island Grower*, which has helped her develop ideas, and discover which plants grow well on Vancouver Island, and recently paid a visit to Phoebe Noble's garden, leaving it a convert to the principles of 'layer-cake' gardening, and convinced of the benefits of mulching.

52C

Review

A

The construction of the timber house avoided serious disturbance to the ground, and a number of fine specimen deer and sword ferns, as well as vanilla leaf, shallon and other forest floor plants, still grew beneath the trees. Huckleberries and rattlesnake plantains sprouted naturally on old, rotting stumps.

B

The presence of the mature trees had major effects on the preparations necessary before planting: the plants chosen, and subsequent management; but once attended to, the trees

have become valuable attractions.

C

The advantages of the mild winters, when temperatures seldom fall below -5°C (23 °F), and the rarity of spring frosts, are offset by occasional short interludes of savagely severe weather. Similarly, periodic droughts during the summer have to be reckoned with when choosing plants.

D

This is not a large garden, and she has time, energy and enthusiasm to spare, enabling her to give plants the individual attention they need to grow well.

52A, B & C. Gardeners have scarcely explored the possibilities of lichens, liverworts and club mosses. The former produce decorative and colourful matrices naturally (top left) or spontaneously in gardens (top right), but in most settings these matrices would be fragile and difficult to maintain. Club mosses (bottom left), by comparison, are relatively robust plants which occur naturally in a great variety of situations, and can contribute forms and textures scarcely ever seen in our gardens.
Parque Nacional Queulat, Puyuhuapi, Aisen, Chile. Forde Abbey, Crewkerne, Dorset, England. Near Kutusova, Ussuriland, Far Eastern Region, Russia.

Outcome

A

The structure and profile of the soil, built up over many years beneath the forest trees, was practically intact – assets which would have been destroyed by digging; therefore, surface treatments were used instead.

The surviving wildflowers suggested a rather natural style of planting, using native species supplemented with woodland plants from other parts of the world.

B

The trees provide shelter rather than shade, because their canopies are high above the ground. The only attention required was the removal of a few of the lower branches to lift some of the crowns a little higher.

Pockets of humus amongst the roots were boosted by mulching all beds before planting with a 7.5 cm (3 in) layer of composted bark, infilling between the plants afterwards with a 4 cm (1.6 in) layer of bark chips.

Immediately before planting, a semi-organic top dressing of 125 g/sq. m of blood, fish and bone manure, incorporating rock potash, was scattered over the surface of the composted bark to help the young plants become established. (Note that blood, fish and bone manure is naturally deficient in potassium, but proprietary brands are available in which the levels are supplemented by additions of this mineral.)

C

The choice of trees, shrubs and the more permanent perennials had to take into account occasional very cold spells during the winter. The warm, dry summers are ideal for many short-lived or dubiously hardy but easily-replaced, colourful perennials, and these were used liberally in sunlit areas to follow the spring display of the woodland plants.

D

The wife very soon set up a small propagation unit, with a greenhouse and cold frames and a standing-out area for containers filled with plants. She used this to grow plants not readily available from nurseries from seed, and to propagate tender perennials needed for beds near the house, and in troughs and hanging baskets.

The plants

The absence of spring frosts, and the sheltering canopy of the trees made the garden particularly favourable for woody plants with flowers or young leaves that are sensitive to frost, and amongst those planted were *Acer circinnatum* and cultivars of *A. palmatum* including 'Bloodgood', 'Margret B' and crimson and green forms with dissected leaves; several of the Kosar-DeVos *Magnolia* hybrids, including the deep-pinky-purple 'Ann' and rosy-lavender 'Ricki', and *Magnolia* X *soulangeana* 'San Jose, *Styrax japonica* 'Carillon' and 'Pink Chimes' also grew well. These were supplemented with other shrubs, some quite low-growing, to thicken the lower parts of the matrix and provide sheltered, humid conditions for the ferns: amongst them were *Amelanchier alnifolia*, *Nandina domestica* 'Firepower' and *Aronia arbutifolia* 'Brilliant' (for their autumn foliage). *Holodiscus discolor* introduced itself to the garden, and other natives planted included *Mahonia aquifolium* 'Apollo' and *Philadelphus lewisii*; with *Ribes laurifolium*, *Pieris japonica* 'Daisen' and 'Pink Delight', *Stephanandra tanakae* and *Vestia foetida*.

She adopted the idea of 'layer cake' planting for the perennials, mixing them with several bulbous plants and ferns, and starting with a scattering of upright or moderately tall plants with clumps of *Aruncus sylvestris*, *Filipendula palmata* and *Aconitum* X *cammarum* 'Bicolor' amongst ribbons of *Smilacina racemosa* and *S. stellata* and the giant Solomon's seal, *Polygonatum commutatum*. Other, taller emergent plants included *Lilium columbianum*, *L. pardalinum* and *Arisaema speciosum*.

Below these was an intermediate layer of clump-forming plants, many of which had compact hummocks of foliage for much of the year, with taller spikes of flowers. Hostas and hemerocallis were prominent, and also *Agapanthus* 'Castle of Mey' and 'Isis'. Several eastern north American natives were used too, including *Heuchera americana* 'Molly Bush' (with bronze and purple foliage), *H.* X *brizoides* 'Widar' (with brilliant-red flowers), and *Mitella breweri* and *Tellima grandiflora* 'Purpurea'. Other clump-forming plants included *Erythronium oregonum* (which self-seeded itself freely), and *E.* 'Pagoda' and *E. revolutum* 'Rose Beauty'. She tried *Cypripedium pubescens*, and *C. reginae*, without much success.

The lowest level of the matrix was made up of creepers and infiltrators, including the deeply shade-tolerant *Asarum canadense* and *A. shuttleworthii* 'Callaway' (with glossy, silver, marbled leaves) and *Arisarum proboscideum*; *Cornus canadensis* was interplanted with *Clintonia borealis* and *Maianthemum bifolium*, and there were several patches of the runnering *Duchesnea indica* and *Saxifraga cuscutiformis*. She also planted drifts of *Tiarella wherryi* and *T. cordifolia*, including 'Oakleaf' and 'Echo Red Heart', with crimson-centred leaves.

Ferns became a notable feature of the planting; amongst them were drifts of *Adiantum pedatum* and the copper form of *Onoclea sensibilis*, and fine individual specimens or small clusters of *Blechnum spicant*, the crimson-flushed *Dryopteris erythrosora* and *D. goldiana*, and *Polystichum aculeatum*, *P. munitum* and *P. vestitum*.

London 'barrister's' suburban play-pen

This garden round a mock-Tudor villa in Northwood in the western suburbs of London lies on heavy clay – claggy in winter, brick-hard and riven by cracks in dry summers. Comparatively large for the neighbourhood, its owner likes to refer to it as 'two acres' – in fact, at 0.4 hectares, it is exactly half that.

He is the recently-retired clerk of a barristers' chambers in the Temple, sometime divorced, who spends much of his time at a local golf club, where he is angling for election as chairman of the Greens Committee. He employs a gardener to do the work, but is not averse to pottering about in the garden, and has strong ideas about how it should look. A collection of hybrid tea roses in formally laid-out beds is his pride and joy. He is pernickety about his lawns, hates ivies in any form, anywhere, and appreciates the well-groomed, sexy shapes of dwarf conifers in bed with brightly-foliaged heathers.

In retirement, he throws a popular line in barbecue parties, at which he enjoys playing the chef, and for which he has built a 'barbecue garden'. These affairs, with secluded seats and shelter from showers and cold night airs, have become much sought after by his pals at the golf club, who appreciate opportunities for a little partner swapping to revive jaded appetites in their declining years.

Review

A
The barbecue garden was wanted as soon as possible. There was no question of waiting years while shelter and seclusion develop.
B
It has to provide a visually exciting setting for his parties, and overhead shelter and cover without losing the *al fresco* atmosphere.
C
The clay soil was a particularly unsuitable substrate for party shenanigans. When wet, its cloying properties guarantee that it sticks to anything it touches and climbs up anything that moves.
D
The planting had to take account of the affects of numerous feet – not always well controlled – and the probability of party horseplay, while providing secluded nooks and arbours for more intimate moments.

Outcome

A
Instant height was achieved with a pergola-like framework of timber, fronting on to the lawn and enclosed on two sides by trelliswork, which also formed arbours and secluded corners. Solid timber posts supporting the pergola were a feature of the design, simulating the effects of tree trunks below the overhead canopy of this synthetic wood.
B
Spaces between the cross-members of the pergola near the house were glazed with polycarbonate acrylic to reinforce overhead cover; further out, they were left open. Vines and other climbers grown over the timber framework and on the trellises provided a quick solution to the need for a sheltering canopy.
C
The clay soil was removed to a depth of 15 cm (6 in) and replaced with hardcore and quarry rubble, over a woven polypropylene membrane, to form a well-drained, level surface on which a

pattern of brick paviors and non-slip, reconstituted stone slabs was laid. Planting spaces were left at the bases of the pillars and along the bottom of the trellis.

A small ornamental pool and fountain with submerged lighting was built in a space open to the skies in the centre of the garden as a focal point .

D

In spring and early summer, when parties took place at midday and the vines and climbers were mostly leafless, woodland perennials and bulbs planted in spaces between the paving and in containers provided colour.

Later, parties tended to be held after dark, and plants at ground level became too vulnerable to damage. Colour was provided by plants specially grown in large containers, and by the foliage, flowers and fruit of the climbers.

A lean-to greenhouse against a high south wall was used as an 'orangery' in which to overwinter tender plants in containers.

The plants

The first climbers planted were cultivars of *Wisteria floribunda* and *W. sinensis* – these were rigorously pruned to encourage spurring and control their size. *Vitis vinifera* 'Purpurea' was grown on the trellises, and the small, sweet 'Himrod', and 'Baco Noir' were trained as rods across the pergolas – the latter for its innumerable colourful bunches of rather sour grapes that tended to be left because they were not too tempting a target for party-goers. There were numerous clematis, amongst them *C. florida* 'Sieboldii', which did well under cover by the house, and 'The President' for its double flowering season; late-flowering 'Madame Julia Correvon', 'Madame Edouard Andre' and 'Huldine' were winter pruned to about 60 cm (2 ft) from the ground. Honeysuckles, golden hop, *Ipomoea purpurea* and jasmine were planted on the trellises, but the thorns on climbing roses made them so unpopular with guests they had to be removed, leaving only the thornless 'Veilchenblau', 'Zephirine Drouhin' and 'Kathleen Harrop'. Several bougainvilleas, amongst them the salmon 'Miss Manila', bright, glowing red 'Scarlett O'Hara' and pink 'Blondie', grown in pots overwintered under cover, and pruned annually to a narrow, upright

framework, were used with dramatic effect for late summer colour amongst the vines.

Spring-flowering woodland perennials planted in narrow beds and spaces at the base of pillars included *Corydalis flexuosa, Arum italicum* 'Marmoratum', several pulmonarias, *Mertensia virginica*, polyanthus hybrids, *Dicentra formosa* 'Langtrees' and 'Luxuriant', and wallflowers. Either they were cleared away, or their foliage died down before evening parties exposed them to trampling feet. These were supplemented by bulbs, particularly large and flamboyant ones like the Darwin hybrid tulips 'Apeldoorn Elite', 'Gordon Cooper' and the multi-hued 'Gudoshnik', and 'Blue' and 'Flaming Parrot'; a selection of orchid-flowered daffodils included 'Baccarat' and 'Lemon Beauty', and – his favourites – the doubles 'Tahiti', 'Texas and 'Acropolis'. *Fritillaria imperialis* 'Aurora' and 'Maxima Lutea' produced suitably impressive flowers, and a distinctive odour that contributed nothing to the enjoyment of food. They were used only once.

Later on, the display in containers owed much to cultivars of argyranthemum and pelargonium – including those with fragrant foliage, supported by other aroma-contributors like *Heliotropium peruvianum, Humea elegans, Lilium regale* and *Nicotiana* 'Evening Fragrance'. Large dragon pots filled with *Zantedeschia aethiopica* and the cultivar 'Green Goddess' featured round the fountain. Height and a 'tropical atmosphere' were contributed by several half-barrels containing the giant, brightly silver-edged reed *Arundo donax* var. *versicolor*, *Phormium tenax* 'Purpureum' and the brilliant scarlet, yellow or orange flowers of cultivars of *Canna indica*, including 'Purpurea' and 'Variegata'. The superb *Brugmansia* 'Grand Marnier' was tried one year, but took up too much space, and had scarcely started to flower before the partying season finished.

New Zealand politician's haven from divisions

The garden belongs to a former farmer and politician, and his wife, on the slopes of Mount Taranaki in New Zealand. The annual rainfall is very high, and the climate mild – in many winters almost frost-free. The garden, of about

2 hectares (5 acres), containing remnants of the original evergreen bush, is on gently-sloping ground a couple of hundred metres above sea level, with fine views to the snow-clad cone of the volcano and across the Tasman Sea. Several lahars (hillocks of clay, stones and ash), the results of ancient eruptions, make the topography of the garden extremely variable.

The owner and his wife both delight in gardening, and he wryly regrets frustrating, and finally disillusioning, years as a politician which could have been better spent as a gardener. They regularly visit the Hollard gardens, and enjoy renewing acquaintance with the large, brindled cat which accompanies them, cradled in their arms. Recently, to their great joy, they have discovered Gordon and Annette Collier's garden at Titoki Point, and find its combination of informality and intention so exciting, that they have returned several times, finding it an inspiration for their own garden. On their first visit, they were amused to be greeted near the gate by two small dogs, which escorted them courteously up the drive, but unlike the Hollard cat, after observing they had paid their dues, left them to make their own way round the garden.

Review

A
The evergreen forest was a crucial asset. It has been damaged by logging, domestic cattle, wild goats, pigs and possums and by Hurricane Bola, but still forms the nucleus of the new garden.

B
The natural vegetation is an extreme example of a temperate forest matrix, and the mild winters, abundant rainfall and fertile, reddish topsoil known as 'Egmont ash' appear to impose few limits on gardening. Finding ways to control exuberant growth that could quickly make the garden almost impenetrable was the main challenge.

C
The husband's taste is for a well-regulated, ordered style of garden. Their discovery of Titoki Point made him more appreciative of subtle styles of co-ordination and design – a change much appreciated by his wife, who has been contending with his preference for order for years.

D
The benign conditions made it possible to combine trees and other plants, with a remarkable diversity of form and texture – opportunities that are still being developed.

Outcome

A
The first years were spent sorting out the bush, fencing out grazing animals, identifying the trees and tree ferns and noting those most worth preserving, forming paths and more open areas, trying to control the possums, and giving the vegetation time to heal itself.

B
Control depended on creating effective matrices within which plants could develop in mutually balanced ways.

This was done by identifying different settings within the garden suitable for a variety of plant communities, and by carefully balancing the vigour and other attributes of the plants themselves – otherwise, weaker ones rapidly succumbed to competition.

C
The highly-controlled patterns of the Hollard garden were not applicable to this situation, and although the topography matched Titoki Point better, other conditions were too different to make that an easy model to follow.

In the end, the use of central cores of native bush, providing a background and sheltering rides and glades planted with rhododendrons and other shrubs and perennials, like the nearby Pukeiti Rhododendron Trust Gardens, was adopted as a guide.

D
The husband was uneasy at first with the lack of formality and definition, feeling insufficiently in control of the garden and the way it was developing.

These feelings were at least partially relieved by careful attention to visual logic. Harmonies and contrasts within the planting were very carefully devised – the former to create quiet areas, the latter to emphasize transitions from one part of the garden to another. Repetition was used to establish patterns that emphasized elements of the design, and linked different areas. Routes through the garden were defined by using plants and shapes to signal approaches to steps, viewpoints and links between one setting and another.

The plants

The bush, battered but now regenerating, forms an impressive part of the garden, where tall trees, their upper limbs crowded with epiphytes, loom out of the densely-foliaged layers of evergreens beneath them. These tall, emergent individuals are wind-blown and decayed, their crotches stuffed with pubic astelias, their superstructure of branches draped with lichens, ragged with clustered foliage at the tips of some branches, others reduced to gaunt, dead limbs pointing grotesquely towards the sky. The evergreen foliage below is a dense, green, amorphous mass, relieved only by the striking forms of the cabbage trees and tree ferns or the bright white splash of a clematis in flower, and creating constant, almost unrelieved shade on the dim, humid floor of the forest, where only scattered ferns, fallen astelias, mosses, liverworts and filmy ferns can make a living.

A 'hedge' of ancient *Phormium tenax* and a row of gnarled and contorted *Cupressus macrocarpa* provide shelter near the house and a setting for a small, more ordered, more formal garden, where there are mixed borders in which the upright grass tree *Dracophyllum latifolium* and the spiky foliage and giant inflorescences of *Beschorneria yuccoides* stand out in exotic contrast to a ground-covering matrix of perennials. These include broad, mounded clumps of ligularias, hostas, astilbes, rodgersias and hellebores, enlivened by the vertical accents of Siberian iris and arching Solomon's seal. Japanese anemones, epimediums, Spanish bluebells, dicentras, navel wort and a variety of candelabra primulas occupy spaces between them, and the crimson, purple or variegated foliage of ajugas, and the bright-blue pea flowers of *Parochetus communis* fill any spaces that appear at ground level.

Amongst the most impressive trees in the remnant of bush are conifers like Dacrydium cupressinum (rimu), *Phyllocladus trichomanoides*

and *Prumnopitys ferruginea*, all fruitful supporters of the native birds. Broad-leaved trees include titoki (*Alectryon excelsus*), a small glade of the deciduous *Fuchsia excorticata, Griselinia lucida*; a number of tall, upright *Knightia excelsa* regenerating vigorously in gaps in the canopy, the brilliant *Metrosideros robusta*, spectacularly covered with scarlet flowers in the years when it blooms well, and *Pittosporum crassifolium* with numerous *Weinmannia racemosa*. Contrasting forms and foliage are introduced by palms, including several mature *Rhopalostylis sapida*, and a few slowly-developing juveniles, and tree ferns such as *Alsophila medullaris*, with its glossy, black rachises, the silver fern *Cyathea dealbata*, and numerous *Dicksonia squarrosa*.

Shadowed areas beneath the tree canopy are already occupied by numerous ferns, especially the unpalatable *Polystichum vestitum*, and these were supplemented with new planting, reinforced with small groups of bromeliads for their contrasting foliage. Amongst the ferns are the giant *Marattia salicina* (which had been exterminated by wild pigs in search of its starchy tubers), and the large, graceful *Asplenium bulbiferum* (which had been similarly reduced by goats). *Leptopteris superba* (the Prince of Wales's feather) established well in some of the cooler, moister gullies, in company with the almost monotone, slightly glaucous fronds of *Histiopteris incisa* and mats of the kidney-shaped fronds of the filmy fern (*Trichomanes reniforme*).

Useful occupiers of ground, amongst ferns, in semi-shaded, partially-sunlit glades are bromeliads, which included the rare *Ochagavia carnea* (found naturally only on Juan Fernandez Island), *Nidularium rutilans* (with deep-crimson bracts in the centres of the rosettes) and *N. innocentii* 'Striatum', whose variegated leaves gave an impression of dappled sunlight.

Fig. 13. New Zealand politician's haven from divisions Native woodland, bush or spinney can provide very friendly conditions in which to make a garden. Here, existing trees, shrubs, climbers and ferns have been used as the foundation of the garden. Other native and non-native trees and shrubs have been planted, and numerous woodland herbaceous perennials introduced.

Native trees and shrubs include pittosporums, fuchsias,

rimus, rewarewas, celery pines, cabbage trees and clematis. Perennials planted below include hostas, Siberian iris, Solomon's seal, bugles and primulas – highlighted in places with bromeliad's growing epiphytically on tree stumps and branches.

Spiky-leaved plants are repeatedly used as a contrast to the heavy evergreen leaves of many of the native trees and shrubs – sometimes to highlight routes through the garden, sometimes to emphasize changes of atmosphere within it.

Conclusion

'Matrix planting' is a phrase that I believed had occurred to me spontaneously, until I came across an article by an old friend, and fellow student at Wye College, E.C.M. Haes, in the quarterly bulletin of the Alpine Garden Society. He employed the term to describe alpines growing in intermingled mats in a corner of his garden. Long forgotten though it was, I would certainly have seen that article, and perhaps the name had lodged in a hidden corner of my memory, to be recalled when I needed a concise way to describe a method of gardening in which plants are intended to meld together in more or less self-sustaining communities.

It may seem to some that this is just another term for 'ground cover' – an attempt, perhaps, to revive an image tarnished, a little unfairly I think, by too many examples of unimaginatively chosen plants in uninspired settings masquerading as ground cover. Many of the principles, and the plants used, on which the success of one depends apply to the other. But matrix planting is concerned with the successive layers of vegetation, one above the other, through which plants form multi-dimensional communities, not only in the space above the ground, but also in time as the seasons change, and one year gives way to the next. Few would refer to the stratified vegetation of a wood as 'ground cover' (though from a bird's-eye view the cover is most effective), nor the complex mixtures of grasses and herbs that form long-lived, self-sustaining communities in meadows. The growth patterns of the plants that grow in and around ponds would not form part of a dialogue on ground cover, but the communities that are sustained by these relationships are a part of matrix planting.

More recently, we have learnt about habitat planting – which also has much in common with matrix planting. Both adopt as models the natural behaviour of plants, the places where they grow, and the ways they use the opportunities and cope with the problems of different situations. Some garden settings are inextricably linked with habitats where plants grow naturally – in the shadow of trees and buildings, for example, success depends on a close match between the setting and the nature of the plant. But that is not always so. Mixed borders in open situations on neutral soils – amongst the the commonest of all garden settings – are undoubtedly habitats, but they would accommodate with equal prospects of success plants adapted to a variety of different situations and conditions in nature. In such settings the natural origins of garden plants become less significant; their ability to form self-sustaining matrices of stems, foliage and roots becomes critical. In some situations careful matching of habitat and setting is the key; in others, attention must be paid to compatability between the members of the community.

Many gardeners will feel that matrix planting reduces their power to control what goes on in their gardens. Calendars, books, magazines and television present us with picture-book gardens filled with beautifully-posed, meticulously-selected plants, sometimes in carefully-controlled groups, sometimes in more natural-looking communities, but under control in a framework of weed-free borders and paths, mown grass and clipped hedges. They convey the message that garden in whatever way we may, we should all obey the commandment that 'Thy garden shall be immaculate.'

These reassuring signs of control are part of our defences against nature, and our attempts to dominate everything that goes on around us. Attempts that, it seems to me, increasingly take the form of obsessive attention to tidiness and order, and the elimination of anything that interrupts this order, too often at the expense of individuality, atmosphere and sense of place. Matrix planting depends for its effects on imagination rather than tidiness. Clear-cut distinctions between weeds and garden plants are less easily made; it is better to leave insects alone and rely on natural balances between predator and prey than attack with poisonous sprays; dead leaves are a source of humus and part of the natural cycle of growth and decay on which success depends.

Some time ago, a friend of a friend invited me over for a tour of his garden. Later, sitting on a chair on his impeccably-maintained lawn, chatting over a drink, I automatically flicked the stone from an olive into the nearest border, where it landed on the finely-tilled soil between the perfect dome of a dwarf rhododendron and a carefully-combed clump of irises. It lay there, reproaching me for my sluttishness – seemingly the only unintentional object in the immaculate order of the garden. A calling card, left by my dog, on my host's lawn would have been only marginally more shaming.

If you are dedicated to gardening as a form of housework, you will not find matrix planting an appealing alternative. If you prefer more relaxed styles, where happenstance plays its part, if you do not measure the success of your gardening by the regimentation of your plants, if you could be content with a garden where a discarded olive stone would pass unnoticed, you might find matrix planting a rewarding path to follow.

Index

This index includes the names of plants referred to in the main body of the text and accompanying lists, and provides the Latin equivalents of all vernacular names used.